A Military History of the
English Civil War, 1642–1646

A Military History of the English Civil War, 1642–1646

STRATEGY AND TACTICS

Malcolm Wanklyn and Frank Jones

Harlow, England • London • New York • Boston • San Francisco • Toronto
Sydney • Tokyo • Singapore • Hong Kong • Seoul • Taipei • New Delhi
Cape Town • Madrid • Mexico City • Amsterdam • Munich • Paris • Milan

PEARSON EDUCATION LIMITED

Edinburgh Gate
Harlow CM20 2JE
United Kingdom
Tel: +44 (0)1279 623623
Fax: +44 (0)1279 431059
Website: www.pearsoned.co.uk

First edition published in Great Britain in 2005

© Pearson Education Limited 2005

The rights of Malcolm Wanklyn and Frank Jones to be identified as authors
of this work have been asserted by them in accordance with the
Copyright, Designs and Patents Act 1988.

ISBN 0 582 77281 8

British Library Cataloguing in Publication Data
A CIP catalogue record for this book can be obtained from the British Library

Library of Congress Cataloging-in-Publication Data
Wanklyn, Malcolm.
    A military history of the English Civil War, 1642–1646 : strategy and tactics / Malcolm
Wanklyn and Frank Jones.—1st ed.
        p. cm.
    Includes bibliographical references (p.) and index.
    ISBN 0–582–77281–8
    1. Great Britain—History—Civil War, 1642–1649.   2. Military art and science—Great
Britain—History—17th century.   3. Great Britain—History, Military—1603–1714.   I. Jones,
Frank.   II. Title.

DA415.W325 2004
942.06′24—dc22

                                                                                2004048627

10 9 8 7 6 5 4 3 2 1
08 07 06 05 04

Set by 35 in 9/13.5pt Stone serif
Printed by Biddles Ltd, King's Lynn

The Publisher's policy is to use paper manufactured from sustainable forests.

To Professor Austin Woolrych, and to the memory of
Brigadier Peter Young DSO MC MA FSA

Contents

Preface

Returning to full-time research into the military history of the English Civil War after a period of almost forty years has been like returning home after a long absence, a joyful but in some respects disorienting experience. It was delightful to find catalogues in the Duke Humfrey Library on exactly the same shelves as they had been in 1965. On the other hand, advances in information retrieval have made the mechanics of research so much easier. Being able to view the Thomason Tracts on microfilm at Birmingham Reference Library, and to search catalogues in distant libraries and record offices via the Net, shortened the research programme by several months and massively reduced its cost. However, other things were subtly and disturbingly different. Even under a bright summer's sun the battlefield at Naseby had a menacing air as a wind pump set up in the middle of Broadmoor let out a quiet metallic clang every time it rotated in the light breeze. Cheriton too was not as I remembered it. Jean and I visited the chalk downs over which the battle was fought on the brightest of all summer mornings, but I cannot recall having appreciated the sheer beauty of the place on previous visits or the deep sadness that hangs over it.

But why revisit the Civil War after so long an absence and in a manner that necessitated extensive archival research? I had felt no strong impetus to return to my first love as I approached retirement. Indeed, when I reviewed my career in *Living Economic and Social History*, a book published in 2001 to celebrate seventy-five years of the Economic History Society, I declared myself a thoroughgoing economic historian and dismissed the idea of returning to military history in the future. However, I had taught an undergraduate course on the period 1630 to 1660 for the past thirty years, and whenever I revised my lecture notes on the 1640s using the most recent publications, the more my dissatisfaction grew as historians failed to engage head-on with what I had always seen as one of the three central issues of the decade – why Parliament rather than the king won the First Civil War – the others being why civil war broke out in 1642 and why the parliamentary coalition fell apart in 1647. I had also been irritated by the flagrant disregard for factual accuracy that marred some of the book-length studies of the war and by the failure to apply the tools of critical analysis to some of the most venerated primary and secondary sources. I hope that my irritation is not too obvious in the pages that follow. However, I do need to put it on record that my disquiet about published research is narrowly focused. I hold much of the work that others have published during my long absence in great respect, most particularly that of Martin Bennett and John Morrill, and I am looking forward with great anticipation to Richard Cust's new biography of Charles I.

It is not our intention to inflict on the world yet another analysis of the politics of the 1640s or a further detailed study of some aspect of military administration. We will also be deliberately avoiding certain well-trodden paths within the war itself, namely the support for one side or the other (or neither) in 1642, the Clubman uprisings of 1645, and the fighting in those parts of England and Wales that was not of direct significance to the operation or effectiveness of the field armies. All are important topics in their own right, but they are also to a greater or lesser extent tangential to a discussion of how the war ended when it did and how it did. Admittedly, Chapter I includes an account of the origins of the civil war, but this has been kept as succinct as possible so as not to restrict the space devoted to the main thrust of the book. It is almost certainly too short for its own good, but those who find what they perceive as gaps in our argument, or who bridle at our sweeping generalizations, should take note of the limited claims we make for it. Chapter II, on the other hand, is of fundamental importance as it provides the justification for the rest of the book. It draws together material that suggests strongly that a Roundhead victory was not inevitable in the summer of 1645 because by that stage in the war the supporters of Parliament enjoyed an overwhelming superiority in resources over those of the king. Indeed, it will be suggested that the disparity between the two sides may have been less pronounced then than it had been earlier in the war. The clear inference from this is that historians should be looking primarily at operational factors to explain why the war ended when it did. The remainder of the book therefore concentrates on two very important facets of military operations, strategy and battlefield tactics. I hope to cover other aspects in subsequent books.

The structure of the book may appear somewhat unusual, redolent more of past rather than current ways of presenting seventeenth-century English history. However, since the strategies employed by the king, the Parliamentarians and the Scots evolved as events unfolded, they can be explained only within a chronological framework in which description and analysis are combined. This is the custom in strategic studies of complex wars whatever the time period, but is doubly essential in the case of the Great Civil War given that historians still rely for their basic narrative on S.R. Gardiner's four-volume account published in the reign of Queen Victoria, which is unsatisfactory in a number of important respects. It is therefore an almost accidental feature of this book that it provides a revised version of the narrative of the fighting in England and Wales between 1642 and 1646, although it is one that has been constrained by the need to focus exclusively on the operations undertaken by the field armies.

Finally, I would like to thank a number of colleagues for their assistance in the inception, the research for and the writing of this book. I cannot overemphasize the importance of the direct and indirect contribution of my co-author Frank Jones. Frank was an undergraduate student of mine who then undertook part-time research under my supervision. The result was a thesis that increased understanding of the tactical innovations that enabled Parliament's generals to defeat the king's horse on the battlefield. A revised version of Frank's argument is presented in Chapters III and XXIII. This is his principal contribution to the book. Had he not been earning his living in Beijing for much of the last two years, he would have written far more. Second, tutorials with Frank kept my interest in the military history of the Civil War alive during the 1990s, when my own personal research had travelled furthest from it.

I also owe a considerable debt to my colleagues on the War Studies degree programme, John Buckley, Toby McLeod and Stephen Webley, who, as we talked during quiet moments in the battle of Normandy field trips, gave me the courage to don my armour for one more fight in the historical arena. I also owe a great debt to John Buckley for commenting on the military narrative chapters of the book, and to Drs Richard Cust and Peter Edwards, who have done the same for the two introductory chapters, although I apologize to them both for ignoring some of their suggestions. I would like to thank my university for providing me with a contract that allows me the time, and also the resources, to complete large-scale publications. Here I feel that I owe a bigger debt to my deans, Jean Gilkison and Geoff Hurd, and to my vice-chancellor, John Brookes, than they will acknowledge. I would also like to thank the staff of Birmingham Reference Library, the Bodleian Library, Oxford, the British Library, and the Wiltshire County Office in particular for their assistance and for their constructive responses to questions that were sometimes poorly phrased. I would have found it difficult to visit distant archives and battlefield sites without the help of my wife Jean's driving skills. Her reward is that research and writing keeps me out from under her feet. Finally, I owe an enormous amount to Brigadier Peter Young and to Professor Austin Woolrych for their help in my early years as a scholar, and for the inspiration that their writings and their enthusiasm for the Civil Wars have given me from then to the present day.

Malcolm Wanklyn

Illustrations

Maps

Figures

Abbreviations

BL   British Library
CJ   Journal of the House of Commons
CRO   County Record Office
CSP   Calendar of State Papers
HMC   Historical Manuscript Commission
LJ   Journal of the House of Lords
PRO   Public Record Office
TT   Thomason Tracts, British Library

PART I

Introduction

chapter 1

The nature and origins of the Great Civil War: a brief overview

The middle years of the seventeenth century witnessed the greatest concentration of armed violence in the recorded history of Britain and Ireland. More men died of wounds during the 1640s in these islands than in any other decade in our history, and one-third to a quarter of those between the ages of 16 and 60 were in arms for part or all of the time, whereas most of the major towns were garrisoned and a substantial proportion besieged.[1] For those of us who live in England and Wales, the central image is of epic battles between the Cavaliers, the supporters of King Charles I, and the Roundheads, who followed Oliver Cromwell. However, bitter internecine warfare rarely emerges out of nothing, and the First Civil War of 1642[2] to 1646, which ended in the comprehensive triumph of the king's enemies, was no exception. It was the second of three stages in the disintegration of the traditional political institutions of England and Wales and of the social control based on land ownership that underpinned them. The first stage was military defeat by the Scots in 1640 in the so-called Bishops' War and its constitutional aftermath, which are described briefly later in this chapter; the last the revolution of 1647, when ultimate power passed into the hands of the victorious Roundhead army. But that was not the end of the fighting. Associated with the bedding in of the revolution was a revival of internal conflict in England and Wales. This has always been seen as a second civil war. However, it was more than a civil war. Without the very strong prospect of a Scottish invasion, it is unlikely that Charles's English and Welsh supporters would have taken up arms on his behalf.

Quite recently, historians have begun describing the warfare that convulsed all but the south-eastern parts of the British archipelago between 1649 and 1652 as a third civil war. With this term we fundamentally disagree, as also with the emerging fashion for describing the whole of the fighting that took place between 1638 and 1652 as a British Civil War or Wars.[3] Although England and Wales, Scotland and Ireland were all ruled by Charles Stuart in 1638, they were separate kingdoms with separate governments, separate parliaments, separate religious traditions and separate legal systems, although the English government had considerable control over law making in Ireland. As there was not a united kingdom of Great Britain,[4] how could there be a British War? Also, there were significant differences between the three nations' experience of warfare between 1638 and 1652. What occurred in Ireland throughout the 1640s and beyond was more a war of liberation aimed at achieving freedom of religious practice for Roman Catholics and the end of English domination of Irish institutions than a civil war.

What happened in Scotland is less clear-cut, but it cannot be described as civil war. The campaigns of the Marquis of Montrose on the king's behalf during 1644 and 1645 were spearheaded by an invading force from Ireland, which received some military assistance from some of the Highland clans but very little support elsewhere in the country. In 1648, when the Duke of Hamilton's supporters carried out a major invasion of England, there was very little fighting in Scotland itself, despite considerable opposition to the undertaking, until after Hamilton had been defeated.[5] Scotland's experience can best be seen as a series of attempts to defend itself against its southern neighbour as first the king, then the republic, attempted to take control of its political institutions and subvert its religion.

In England, on the other hand, what was experienced between 1642 and 1648 was without question civil war. However, the wars of 1639–40 and 1649–52 were fought against other nations, first the Scots and then the Irish and the Scots separately.[6] Wales's experience of warfare throughout was very similar to that of England, that is intermittent civil war for six or so years fought over the same issues. This is not surprising, as the two countries had existed as a unitary state with identical or very similar political, administrative, legal and religious institutions for a hundred years. Moreover, at no stage is there any significant sign of the war being seen as an opportunity for a repressed people to throw off their English yoke.[7]

In the twentieth century, the debate between historians over the causes of the crisis of the 1640s was marked by considerable acrimony. However, a kind of truce now exists based on a shared understanding that it was multi-causal and not predestined by the inexorable march towards a classless society, parliamentary democracy or the freedom of the individual. Crisis there would probably have been in England at least whoever had been monarch, but an accidental factor, the personality of Charles I, is recognized as having had a profound effect on the immediate causes of the crisis and its subsequent course. The increasing cost of central government ran full pelt into the determination of taxpayers and their representatives in Parliament not to dig more deeply into their pockets. One response of English monarchs to this had been to attempt to raise money without Parliament's consent. This led to charges of abusing the law and trampling on the fundamental liberties of the subject, but Charles went much further than Queen Elizabeth or his father King James, and he reaped the consequences when he tried to fight a war against his Scottish subjects in the summer of 1640.

There were also two other areas of policy where previous monarchs had displayed a capacity to avoid confrontation. In England the incomplete reformation in religion of the sixteenth century, if not bound to result in conflict, was a potential powder keg if the monarchy, which had gained control over the Church in England without purging it of all elements of Roman Catholicism, did not pursue a religious policy at home that persecuted the Catholics while behaving with more circumspection towards those within the state Church who would have liked the Reformation to have gone further. The monarch was also expected to conduct a foreign policy that supported Protestantism overseas wherever it was threatened by international Roman Catholicism. Charles, however, broke with the past. He had given his enthusiastic support to a High Church faction in the English clergy, some of whose ideas about theology and the practice of religion could be confused with Roman Catholicism. In addition, Charles had given a measure of toleration to English Catholics while allowing his bishops to harry, if not persecute, Protestants who refused to obey the rules of the Church to the last letter. He had also pursued a foreign policy that favoured Catholic Spain in its war against the Protestant Dutch.[8]

Second, monarchs had to take account of the different histories, institutions and cultures of the multiple kingdoms of the British archipelago when introducing innovations in government. Here caution and playing the long game were crucial to success. Charles, however, tended to disregard the example of his predecessors, most particularly that set by his father, and to push ahead regardless, in the absolute conviction that it was his subjects' religious duty to obey his commands as much as God's, by whose will he was king of England, Scotland and Ireland. Moreover, his reputation in all his dominions for duplicity when unable to browbeat opposition or overcome it by force meant that when he did eventually give way under pressure it was seen as mere subterfuge. The king's reputation for double-dealing, combined with fears of Catholic influence on him through his queen, Henrietta Maria, and some of his courtiers, not only helped to precipitate the crisis but also made it more difficult to resolve at every stage, as it was widely believed that in the future he would renege on any concession he had made, given the opportunity.[9]

Trouble began in 1637, when Charles attempted to bring about uniformity in the practices of the Scottish church by royal decree and against the advice of many of his Scottish ministers and advisers. A new prayer book, prepared in England largely by English theologians, aroused grave fears both for the purity of Presbyterianism, the more radical form of Protestantism that had taken very strong root in the Lowlands and parts of the Highlands, and for Scottish political and constitutional independence from England. It also lit the fires of nationalism among all classes, from the servant girl who threw a stool at the minister in St Giles's cathedral to the leading members of the Scottish nobility. Attempts by the king's envoy to Scotland, the Marquis of Hamilton, to achieve a negotiated solution over the next year or so failed. A military confrontation in 1639, for which neither side was fully prepared, was followed by outright war in the following summer. The Scots were able to raise an army and invade England before Charles had assembled enough troops at York to meet them on equal terms. They crossed the Tyne after defeating a small force of English infantry and cavalry at Newburn, and occupied Northumberland and Durham. However, unlike almost all their predecessors, the Scottish soldiers did not rape and pillage. They also did all they could to reduce casualties by allowing the detachment defeated at Newburn and the garrison of Newcastle to escape across the Tees without serious harassment. Such behaviour was intended to assist opposition to the war in England, which was apparent in the reluctance of the English Parliament that Charles had summoned in the spring to vote taxes to help finance the war, and in the subsequent behaviour of his subjects when he tried to collect taxes without Parliament's consent.[10] It was also evident in the slowness with which Charles's army had come together (raised as it was by the lord lieutenants and their deputies, who had themselves sat in the recent Parliament or helped to choose the members of the House of Commons) and in the lawless behaviour of some of the troops on their way to York.[11]

Unwilling to use his apology for an army for fear that it would disintegrate, the king was obliged to negotiate a truce in September 1640, the financial clauses of which made it essential for him to call a new Parliament to vote taxes to pay for the cost of maintaining both armies. This the new Parliament did, but it also tried and executed the king's chief minister, the Earl of Strafford, began legal proceedings against High Church clergy and other royal officials, and gained Charles's consent to a number of laws restricting royal power over taxation and over the length and timing of parliamentary sessions. The king gave way reluctantly, but he had no option. If he sent Parliament packing, the Scottish army would brush aside his own army, advance towards London and impose greater concessions on him by force. In such circumstances, civil war was most unlikely provided that the Scottish leadership did not lose control of its troops. There was no sign yet of a 'king's party' ready to fight for him, and no reason for any of his English subjects to take up arms against him.

However, for Charles matters began to improve from August 1641 onwards. A peace treaty with the Scots signed in the late summer was followed by the disbandment of both armies. As a result, the king and those of his English subjects who wanted further constitutional and religious changes were on level terms insofar as military muscle was concerned. The king was also gaining support. He benefited from attacks by Protestant radicals in Parliament and the country on two fundamental aspects of state religion as established in England and Wales in Queen Elizabeth's reign, the Book of Common Prayer and the government of the Church by bishops. Moreover, under the influence of new advisers, he had begun to promote Low Church clergy to vacant bishoprics and to endorse Protestantism overseas by betrothing his eldest daughter to the son of the ruler of the Netherlands. At the same time, massed demonstrations outside the Palace of Westminster, the spread of lawlessness and growing disorder in the Church as radicals and traditionalists struggled for control of the pulpit were highlighting the advantages of strong monarchical government.

However, powerful individuals and groupings in Parliament, the city of London and some other parts of England were determined to make the English Church more Protestant and to restrict the king's powers still further by wresting executive authority from him. Their programme was set out in the Grand Remonstrance, a lengthy document debated most acrimoniously in the House of Commons in November and only approved by a small majority. Constitutionally, the crucial clauses were those that would have deprived the king of his rights to appoint ministers without consulting Parliament and to enjoy unfettered command and control over the militia of the realm, a term that embraced not merely the army and the navy in time of war, but also the home defence forces in the counties and towns of England and Wales, the so-called trained bands.

What would have happened had external factors not intervened can only be a matter of conjecture, although the longer the king resisted attacks on his remaining powers and the more vociferous the religious radicals became, the more likely was the consensus in Parliament and the country to unravel totally and a king's party to emerge. However, events in Ireland brought the matter of sovereignty to a head in a most acute form. A Catholic revolt had broken out in October; thousands of Protestants were dead and thousands more refugees; an army had therefore to be raised at once to put down the rebellion. Traditionally, English armies were raised by the king and commanded by his nominees, but to allow the new army to take orders from Charles was seen as foolhardy by his opponents in Parliament and the country. To force him to agree that the new army should be under Parliament's control, rumours were put about that the queen was privy to some aspects of the uprising and might therefore be charged with high treason. It was probably this that pushed the king into attempting to arrest six of his leading opponents in Parliament on 5th January 1642 on the grounds that they had been in treasonable correspondence with the leaders of the revolution in Scotland.[12] When the attempt failed, he and Henrietta Maria quickly left London. She sought safety in France, while he remained in the Home Counties until he had managed to secure his eldest son's escape from London.

Thus central to the transition from the first stage of the crisis to the second was a struggle for control of the armed forces. For the next six months, King Charles and his opponents in the Commons and the Lords moved towards war over this fundamental issue of sovereignty, each hoping that the other would back down through political pressure or the threat of overwhelming military force. During this period, the king was able to convince many of his English and Welsh subjects that he stood for defence of the traditional constitution and Church doctrine and government as established by Queen Elizabeth and her first Parliament in 1559, and that his authority alone could stop the slide towards social and religious anarchy. The opposition at Westminster on the other hand (from now onwards often described for convenience's sake as Parliament, although they comprised only about two-thirds of the Lower House and less than a third of the Upper) was determined to deprive him of almost all his remaining constitutional powers, as he could not be trusted to exert them in the interests of Protestantism and the safety and security of the realm. This attracted support, as did their undertaking to oversee a programme of religious reform, although how far this was to go and how fast was unclear.[13] In the end, to the surprise of Parliament if not the king, both sides attracted sufficient support for civil war to become a reality.

Notes

1 This is a paraphrase of the first sentences of John Morrill's introduction to *The Civil Wars: A Military History of England, Scotland and Ireland 1638–1660* (J. Kenyon and J. Ohlmeyer (eds)).

2 We see it as an unfortunate term, as there had been several civil wars during the reigns of the Plantagenet kings. We prefer the Great Civil War, as it lasted much longer than the rest, even the Wars of the Roses, which was a succession of little civil wars spread over more than thirty years.

3 e.g. Kenyon and Ohlmeyer, *The Civil Wars*, 32, and Bennett, *The Civil Wars in Britain and Ireland*, xi lines 6–8; but see the authoritative and incisive discussion in Gaunt, *The British Wars*.

4 When he succeeded to the throne of England, James I had tried to get accepted the notion that he was king of Great Britain, but legal opinion held that creating a united kingdom by royal decree would invalidate the existing laws of England and Scotland. He had 'retreated from the attempt by 1607' (Russell, 'James VI and I', 159–62).

5 Edward Furgel in Kenyon and Ohlmeyer, *The Civil Wars*, 55–64.

6 Admittedly there was an abortive uprising against the republic in parts of Lancashire in 1651, but the invading Scottish army received very little assistance from supporters of the monarchy elsewhere in England and Wales.

7 Roland Hutton has discovered what appear to be nationalist sentiments expressed in South Wales right at the end of the First Civil War, when an invasion by Parliamentary troops threatened, but the evidence is problematic and the call to arms, if that was what it was, was ineffective. (Hutton, *The Royalist War Effort*, 195).

8 Foreign affairs could also cause tension between Charles's kingdoms. War with France in the 1620s, for example, caused resentment in Scotland because of that country's close historical and trading links with France.

9 The most recent lengthy summing up of the secondary literature on the origins of the crisis is in Young, *Charles I*, but the analysis here relies heavily on Russell, *Causes of the English Civil War.*

10 Indeed, there is evidence of contacts between the leaders of the opposition in England and discontented members of the Scottish aristocracy from about 1635.

11 Fissell, *The Bishops' Wars*, 59–60; MacInnes, *Charles I*, 197.

12 This incident is usually described as the Arrest of the Five Members, but that was merely the number of members of the House of Commons named in the indictment. There was also a sixth man, who sat in the House of Lords, Lord Mandeville, the future Earl of Manchester (Gardiner, *Constitutional Documents*, 236–7).

13 Young, *Charles I*, 147–53; Ashton, *The English Civil War*, 140–56; Fletcher, *Outbreak of the Civil War*, 283–321, 408–18; Russell, *Fall of the British Monarchies*, 465–6.

chapter II

How was the Great Civil War won?

The intense interest in the Great Civil War is clearly shown by the avalanche of books devoted to it over the past forty years. At least a dozen new narratives of the war have been published, as well as detailed studies of most of the major battles and some of the principal commanders; the administrative machinery put in place at local, regional and national level to support and sustain the war effort has been thoroughly investigated insofar as the sources allow, and its effectiveness assessed; and the intellectual preoccupations of the second half of the twentieth century from quantification through women's rights to postmodernism have opened up new insights into how the war was experienced by those living at the time. Given that the research underpinning this body of work has involved historians in picking through the archives with the finest of toothcombs, it goes without saying that more is now known about almost every aspect of the war than was the case in 1960.

However, discussion of the central issue – why Parliament won and the king lost – has been very restrained, and it would not be too wide of the mark to say that Clio's chariot has ground to a halt with one wheel stuck firmly in the rut of a determinist explanation formulated in the distant past, namely that Parliament's victory was inevitable because of its overwhelming superiority in resources. This view is at its clearest in textbook-type studies,[1] where the factors listed are very similar to those that one of us learned at school in the 1950s from reading books written in the 1930s: the navy; a preponderance in military supplies of all sorts; the assistance of a Scottish army 20,000 strong from January 1644 onwards; undisputed control over London and the wealthy and populous south and east of England; and above all else the wit to learn how to put such assets to best use, culminating in 1645 in the establishment of a national army, the New Model, which achieved decisive victory within three months of its formation.[2]

More specialist studies published over the last fifteen years have revealed flaws in some facets of the determinist model, but they fight shy of discussing why the war ended when it did in a Royalist defeat. Comments tend to be tucked away in subordinate clauses but, despite being aware of some of the weaknesses in the determinist case, their underlying message is still largely determinist in flavour.[3] Barratt's *Cavaliers* is the only major publication to incorporate a full discussion. His conclusion is also unremittingly determinist, but this is not surprising as he focuses on the weaknesses and strengths of the Royalists, taking no real account of the other side's political divisions and administrative problems, which were becoming increasingly apparent in late 1644 and the first half of 1645.[4] The first objective of this chapter is therefore to submit the determinist model to rigorous reappraisal, giving due weighting to the resources possessed by both sides.

There is no doubt that control of the navy was important in helping Parliament not to lose the war in the first eighteen months, but the role it played in the decisive 1645 campaign was indirect at best.[5] Without the navy to transport troops and supplies to beleaguered ports, Parliament would almost certainly have lost control of Plymouth in the winter of 1643, which would have freed several thousand Royalist troops to take part in a formidable attack on London from the south and west in early 1644. Hull may also have surrendered in the autumn of 1643 without supplies brought in by sea, thus removing the sole obstacle to the king's Northern army invading East Anglia, which was not only second to London in supplying the enemy cause with taxation revenue and recruits for the army but also the capital's principal source of basic foodstuffs. However, as a European statesman remarked several centuries later, the English navy did not run on wheels. As a result, its impact on warfare on land was strictly limited even in the southwestern peninsula, surrounded as it was by the sea. In August 1643, the Earl of Warwick, Parliament's high admiral, was unable to force his ships through to Exeter and relieve the besieged garrison because of Royalist heavy artillery at Topsham. In the following year he was unable to supply the field army of the Earl of Essex, the Parliamentarians' lord general, when it became trapped in Cornwall, and in 1645 the navy was unable either to assist in any major way in the successive attempts to relieve Taunton or to intercept infantry regiments sent from South Wales to Somerset by sea after the battle of Naseby to reinforce the last Royalist field army.[6]

Moreover, the navy had limited success on its own element because of the small number of ships it could deploy and the huge area of coastline it had to patrol. As a result, it was only intermittently successful in blocking communications with Ireland and was singularly unsuccessful in preventing troops leaving there to reinforce the Royalist war effort in the northwest and the southwest of England between November 1643 and January 1644. It failed to intercept Queen Henrietta Maria either when she set out from the Continent for the north of England in January 1643 or when she returned there from Falmouth in June 1644. If she had fallen into Parliament's hands on either occasion, Charles would have been under intolerable pressure to sue for peace, as the charge of complicity in the Irish uprising still hung over her head. Finally, despite the occasional success, the navy was unable to stem the flow of military supplies from the Continent in the last two years of the war, without which the king's armies could not have continued the fight. Lack of gunpowder had almost forced Charles to abandon the south of England in May 1643, and it had cost him what might have been the decisive victory at Newbury in September, but from then onwards, with many of the West Country ports under his control, it proved impossible for Parliament's fleet to stop the flow of imports from the Continent. As a result, Charles's armies were very well provided with gunpowder in the 1644 and 1645 campaigns. Despite expending large quantities in the storming of Leicester and at the battle of Naseby, there were still forty full barrels in the king's artillery train when it was captured after the battle. Moreover, shiploads continued to arrive in the west coast ports until almost the end of the war. As a result, when the last battle of the war in the southwest was fought at Torrington in February 1646, the Royalist general Lord Hopton had fifty barrels of gunpowder in reserve in addition to that which had been distributed to the troops before the fighting began. Only in the case of the loss of Lancashire in August 1644 was shortage of powder a possible reason for military failure. Moreover, enemy forces could suffer from similar problems of supply. In June 1645, the corps of the New Model Army that had relieved Taunton, unable to face Royalist troops in the open because of a lack of ammunition, was forced to shelter behind the town's fortifications.

The same argument applies to armour, weapons and other military supplies. In 1642 and for much of 1643 the king's field army was indifferently equipped. However, the Royalist armies that took the field in 1645 were very well supplied, as shown by what was captured on the battlefield and in their army bases, such as Shrewsbury and Bridgwater, when they fell into Parliamentary hands. As late as February 1646, the New Model Army cavalry found it difficult to pursue Hopton's army through the streets of Torrington because of the huge number of muskets the Royalist soldiers had dropped as they ran.[7] The quality, as opposed to the quantity, of the weapons and supplies the two sides possessed is more problematic. Edwards's recent work has shown how well equipped Parliament's armies were in the last year of the war, but at the same time he suggests that the Royalists also achieved a considerable level of success. Moreover, being well armed and well horsed was not a guarantee of success in battle. Sir Arthur Haselrig's 'lobsters', so-called because they wore full suits of armour to the knee, performed badly at Roundway Down in July 1643, while a London journal, commenting on the poor performance of Eastern Association horse at Naseby, described them as 'better armed than hearted'.[8] There is thus no evidence whatsoever to suggest that Charles lost the Civil War in 1645 through lack of military supplies.

The contribution of the Scottish army to victory in 1645 was similar to that of the navy. Parliament might have lost the war in 1644 without direct Scottish military assistance (although the actual contribution of the Scottish army to the victory at Marston Moor was a matter of dispute at the time and has been ever since), and the military experience of Scottish professional soldiers was an extremely valuable asset to all three of its field armies throughout 1643 and 1644. By the spring of 1645, however, the Earl of Leven's field army was probably only half the size it had been a year earlier. Starved of resources and worried that the king would increase the threat to his rear by sending troops from England into Scotland to assist the Marquis of Montrose, Leven withdrew his army from Yorkshire into the Eden valley, where it could easily combine with the infantry regiments besieging Carlisle to resist a Royalist incursion. As a result, despite hurriedly marching south during June, the Scottish army was still over sixty miles away when the battle of Naseby was fought. It then moved into the Welsh borderland to prevent the troops that had survived the battle and escaped into South Wales from attacking the New Model Army's rear as it advanced into the southwest of England. However, not only was it unable to prevent their escaping to join the king's forces elsewhere in England, it also abandoned the siege of Hereford when the troops it had failed to intercept returned to relieve the city. Moreover, Scottish officers were much less important to the Parliamentary war effort in 1645. Although some continued to play a role in the provincial armies, those who were offered commissions in the New Model withdrew before it could take the field. This was largely because the Scottish leadership resented the fact that the New Model was to include officers who wanted religious toleration in England and Wales for a range of Protestant opinion, not the enforcement of a state religion based on Scottish Presbyterianism.

Troops from Ireland have been seen as playing a similar but much less successful part in support of the king, but their true role has been obscured by exaggeration. Malcolm has claimed that the Royalist war effort could only be sustained from 1644 onwards because of the arrival from Ireland of over 20,000 troops, some English but mostly Irish, who had been released for service in England and Wales by a truce concluded with the rebels by the king's representatives the previous summer. This number is a gross exaggeration caused by uncritical reliance on Parliamentary propaganda. We calculate that only about 11,000/12,000 men crossed the Irish Sea, somewhat larger than the figure recently proposed by Barratt but not that much smaller than the number of Scottish troops that fought at Marston Moor.[9] However, although they arrived in different ports at different times and were initially divided between four Royalist armies, their impact on the fighting in England in 1644 was far from negligible. For example, without them Prince Rupert would have found it impossible to organise the major expedition to relieve York that culminated in the battle of Marston Moor.[10] On the other hand, in the decisive campaign of the war, that of 1645, the contribution of troops from Ireland to the king's cause was almost as limited as that of soldiers from Scotland to Parliament's.[11] Admittedly there were at least five 'Irish' infantry regiments and one cavalry regiment at Naseby, but the losses the infantry had sustained at the battles of Nantwich, Marston Moor and Montgomery in the previous year make it likely that most of the rank and file were newly pressed men from the Welsh borderland rather than veterans of the war in Ireland.

Neither side in the Great Civil War obtained direct support from other European powers, although both received extensive indirect support in the form of military supplies and experienced infantry, cavalry and artillery officers, both mercenaries and volunteers. However, rank-and-file soldiers from Europe appear to have been rare. Despite Henrietta Maria's influence, there was only a single regiment of French volunteers in the whole of King Charles's armies.[12] However, her influence in Europe was such that she was able to assemble a very large quantity of arms and ammunition in the Netherlands and convey it to Yorkshire in January 1643. In this undertaking she received vital assistance from the Dutch fleet, which forced a squadron of English ships to desist after it began bombarding the house where she was sheltering after landing at Bridlington. A Dutch vessel also helped her to return to the Continent from Falmouth in 1644. This support probably owed more to the alliance between her brother, the king of France, and the Dutch in the war against Spain than to friendly relations established by the marriage treaty between the House of Orange and the House of Stuart in 1641.[13]

Parliament's control over London and its suburbs has always been seen as one of the strongest, if not the strongest, element in the determinists' case. The benefits were numerous, but the most significant were its wealth, derived largely from overseas trade, which enabled its citizens not only to pay high taxes to support the war effort but also to provide loans against the security provided by future tax revenues; its population of over 300,000, which made weapons and supplied uniforms and were a convenient source of recruits for Parliament's armies; and its well-trained and well-motivated part-time militia, the trained bands, which reinforced those armies at crucial points during the war.[14] In our opinion, London was of immediate and continuing value to the Parliamentary cause in terms of men, money and morale. In the summer of 1642, Londoners volunteered to fill the ranks of the Earl of Essex's army. The city raised more men that winter, in April and August 1643, and again, more grudgingly, in April 1644. It also helped Sir William Waller to build up a new army in September 1643 after he had lost his first one at the battle of Roundway Down. Moreover, without the support of London's trained bands Essex would not have been able to relieve the besieged city of Gloucester in September 1643 nor Sir William Waller successfully defend Sussex, Surrey and Kent against Lord Hopton's army between November 1643 and March 1644. However, the problems of conducting campaigns with regiments that were only available for fixed periods of time before others replaced them became blatantly obvious during the summer, when they ruined Waller's army as a fighting force. In 1645 London's military muscle was of less direct significance, as the trained bands took part in neither the Naseby nor the Langport campaign. However, Sir Thomas

Fairfax drew on its male population to fill the infantry regiments of the New Model Army, although this time with impressed men, not volunteers.[15]

The steadfastness of the support provided by the city's financial elite was a powerful reassurance to the leadership of the two Houses of Parliament throughout the war. So also was the unflinching loyalty of most of London's population, particularly in times of acute danger such as November 1642 and August 1643. However, factional strife within Parliament and the city fed on one another, causing tensions and mistrust that reached a peak when the military situation deteriorated or appeared to deteriorate, as in June and July 1643, November 1644, and early June 1645.[16] Also, the city corporation used its financial power at times for political ends. This is best illustrated by its behaviour towards the Earl of Essex's army from early 1643 onwards. The reaction against the unrestrained enthusiasm of the previous year for what was primarily an army of Londoners had its roots in Essex's failure to deliver a decisive victory at the battle of Edgehill in October or at Turnham Green in November. A powerful group in the corporation and in the city as a whole had come round to the view, which hardened as the year progressed, that the lord general and his close associates would prefer a negotiated peace with the king to outright victory and were waging war with that in mind. They were even more suspicious of Essex's professional officers, who often lacked ideological commitment to the cause and were seen as wanting to prolong the war so as to line their own pockets. Instead of indulging them, London's rulers began to target their resources towards those who appeared to want to achieve an outright victory, first Sir William Waller and then the army of the Eastern Association under the Earl of Manchester. There is therefore some justice in Essex's claims in the summer of 1643 and in the spring of 1644 that his army could not take the offensive because it was being starved of recruits and military equipment while others were not.[17]

Another advantage that Parliament is said to have enjoyed over the king was that by the end of 1643 it had put in place a system for supplying its armies with money, men and materials, and that this worked largely because of the wealth of the southeast of England. The king, on the other hand, was supposedly unable to put a similar system in place in the part of the country he controlled because of its relative poverty.[18] The Eastern Association has been seen as providing the best example of a successful system of military administration in the provinces, and this is true in many respects. It was able to raise a completely new army during 1643, which, after an inauspicious start, fought very well indeed and for most of the time beyond the bounds of the region that raised and maintained it. However, it was the vagaries of war, not just wealth, that help to explain why the king had no equivalent to the Eastern Association. People on both sides claimed that the counties of the southwest of England conquered by the Royalists in the summer of 1643 had the potential to do for the king's cause what the Eastern Association was doing for Parliament's.[19] However, an important reason why an effective Western Association did not come into being was that Somerset and Dorset and, to a lesser extent Devon and Cornwall, had their administrative machinery and their economic life and infrastructure disrupted by invasion in 1644 and on several occasions in 1645.[20] Parliament was fearful that the Eastern Association would suffer in a similar manner but, although the Royalist high command on several occasions came very close to ordering a full-scale invasion, it never came to the point of doing so.

However, it is also now reasonably clear that the difference between the two sides was less than previously thought. Royalist efforts to raise money on a sustained and regular basis achieved a considerable measure of success in some areas and, more importantly, until the autumn of 1645 the Royalist field armies received sufficient food and pay to maintain their battle-worthiness while campaigning.[21] There are also numerous examples on both sides of the effectiveness of administrative systems being severely hampered by demarcation disputes between competing jurisdictions compounded by personal and ideological differences.[22] Moreover, Parliament found that administrative bodies that were successful at county or regional level were not necessarily as committed to supporting the war effort at the national level. Most taxation that was raised locally for the war was spent locally. Morrill, for example, calculated that 98 percent of the revenue raised in Cheshire for the Parliamentary cause was spent in Cheshire, while Warwickshire sent nothing to London until 1645 at the earliest. Similarly, the king at Oxford received less supplies from the provinces than he would have wished, particularly after the end of the first year of the war.[23]

Both sides also found difficulty in persuading regional authorities to play a full role in supporting strategy at the national level. Regional commanders tended to put the interest of their own part of the country first, which, after all, paid them and supplied them with food and other essentials. In September 1644, a strategy to prevent the king returning to Oxford from the West Country before the end of the campaigning season was luckily wrong-footed by the Earl of Manchester, one of whose arguments was the need to protect his regional association, although his most important objection was almost certainly a more fundamental one. A year earlier, attempts by the Earl of Essex to block the passage of arms convoys between the north of England and the south were frustrated by intra-regional rivalries combined with lethargy. The Royalist high command suffered even more severely from regional insubordination. The failure of the Northern army to invade the Eastern Association in the late summer of 1643 and disrupt the Earl of Manchester's administrative arrangements before they could take root was because the Earl of Newcastle's lukewarm support hardened into outright opposition when he learned that his Yorkshire regiments would not march until Hull had been captured. In 1645, the Prince of Wales's council played a significant, if indirect, role in bringing about the king's final defeat by disputing orders for the army it controlled to join the main field army in the Midlands.[24]

A very recent addition to the determinist argument is the allegation that the success of the Parliamentary system of military administration, and the culture embedded in the Parliamentary cause, enabled its soldiers and officials to retain the loyalty of the civilian population in the areas they controlled by resolving conflicts when they occurred. On the Royalist side, however, the inadequacies of the administrative system, and the concept of obedience based on hierarchy that underpinned it, resulted in irreconcilable divisions between soldiers and civilians. As a result, the king's forces had to resort to plunder, thus totally alienating the civilian population in the areas they controlled. By 1645, non-cooperation had turned to violence, which was met by yet more violence. As a result, the king's officials found it increasingly difficult to pay, recruit and provision their armies, which affected the armies' discipline. However, Hutton has argued with regard to Wales and the Welsh borderland in the spring of 1645 that brute force was a most effective instrument for obtaining men, money and supplies, while Smith has pointed out that Parliament's efficiency in gathering taxes 'produced enormous resentment amongst the civilian population'. However, Hughes has replied by firmly restating the determinist argument, claiming that by 1645 at the latest 'the vicious circle of war weariness and military defeat in their heartlands' had damaged the Royalist cause beyond repair.[25] The issue of allegiance, its shifting patterns and its real effect on the decisive campaign of the war, is therefore a disputed area that is very worthy of consideration in a later publication. All we can do for the present is to survey the wider picture as it has emerged since the 1960s.

In the Edgehill campaign both armies appear to have consisted very largely of volunteers,[26] but the initial popularity of king or Parliament in a town or county did not necessarily continue once the war was under way. It can even be argued that in the first months of the war it was armed force that mattered, not sentiment, in determining allegiance, and that vocal and material support for the first armed body to appear in an area may have been no more than a tactical ploy designed to prevent its towns and villages being plundered. Moreover, those who volunteered in 1642 were not necessarily enthusiastic Parliamentarians or Royalists but may have been induced to join the army by threats and promises, the nature and extent of which we can never be fully aware.[27] Thereafter, whoever controlled a patch of country tended to keep it unless evicted by enemy troops. Nowhere did an uprising against an occupying power result in anything other than the short-term expulsion of the occupying force, as, for example, in Kent in 1643, at Barnstaple in 1644, in the Fenlands in both years, and in the Welsh borderland counties in early 1645.[28] Finally, there are signs that enthusiasm was a passing mood, which was soon followed by indifference or hostility caused by the experience of war, particularly in areas that had direct experience of fighting.[29] When the military reconquered a part of the country known to have been sympathetic to their cause in the early months of the war but that had then been lost to the enemy, they were often disappointed by the response of the civilian population, as the Earl of Essex found when he invaded Devon and Somerset in 1644 and Prince Rupert to a lesser extent when he overran Lancashire earlier in the same year.[30]

However, what is really significant in all of this is not who supported whom and when, but the relative success the two sides achieved in putting armies into the field at the start of the decisive 1645 campaigning season. Surprisingly, the Royalists appear to have achieved more success in their recruiting operations in the winter and early spring of 1645 than at any time since the autumn of 1642. Of the 20,000–25,000 men the king could have had in his field army for the Naseby campaign, at least 2,000, and possibly as many as a quarter, had been raised since October. Sir Thomas Fairfax, on the other hand, although apparently facing an easier task given the high population of southern and eastern England, found difficulty in filling the ranks of his New Model Army infantry regiments.[31] Troops raised via impressments came in slowly because he could not, or would not, employ brute force to speed up the process. He was therefore reliant on the strengths and weaknesses of the administrative system that Parliament had put in place.[32] As a result, we do not find Hughes's argument at all convincing.

Finally, what of the New Model Army itself? The claim that it alone won the decisive victories in June and July 1645 is correct in one respect, as it received little assistance from other Parliamentary troops that took part in the campaign. At Naseby, the ancillary cavalry's activities were confined to mopping up operations, whereas at Langport the Western army failed to take part in the engagement because it was badly deployed. However, it has been argued that victory at Naseby in particular owed more to Royalist mistakes before the battle took place than to any exceptional qualities displayed by the New Model Army. It has also been implied that attributing Parliament's decisive victories to the New Model lays the historian open to the charge of hindsight, that is taking into account knowledge of a reputation that had yet to be acquired. With this we do not wholly agree. Many of the New Model foot soldiers were men impressed during the spring; some of the veterans resented being placed under new commanders; and the performance of some of the troops at Naseby was rather disappointing.

However, although many of the infantry were new recruits, this was not true of the cavalry. It comprised the best units in the army of the Eastern Association, which had been victorious at every engagement in which they had fought apart from the second battle of Newbury, and the best regiments of the Earl of Essex's army, whose quality had steadily improved during the course of 1644. The body of horse on the right wing under Cromwell's direct command, which won the battle of Naseby and broke Goring's army at Langport, consisted almost exclusively of regiments that had been victorious at Marston Moor. Yet what is really significant is that the king failed to concentrate his best cavalry in the same manner. The regiments that worsted Waller's army at Cropredy Bridge and turned the tide at the second battle of Newbury were in Somerset when Naseby was fought. Over three-quarters of the force facing the New Model cavalry was made up either of regiments routed at Marston Moor or of garrison horse with limited experience of set-piece battles.[33]

We conclude that the advantages that both sides enjoyed in terms of resources ebbed and flowed as the war progressed and were not overwhelmingly weighted in Parliament's favour by the start of the 1645 campaigning season. Investigation into why the war ended when it did, and not before or after, must therefore concentrate on the ways in which both sides used the resources they had at their disposal between July 1642 and July 1645. Here generalship is one obvious key factor, and in some respects it is now possible to make more informed comparisons of the strengths and weaknesses of the commanders on both sides than it was in the 1960s. Studies of Prince Rupert have focused on aspects of generalship that went beyond commanding troops in the field, but the picture that persists is still a flawed one with his skills as an administrator and an inspirational leader of men being offset by his failings as a politician and a trainer of cavalry.[34] The king, on the other hand, has been commended for his generalship in the campaigns in southern England in the summer and autumn of 1644.[35] However, Sir Thomas Fairfax's reputation, refurbished by Woolrych and Burne and Young in about 1960, has received little attention since, and he still lacks a full-scale military biography based on primary research, as do Newcastle, Manchester and George Goring. Snow's biography of the Earl of Essex has done little to alter the traditional assessment that he was personally brave and stoical on the battlefield, but lethargic, lacking in initiative and caught up in the stately quadrille of warfare as practised in the Netherlands in the first thirty years of the seventeenth century, where he had learned his craft. Adair's excellent account of the life of Waller has in some respects reduced 'William the Conqueror's' reputation as a commander of large bodies of troops, whereas Edgar's biography of Lord Hopton is overly dependent on 'friendly' sources, namely Hopton's own accounts of his major campaigns and the works of his friend Edward Hyde, Earl of Clarendon. Finally, although Oliver Cromwell has been the subject of at least twelve full-length biographies since 1960, all focus very heavily on his political career.

If works published since 1960 allow a more informed, if incomplete, assessment of the generalship on both sides to be made, the same cannot be said of strategy. The only recent accounts of this aspect of warfare are a few pages in *Cavaliers*, which are largely based on secondary sources; some comments in a study of the New Model Army, which cover only the period from April 1645 onwards; and a chronological account by an American scholar whose expertise lies in the contemporary conflicts in Scotland and Ireland.[36] What is remarkable about all recent discussions of strategy is the reverence still shown towards S.R. Gardiner's *The Great Civil War*, written well over a hundred years ago. Gardiner's book was a masterpiece for its time, but only the greatest historical classics do not have a sell-by date, and *The Great Civil War* is not one of these. Christopher Hill was right to praise

Gardiner for his attention 'to getting the facts right and rightly arranged',[37] while his battle narratives are quite sound given that he did not have access to the full range of sources. However, his account of the strategies pursued by both sides owes more to the shortcomings and enthusiasms of armchair generalship than to his skills as a professional historian. In the first place, his coverage of strategy is inconsistent over time, a sure sign of the amateur enthusiast who focuses only on those things that interest him. For instance, he makes no attempt to explain the Earl of Essex's strategy in the first campaign of the war. Second, his judicious reading and weighing of the historical evidence deserts him at times, the best example being his firm belief that the king intended to attack London from three directions in the summer of 1643.[38] Third, his attention to detail is less sure than in his political narrative.[39] Finally, his interpretation of the fighting in the Great Civil War, and his assessment of the men associated with it, is distorted by hero worship of Oliver Cromwell. Regrettably, this Achilles heel in Gardiner's scholarship has not been widely noticed. Political historians who have followed him, reassured by his command of the chronology in the volumes covering the period 1603 to 1642, and not themselves particularly interested in military history, have reproduced his errors parrot fashion down the years to the confusion of us all.

On the other hand, research into battlefield tactics, largely undertaken by historians who do not work in universities, has made considerable progress, but what is in the public domain is still rather bitty. Much more is known about military science and battlefield theory in the mid-seventeenth century through the intensive study of the books published at the time or soon afterwards, and also about the way that such theory did or did not inform the ways in which generals waged war. It is also clear that neither side enjoyed superiority in military technology. Such developments, as for example the use of mines in siege warfare, introduced by Prince Rupert were quickly copied.[40] However, recent reinterpretations of the major battles of the Great Civil War, although full of invigorating insights, have tended to see the way forward as being to extend and elaborate the battlefield narratives using newly discovered archaeological data and neglected written sources.[41] This approach can be of great value, but only after such sources have been critically evaluated. Until a new piece of historical data has been thoroughly appraised, nobody can be sure of its true value or significance. Similar types of weakness are also apparent in the ways in which well-known texts are used by a much larger range of writers. Not only is it odd that

Clarendon's *History of the Great Rebellion* continues to be regarded as an impartial source of evidence about the Royalists' conduct of the war despite the devastating critique of it published by Sir Charles Firth over a century ago, it is also amazing that other narratives, such as those written by Hopton, Walker, Wogan and Sprigg, have not been similarly evaluated.[42] Historians also need to find out more about the interdependence of sources, but these interesting lines of enquiry unfortunately cannot be pursued in the present book.

To conclude, the partial collapse of determinist explanations of the outcome of the Great Civil War makes it most important for the purely military aspects of the war to be dusted down and reappraised rather than being allowed to remain in the corner like discarded toys. The principal purpose of this book is to begin the process of re-evaluation by discussing strategy and battlefield tactics within the parameters described in the Preface. Accounts of the major engagements will be kept short, with the principal focus being on their strategic significance and on the crucial tactical decisions taken by the opposing generals. However, this does not mean that we believe that detailed battle narratives are not worthy of being included in the mainstream of mid-seventeenth-century studies. In fact we hold the contrary view. In this postmodernist age there should be no prioritization or 'sniffiness', with some aspects of historical investigation being regarded as canonical and others not. By this yardstick, filling gaps in the order of battle or identifying exactly when and where an incident took place is in no way inferior to adding detail of a similar nature to the political narrative. I therefore intend to give battlefield narratives the attention they deserve in a future book.

Notes

1 The most outright determinist is Seel in *The English Wars and Republic*, 32–8, a book seemingly intended for school sixth form students and first-year undergraduates.

2 These points are taken from Aylmer, *Struggle for the Constitution*, 122–9, and Hill, *The Century of Revolution*, 121–2, both published in the very early 1960s.

3 Bennett, *The Civil Wars*, 167, 382n; Bennett, *The English Civil War*, 63, 64, 65; Gaunt, *British Wars*, 55; Kenyon and Ohlmeyer, *The Civil Wars*, 141–2.

4 Barrett, *Cavaliers*, 215–18. For a contemporary view of the fissures that were opening up, see Juxon, *Journals*, 80.

5 It is surely significant that Capp in Kenyon and Ohlmeyer devotes less than a page to the naval campaigns of 1645, and much of that consists of generalizations.

6 TT E64 11 and below Chapters XVII, XVIII, XXII.

7 Carte, *Letters*, 111–14; Bodleian Carte ms XII, 140; Foord, *Naseby*, 318; TT E324 6.

8 Edwards, *Dealing in Death*, 40, 125; Thomason Tracts E 288 33.

9 Malcolm, *Caesar's Due*, 114–16, 118; Barratt, *Cavaliers*, 138–9.

10 *Ibid.*, 138.

11 No more than a trickle of troops from Ireland reached England in the first half of 1645.

12 It fought in the Western army under Prince Maurice and Lord Goring in 1644 and 1645 and was commanded by Bertrand Rosson de la Pleine (TT E292.27; BL Harleian ms 6802, 277; Trelawney Papers, 248–9).

13 Wedgwood, *King's War*, 174–7; Mackay, *Little Madam*, 240–1; Dugdale, *Diary*, 47; Green, *Letters*, 166–7.

14 These points are taken from Porter, *London and the Civil War*, 9–10, and from Aylmer, *Struggle for the Constitution*, 122; Edwards, *Dealing in Death*.

15 See below Chapter XIX.

16 There is very clear evidence of this in the contents of weekly newspapers published in London that held different political positions, and in Juxon's *Journal*.

17 See below Chapters VII, VIII.

18 E.g. Holmes, *Eastern Association*, 224; Barratt, *Cavaliers*, 215–18.

19 See above.

20 Wanklyn, *King's Armies*, 270. Having to maintain troops to blockade the garrisons of Plymouth and Lyme also restricted what the Western Association could have achieved, but this can be exaggerated. For much of the time Plymouth was guarded by troops that would not have been used elsewhere, whereas Lyme's small size and sequestered position between the hills and the sea meant that it was rarely a cause for concern.

21 Wanklyn, *King's Armies*, 107–9; Bennett, 'Contribution and assessment', 7–9; Bennett, *Civil War*, 53–7. See also below Chapter XVII.

22 For the Midlands, see Hutton, *Royalist War Effort*, 100–9; Hughes, *Politics, Society and Civil War*, 208–13, 223–30; Auden, 'Case with the Committee'.

23 Morrill, *Cheshire 1630–1660*, 100; Hughes, *Politics, Society and Civil War*, 212.

24 See below Chapters VIII, IX, XII, XVII, XVIII, and Wanklyn, 'Royalist strategy', 74.

25 Hughes in Cust and Hughes, *The English Civil War*, 264–5, 276; Hutton, *The Royalist War Effort*, 202–3; Smith, *Modern British Isles*, 118–19.

26 Malcolm, 'A king in search of soldiers'; Wanklyn and Young, 'A king in search of soldiers'.

27 See, for example, Phillips, 'The Royalist North'. An interesting example of such an inducement occurred in Cheshire, where Sir George Booth offered to extend his tenants' leases if they were killed fighting for Parliament. Many Parliamentary soldiers came from his estates, but nobody can tell how persuasive the inducement was.

28 Holmes, *Eastern Association*, 72, 160; Everitt, *Community of Kent*, 15, 101–16; Andriette, *Devon and Exeter*, 109, 114.

29 Roy, 'English Civil War'.

30 See below Chapters XV, XVII.

31 Gentles, *New Model Army*, 31–5; Roy, 'England turned Germany?', 142–4; Hutton, *The Royalist War Effort*, 173–4; Stoyle, 'Grenville's creatures', 28.

32 Admittedly, if garrison troops are added to troops in the field, Parliament enjoyed a very considerable superiority over the king in terms of numbers, but Fairfax made no attempt to exploit that resource in the 1645 campaign. He would have learned from his experience of the battle of Marston Moor that large armies had their weaknesses, particularly if they were filled up with troops with little or no experience of the battlefield.

33 Woolrych, *Battles*, 139; Gardiner, *Great Civil War* II, 251; Burne, *Battlefields*, 431. See also Chapters XX, XXI, XXII below.

34 Kitson, *Prince Rupert*, 275–83; Hutton, *The Royalist War Effort*, 129–43.

35 Burne and Young, *The Great Civil War*, 179.

36 Barratt, *Cavaliers*, 83–8; Gentles, *New Model Army*, ch. 3; Wheeler, *Irish and British Wars*.

37 Gardiner, *The Great Civil War* I, xxv–vi.

38 Wanklyn, *King's Armies*, 215; Wanklyn, 'Royalist strategy', 64–8.

39 See, for example, Chapters XIV, XIX below.

40 Kitson, *Prince Rupert*, 124.

41 A good example of a book of this nature is the account of Naseby by Foord.

42 Firth, 'Clarendon's history'.

chapter III

Battlecraft in seventeenth-century Europe

During the course of the seventeenth century there were major changes in battlefield practice, which were seen by Michael Roberts, writing in the third quarter of the twentieth century, as having consequences that amounted to a military revolution. This is not the place to review the twists and terms of the historical controversy that followed, except to point out that the military revolution, if that is what it was, is now seen as extending over a longer period of time and having deeper roots and wider ramifications than Roberts originally suggested.[1] In this chapter, the aim is merely to describe the major changes that relate to mobile as opposed to siege warfare between 1590 and 1640 in order to provide a military technology context for the discussion of strategy and tactics in the Great Civil War that follows, and also to explain some of the technical terms that will be employed.

Seventeenth-century European armies were made up of three arms: infantry, artillery and cavalry. In 1600, infantry formations were drawn up for battle with a *battaile* of pikes in the centre flanked by bodies of musketeers. The pikemen's function was to assault the enemy formation using an iron spike affixed to the end of a pole 16 feet in length. Opposing bodies of pikemen would advance towards one another hoping to break the enemy and cause them to flee by 'push of pike'. The musketeers would attempt to disrupt the ranks of an advancing enemy with their fire, but when the two bodies locked horns, they would drop back level with the rear of the pike *battaile* and continued firing at any available targets.[2] The other function of the pikemen was to keep enemy cavalry away from their musketeers, who had no defensive arms apart from a short sword or their weapon up-ended and used as a club.[3]

The muzzle-loading matchlock, the predominant infantry firearm, was a clumsy, inefficient weapon. Although some contemporaries credited matchlocks with a range of 400 yards, fire was rarely given at ranges above 50–100 yards because of their inaccuracy and their low muzzle velocity.[4] Musketeers using matchlocks also required a constantly lighted length of cord, the match, to fire their weapon, the fuse being a trickle of gunpowder that passed from the pan on the outside of the barrel via a small hole to the charge itself. Such an arrangement made matchlocks useless in wet weather and dangerous to handle in windy conditions. It also precluded surprise in any attack or approach march at night that did not make use of dead ground. Finally, matchlock muskets were slow to reload. Seventeenth-century military manuals listed forty-four separate movements for loading, firing and 'recovering' a matchlock. Not all would be used in every circumstance. Nevertheless, in the early seventeenth century a well-trained man could fire only one lead ball a minute, during which time a squadron of cavalry might have charged 500 yards.[5]

Contemporary writers regarded the accuracy and range of muskets as of secondary importance, provided that the formations of musketeers could deliver a devastating volley. It is therefore not surprising that generals endeavoured to increase their numbers and their rate of fire. However, one authority claimed a misfire rate as high as 40 percent.[6] Also, as musketeers lacked wads and ramrods until later in the century, musket balls were apt to roll out of the barrel when the musket was presented for firing (as happened to the Swedish army at Wittstock in 1636).[7] But there was an alternative to the matchlock. In 1615, the French gunsmith Le Bourgeoys developed the flintlock musket, in which the charge was ignited by a spark produced by a flint 'hammer' striking a small steel anvil. This dispensed with the need for match and significantly reduced misfires. Nevertheless, the flintlock remained uncommon in European armies until the last quarter of the century. Initially they were expensive and difficult to obtain in large quantities, as the locks could be made only by skilled craftsmen. Additionally, the firelock was not as robust a weapon as the matchlock. The lock was easily broken, and the flint needed periodic replacement. Finally, military commanders were not unhappy with the matchlock, which was both cheap and durable. As a result, only a single French regiment was equipped with flintlocks by 1670, and musketeers in the English army were still largely armed with matchlocks at the battle of Sedgemoor in 1685.[8]

The inherent immobility of infantry formations caused by the unwieldy nature of the pikes and the measured pace of the musketeer's *modus operandi* made the foot unsuitable for taking the offensive and winning set-piece battles by themselves, even after the tactical reforms introduced by Prince Maurice of Nassau and King Gustavus Adolphus of Sweden, which are described later in this chapter. Also, although infantry were well capable of defending themselves if protected by walls and hedges, resistance against horse in the open was almost impossible without the protection of their own cavalry, which were therefore usually deployed on the flanks (or wings) of the infantry formation. Better-trained units could often hold out for a time without cavalry support, but everything depended on their keeping in close order. Once the ranks of an infantry formation had been thrown into disorder by fighting, or as it tried to retreat, the enemy could get among the musketeers and pikemen and inflict very heavy casualties, as happened to the Imperialists at Breitenfeld (1631) and the Spanish at Rocroi (1643).[9]

Artillery was even more immobile than infantry. The heaviest field piece was normally the culverin, weighing over two tons and firing solid iron roundshot 16 to 20 pounds in weight. According to Roberts, the culverin's range was 800 yards at most. Eight horses (or oxen) were needed to draw a single culverin, and even much lighter pieces could still require the services of up to five horses. This explains why the Dutch army when on campaign in 1605 required 316 horses to pull its artillery train of fourteen guns and their attended carriages loaded with gunpowder and shot.

To get into action at all, guns had to be deployed on or near a road, and then once deployed they were forced by their weight to remain in the same place for the duration of the battle. They could not therefore respond to any crisis that might emerge as the engagement progressed unless it was in their direct line of fire. To make matters worse, even at the start of a battle, when the artillery were pointing in the right direction, their rate of fire was not rapid enough to deliver an effective barrage. Contemporary accounts specify between eight and ten shots an hour even for skilled gunners; additionally, after forty shots the piece had to be allowed to cool for a time. Otherwise it might burst through overuse.[10] Thus loading and firing were complex, slow and also potentially dangerous operations. Finally, low muzzle velocity, inexact gun casting and boring techniques, gunpowder of indifferent quality, and a lack of rifling meant that hitting a specific target was a matter of luck. It is not therefore surprising that there were relatively few guns in early seventeenth-century armies, usually less than one per thousand men. In the Napoleonic era, four guns per thousand men was considered a minimum ratio.[11] In 1600 and for some years to come, the artillery's principal military value was in battering down the walls of castles and fortified towns, and it is this that largely explains why seventeenth-century armies felt it necessary to haul heavy guns around the countryside with great difficulty and at great expense.

Cavalry was by far the most important arm on the seventeenth-century battlefield. Victory usually went to the side that, having routed the opposing cavalry, rallied and then changed the direction of its attack to take the enemy foot in flank and rear. Thus horse that were trained, disciplined and well led were indispensable for a successful commander. However, even well-trained horse might be capable of performing only a single charge before they lost formation and became a milling mass of horses and men totally incapable of achieving their second, battle-winning, objective.

There were four types of cavalryman in Western European armies in 1600, two heavy and two light. The most numerous were cuirassiers wearing three-quarter-length plate armour, including a closed helmet and often a steel breastplate that was musket ball-proof (in theory). Their weapons were a backsword intended for both piercing and slashing, and anything up to four pistols. Cuirassiers were generally drawn from the nobility and the lesser landowners, as only they could afford the expensive arms and equipment, but continental warfare sometimes presented opportunities for men such as Sydenham Poyntz, formerly a tailor's apprentice, to become troopers and even officers of cuirassiers.[12]

Lancers formed a second category of heavy cavalrymen, but they were on the decline 'because of the scarcity of such as were practised and exercised to use the lance, it being a thing of much labour and industry to learn'. Usually heavily armoured, they were intended to charge the enemy, but it was difficult for them to make any impact against foot armed with pikes, as lances tended to be considerably shorter. Finally, lancers had to be deployed in a single rank in order to be able to use their weapon effectively. As a result, they took up an inordinate amount of space in the line of battle and were liable to suffer heavier casualties as infantry firepower increased. This impaired the weight and the effectiveness of their charge, as there was no second or third line of lancers to make up gaps in the first caused by musket or cannon fire. They could thus only be safely employed in pursuit of a defeated enemy, a task made difficult by their heavy armour.[13]

Harquebusiers were so called because they had originally carried an arquebus, a lighter ancestor of the musket, but by 1600 the individual harquebusier would normally have been armed with a backsword and two pistols or a carbine (a short musket 3 feet in length). His protective armour was less heavy than that of a cuirassier or a lancer. Ideally, he would have been equipped with helmet, back- and breastplate, a buff leather coat, a metal gauntlet or leather vambrace to protect the rein hand, and sometimes a gorgette to defend the neck, but what he actually wore depended on circumstances, such as the ability of an armaments industry to respond to the massive increase in demand at the start of a war. Being more mobile and flexible than either cuirassiers or lancers, particularly on heavier ground, harquebusiers were not only easier for generals to move about the battlefield but also better able to pursue a beaten foe. Moreover, they were heavy enough to act as shock troops, which was particularly important when such tactics returned to favour after Gustavus Adolphus's victory at Breitenfeld.[14]

Finally there were the dragoons, a cross between an infantryman and a cavalryman. Dragoons first appeared in sixteenth-century France, taking their name from the dragon, the short musket that was their primary armament. Their firepower was therefore much greater than that of any other type of cavalryman, but in the mid-seventeenth century they normally fought on foot, not on horseback, armed with matchlocks, not dragons. Their combination of mobility with firepower was valued in a number of continental armies in the first half of the seventeenth century, and they were widely employed as advance guards to seize bridges and narrow defiles prior to the arrival of the main army.[15]

In the late sixteenth century, battles had been fought between massive infantry formations known as tercios, sometimes sixty ranks deep and up to 3,000 strong. They consisted mainly of pikemen with sleeves of musketeers at the corners and sides. Deployed in a single line on the battlefield, the role of the tercio was to move forward, engage its opponents and force them back until they broke and ran. The cavalry would then set off in pursuit, conducting what was known as the execution. However, only the harquebusiers among the cavalry had the strength combined with endurance to carry out a truly effective and bloody execution. Cuirassiers were therefore trained to assist in the process of disembowelling enemy tercios using a drill known as the caracole. They trotted up to the enemy in a succession of small dense columns several ranks deep. On nearing the target the front rank fired its pistols before swinging away in a 180-degree turn to the rear of the column, where it reloaded while moving forward towards the head of the column once more, when it repeated the manoeuvre. The theory was that such continuous fire would eventually open a gap in the tercio, allowing other mounted troops to exploit it.[16]

This orderly and slightly sedate set of tactical routines for infantry and cavalry changed through a series of major innovations that began in the late sixteenth century during the Dutch Wars of Independence. Prince Maurice of Nassau, the Dutch generalissimo, came to the conclusion that his army needed to break from orthodox, but in its case unsuccessful, battlefield practice if it was to defeat its superbly trained and equipped Spanish opponents. Between 1590 and his death in 1625, Maurice, assisted by his brothers, completely reorganized the way in which the Dutch army fought. They also provided, through their published treatises and drill books, a model of infantry and cavalry tactics that was to have a significant effect on other European armies.

Maurice abandoned the tercio. Instead he formed his infantry into battalions 550 strong, in which the pikemen were deployed in linear formation five or so ranks deep rather than in blocks, thus enabling a much larger number to use their weapons against a frontal attack. He also increased the ratio of musketeers to pikemen to six to five. This had an impressive effect on infantry firepower when combined with a new drill[17] by which each rank of musketeers fired in turn and then moved to the rear of the formation to reload, thus producing a rolling fusillade. However, the slowness of reloading meant that musketeers were deployed ten ranks deep, not six as had been originally intended. The battalion structure also meant that infantry enjoyed greater flexibility than when grouped in tercios. This was enhanced by their being deployed in a checkerboard formation, which enabled battalions to provide supporting fire for one another in battle, something tercios were incapable of doing because they were deployed in line.[18]

In the case of the cavalry, Maurice deployed his harquebusiers six ranks deep in close order and armed them with a pistol, a sword and a carbine. However, Dutch cavalry did not charge the enemy; they waited for the enemy to charge them, relying on the weight of their barrage to disorder their opponents to a greater or lesser extent. If their fire disrupted the enemy formation before contact was made, they could countercharge, but at a trot rather than a gallop as it took cavalrymen some time to pick up speed. Additionally, a slower pace meant easier retention of an individual's position within the cavalry formation, thus allowing the shape of the formation itself to be retained and the shock to be more effective when it collided with the enemy. However, if firepower did not prevent contact taking place, the close order and depth of the formation would enable it to absorb the shock. Moreover, the casualties inflicted on the enemy during the charge would have caused sufficient disruption for the Dutch to have the advantage in the ensuing *melée*, in which the two bodies of horse engaged one another in close combat.[19]

The next major tactical innovator was Gustavus Adolphus, who inherited a war with Denmark, Russia and Poland when he succeeded to the throne in 1611. He remained at war with one power or another until his death in battle at Lutzen in 1632. Although influenced by Maurice's reforms, Gustavus found Dutch tactics unsuitable for warfare on the plains of Central Europe, where manoeuvrability and flexible formations were more important, if anything, than firepower.[20]

By 1630, the Swedish king had developed a musket weighing 11 pounds, over 50 percent lighter than previous models. This, combined with the newly devised powder cartridge containing the musket ball and its propellant, meant that the rate of fire of the musketeer doubled, and tactics were formulated to make full use of the improvements. First, Gustavus took advantage of the increased speed of reloading to deploy his musketeers in formations only six deep. He also exploited the three-foot space that was traditionally allotted to each musketeer by training them to 'double their files', that is for the second, fourth and sixth ranks to move into the gaps in the first, third and fifth when they fired. This increased significantly the weight of shot at each delivery, but it also meant that the whole body could produce a single, simultaneous salvo if the front rank delivered it kneeling, the second rank crouching and the third rank standing. In such a scenario, the pikemen became more rather than less important. Equipped with a shorter pike, they were expected to charge the hopefully shaken enemy once the salvo had been delivered, but the latter also looked to the pikemen for protection. Having fired simultaneously, they were all reloading at the same time and thus virtually defenseless.[21]

Gustavus Adolphus's new horse drill probably grew out of the experience of his early campaigns, in which the Swedish army had suffered at the hands of Polish cavalry armed with swords and attacking at the gallop, and also possibly from what he had read or heard about the French tradition of cavalry warfare. Seizing the initiative rather than waiting for the enemy to do so was the fundamental difference between the behaviour of the Swedish cavalry on the battlefield and that of the Dutch. That meant charging the enemy, not waiting for him to charge. Swedish cavalry units, harquebusiers rather than cuirassiers because of the structure of Swedish society, were deployed three rather than six ranks deep (as Dutch doctrine prescribed). Eschewing the carbine as an encumbrance in the charge, Gustavus Adolphus armed them with only a sword and two pistols. Each regiment consisted – at least on paper – of eight squadrons of 125 men, each separated from its neighbour by 20 yards.[22] They would advance towards the enemy at a steadily quickening pace, and 50 yards from contact the flank squadrons would raise the pace to a full gallop and charge home. The remaining squadrons would arrive as the *melée* was developing to deliver the final blow in the centre. On the other hand, the centre squadrons could act as a pursuit force if the flank charges alone had broken the enemy horse, or they could serve as a rallying point if the flank attacks had been repulsed.[23] The charge was always made in a tightly packed formation: 'Those troops that are to give the first charge are to be at their close order, every left-hand man's right knee must be close locked under his right-hand man's left ham . . .' according to a contemporary manual. Close order turned the whole squadron into a single missile, maximizing the shock of impact and preventing individual horses from turning away before contact. The other characteristic of Gustavus's use of cavalry on the battlefield was that Swedish harquebusiers were trained not to use their pistols as they charged but to reserve their fire for the *melée* or the pursuit of the beaten foe, where being at close quarters with the enemy would compensate for the pistols' low muzzle velocity.[24] Finally, the importance of cavalry shock tactics for the success of the army as a whole meant that larger numbers of cavalry were needed if opportunities on the battlefield were not to be missed. In Swedish armies, the ratio between cavalry and infantry therefore rose to one:two, twice that which pertained in the Dutch army.[25]

Changes in Gustavus's use of cannon on the battlefield were considerable, but not that significant in the short run. Swedish skills in metallurgy resulted in the development of lighter pieces of artillery, which were produced in large numbers once they had proved their worth. These were more flexible in use, as they could be pulled by a single horse or manhandled by two or three soldiers. Instead of being kept together in one place on the battlefield like the heavy artillery, they were positioned among the infantry formations to increase their firepower. Nevertheless, it was still difficult to move them about during a battle. Not long after Gustavus's death, however, the Swedish army had achieved sufficient flexibility in the deployment of artillery during an engagement for it to play a major part in their winning the battle of Jankow.[26]

A last feature of Swedish battlefield practice was that Gustavus extended the Dutch checkerboard formation from the infantry to the cavalry. Brigades of both arms were integrated along the entire front so that they could support one another as required. As a result, cavalry stationed in the centre of the reserve line had sufficient space to support the infantry battalions to their front if necessary, while musketeers placed between cavalry squadrons increased their firepower by a considerable margin. However, although the smaller infantry formations were agile enough to change direction and protect the flanks of the Swedish army if required, horse continued to be deployed primarily on the wings, where they might have the opportunity to deliver an attack on the enemy flank.[27]

Swedish tactics were widely copied during the 1630s. However, changes in battlefield practice and military technology developed by the princes of the House of Nassau and the Swedish king were rarely applied in their entirety in other armies. Instead they were adopted in a piecemeal fashion to suit local conditions, and the Royalist and Parliamentary armies were no exception to this.

Notes

1 Parker, *Military Revolution*; Rogers, *Military Revolution Debate*.

2 Oman, *Art of War in the Sixteenth Century*, 568.

3 The bayonet inserted into the end of the musket barrel was not used until the second half of the seventeenth century.

4 Firth, *Cromwell's Army*, 89–90.

5 Hughes, *Firepower*, 3; Young, *English Civil War Armies*, 9.

6 Quoted in Firth, *Cromwell's Armies*, 85.

7 Danskin, 'Battle of Wittstock', 24–7.

8 Dupuy and Dupuy, *Collins Encyclopaedia of Military History*, 572; Gush, *Army Lists 1420–1700*, 36. Earlier in the century, musketeers armed with flintlocks

tended to be used to guard the artillery train, where a length of lighted match carelessly employed could easily cause a catastrophic explosion.

9 Holmes, *Oxford Companion to Military History*, 779; Roberts, *Gustavus Adolphus*, 262–4.

10 Hughes, *Firepower*, 35; Roberts, *Gustavus Adolphus*, 229n.

11 Firth, *Cromwell's Army*, 150, 179; Gush, *Renaissance Armies*, 106; Roberts, *Gustavus Adolphus*, 228n; Hughes, *Firepower*, 75.

12 Wagner, *European Weapons and Warfare*, 32; Poyntz, *True Relation*, 45, 106.

13 Wagner, *European Weapons and Warfare*, 32; Cruso, *Military Instructions*, 26, 30.

14 Wagner, *European Warfare*, 37; Jones, *Role and Efficiency of Cavalry*, 42.

15 *Ibid.*, 32; Gush, *Renaissance Armies*, 21; Tincey, *Soldiers of the English Civil War: Cavalry*, 20.

16 Parrot, 'Military Revolution', 21–7; Dupuy and Dupuy, *Collins Encyclopaedia of Military History*, 116.

17 This originated from Maurice's brother William's reading of texts from the Ancient World in which sling throwers had used such a drill to maintain a continuous barrage of shot.

18 Gush, *Renaissance Armies*, 106; Parker, *Military Revolution*, 18–19; Jones, *Art of War*, 221.

19 Jones, *Role and Efficiency of Cavalry*, 35, 47–9; Dupuy and Dupuy, *Collins Encyclopaedia of Military History*, 575.

20 Gush, *Renaissance Armies*, 106; Roberts, *Gustavus Adolphus*, 254–5.

21 *Ibid.*, 258–9; Hughes, *Firepower*, 10.

22 Gush, *Renaissance Armies*, 114; Tincey, *Soldiers: Cavalry*, 2; Rogers, *Battles and Generals*, 110. Traditionally, Swedish armies had been raised by communities, not the aristocracy, and the heavy cavalry tradition was therefore not strong (Roberts, *Gustavus Adolphus*, 228).

23 Cruso, *Military Instructions*, 26, 97–8; Roberts, *Gustavus Adolphus*, 256–7.

24 Vernon, *The Young Horseman*, 43.

25 Dupuy and Dupuy, *Collins Encyclopaedia of Military History*, 579; Gush, *Renaissance Armies*, 118.

26 Holmes (ed.), *Oxford Companion to Military History*, 915; Roberts, *Gustavus Adolphus*, 230–4, 254.

27 Roberts, *Gustavus Adolphus*, 251; Dupuy and Dupuy, *Collins Encyclopaedia of Military History*, 590.

PART II

Knock-out strategies

chapter IV

Initial strategies

In March 1642, the struggle to control the militia came to a head. The two Houses of Parliament passed a bill that would have deprived the king of his control over the army and the navy, vesting it instead in its own appointees. He vetoed the bill, on the grounds that such powers were, and always had been, fundamental to monarchical authority in England. However, they declared that it was the constitutional duty of the Lords and the Commons, as representatives of the people of England, to do all that was necessary to protect the people's lives and liberties if the king could no longer be trusted to do so.[1] Charles then left for the north of England for fear of being taken back to London by force, thus finally removing the fiction that king and Parliament were cooperating to govern England, but a month passed before either decided to test the other's resolution. The flash point was Hull, where much of the arms and ammunition collected to fight the Scots in 1640 was stored. With the king by that time at York, only 30 miles away, the two Houses made the first move. They declared it their intention to transfer the Hull magazine to London. The justification was that it was needed to equip the regiments being raised to put down the revolt in Ireland.

Charles's reaction was to try to gain entrance to Hull backed by a body of armed men drawn from the Yorkshire trained bands. However, the governor, Sir John Hotham, refused to admit him, on the grounds that Parliament had not given its permission. The MPs and peers at Westminster responded by putting into effect more of the powers they had assumed over the militia. Their first actions were both symbolic and practical. Representatives of the two Houses presided over a formal review of the city of London trained bands, while the lord lieutenant of Lincolnshire was instructed to be ready to go to Hull's assistance with the county trained bands and to supply it with provisions as necessary.[2] The king in the meantime had asked the Yorkshire trained bands for volunteers in sufficient numbers to form a regiment of foot and one troop of horse to serve as his personal bodyguard. The MPs and peers remaining at Westminster took this to be an act of war against the people of England, whom they represented, and whom the king had sworn to defend in his coronation oath. Using precedents from Richard II's and earlier reigns, they decided that, as the king was behaving as if he were constitutionally insane, they as the people's representatives could legitimately exercise all his powers.[3] Preparations for war then gathered pace with both the king and Parliament taking steps to defend their cause. From mid-June 1642 onwards, their supporters ransacked the houses of the gentry and the aristocracy looking for arms and armour, and they set about securing the weapons and gunpowder belonging to the trained bands. This led to struggles for power, most particularly in the county towns, where most trained band magazines were located. Both king and Parliament appointed generals to command their armies in the field, and lesser officers were given commissions to raise regiments of horse and foot. Putting an army together took time, but nevertheless both sides developed strategies by which their respective aims could be achieved using the resources they had to hand.[4]

At this point, it is necessary to discuss briefly how strategic decisions were made during the Great Civil War. The two Houses of Parliament assumed responsibility for the wider picture, grand strategy if you like, but delegated day-to-day conduct of the war to a large Committee of Safety drawn from their members. However, the committee served merely as the mouthpiece of the two Houses, leaving the working out of Parliament's strategic designs to the generals, the Earl of Essex in the south and Lord Fairfax in the north, who then issued commands to their subordinates. However, dissatisfaction with the conduct of the war during its first eighteen months led to day-to-day strategy being placed firmly under the control of a much smaller 'war cabinet', the Committee of Both Kingdoms, which was established in February 1644 to coordinate the allied war effort in England and Wales. Unlike its predecessor, it was to 'order and direct concerning the carrying on the war'.[5] If anything, the committee's control over the generals increased with the formation of the New Model Army in April 1645, a reflection of the occasions on which the Earls of Essex and Manchester had disregarded its specific commands during the campaigns of the previous summer and autumn. The humiliating abandonment of the committee's pet project, the siege of Oxford, at the beginning of June resulted in greater strategic responsibility being vested in the commander of the New Model, but the significance of the move can be overemphasized. Sir Thomas Fairfax may have been freed from direct day-to-day interference, but he continued to ask the two Houses first for their advice and then for their consent over matters of grand strategy.[6]

On the Royalist side the king, as *generalissimo*, had ultimate command over strategy, and indeed he took great interest in that aspect of warfare as his military confidence grew. Before making decisions Charles normally consulted his council of war, whose members included prominent generals, ministers and courtiers, but he also pursued his own agenda at times as, for example, in his instructions to Sir William Ogle concerning Winchester. As the war progressed, the council's direct involvement in strategic decisions seems to have waned, but even after it had been split into three parts in the spring of 1645,[7] the various components, to the king's considerable annoyance, still claimed the right to be consulted about, even to have a veto over, the composition of the field army and the direction in which it was to march.

The decisions that Charles took were sometimes right and sometimes wrong, but he was normally consistent even in the Naseby campaign, when major changes in tack were not signs that he was being blown hither and thither by conflicting advice but reflected the need to respond to day-to-day changes in the military situation. However, he made the serious mistake early in the war of allowing too much discretion to his commanders in the field in the belief that those on the spot knew best. This was a noble sentiment when nothing much was happening, but lack of firm control over regional commanders resulted in important opportunities being lost in East Anglia in the late summer of 1643 and in the south of England in April 1644.[8] It also made fighting the spring 1645 campaign more difficult than it need have been, but provincial insubordination is only a second-order explanation of why the king lost the decisive battle of the war at Naseby in June.[9]

The king's war aims were straightforward – to maintain his position in the constitution, most particularly the authority that he and his ancestors had enjoyed over the armed forces, and to preserve the Elizabethan prayer-book and the government of the Church by bishops. As political solutions had failed, he would need to impose his will on Parliament and its supporters by force. The king's strategy therefore needed to be an active one, and success could not be achieved without an effective army. By mid-August, regiments for the Royalist field army were being raised (or had been raised) throughout the north of England, in the north and central Midlands, in Somerset, and in most parts of Wales. However, having failed to secure the magazine at Hull, arming the recruits was a major problem. The resources of the country houses were limited; his supporters had not been conspicuously successful in gaining control of the county magazines; and importing weapons and gunpowder from abroad was difficult because Newcastle was the only port he controlled facing the Continent. To ensure that it remained in Royalist hands, the Earl of Newcastle was sent there from York in late June. His orders were to garrison the town and to raise a force to defend the four most northerly counties of England against Parliament.[10]

The next best source of arms after Hull was the magazine at Portsmouth, whose governor, George Goring, was willing to declare for the king when the moment was right. However, with a garrison of only about 500 men and the navy firmly under Parliament's control, he would require military assistance. The king's original intention had been to march into southern England once he had raised a decent-sized army. To prepare the way, he sent the Marquis of Hertford south from York in late July accompanied by a body of officers and gentlemen with orders to recruit men in south-central England and to support Goring when he revealed his true allegiance. However, the commander of the Portsmouth garrison, faced with the prospect of being reinforced by troops from London, was forced to declare himself earlier than he had intended. Moreover, Hertford encountered hostility in Wiltshire and considerable opposition in Somerset. After a few weeks, he managed to assemble a force of about a thousand men, drawn mainly from the north Dorset trained bands. He threw them into Sherborne Castle, a fine defensive position, but could not advance towards Portsmouth because a contingent from Parliament's field army under the Earl of Bedford, supported by enthusiastic volunteers from Somerset, was blocking his path. Portsmouth surrendered after a four-week siege on 5th September. Hertford then set about saving what he could. The three troops of cavalry and the only infantry regiment being raised for the field army, Colonel Thomas Lunsford's, retreated through Somerset to Minehead followed at a discreet distance by Bedford's men. At Minehead, the foot embarked for South Wales on coal barges, joining the king in time for the battle of Edgehill, but the number of boats in port was smaller than had been anticipated. As a result, there was no room for the cavalry, which retreated into Cornwall, where there was considerable support for the king's cause, while Bedford's soldiers rejoined Parliament's field army, which by that time was quartered in Worcestershire.[11]

Parliament's war aim was even simpler – to oblige the king to accept its entire programme for constitutional and religious reform. The hope was that the mere threat of force would be sufficient to bring this about. All that was needed was an army so powerful that the king would lose his nerve, as in the Second Bishops' War two years earlier. By the middle of August 1642, all appeared to be going well. The Earl of Essex may have had as many as 10,000 men under arms in London, mainly infantry, whereas the king had at best a quarter of that number when he left York for the Midlands early in the month.[12] Moreover, Royalist attempts to raise troops in the midland counties met with mixed success. Two regiments of foot were raised in Lincolnshire and one in Nottinghamshire, but little headway was made in Leicestershire, where the resident aristocrats, the Grey and Hastings families, who supported Parliament and the king, respectively, were evenly matched, while an attempt to browbeat Coventry into opening its gates was a conspicuous failure. Raising the royal standard at Nottingham on 22nd August (not a declaration of war but a piece of theatre intended to appeal to his subjects' loyalty and thus produce a host of volunteers for the Royalist cause) was also a failure, if not a humiliation. Indeed, after the event Sir Jacob Astley, his infantry commander, is alleged to have said that such was the shortage of troops he could not guarantee that Charles would not be 'taken out of his bed if the rebels should make a brisk attempt to that purpose'.[13]

The policy of deterrence helps to explain why Parliament did not attempt to capture the king at a time when he was militarily very weak, but there were two other reasons. Astley had overemphasized the military threat, if those were indeed his words. The Earl of Essex could not have seized the king by force, as he did not have the right troops available in sufficient numbers. The massive superiority he enjoyed was in infantry, which would have moved too slowly to catch Charles by surprise. His cavalry and dragoons were capable of swift movement across country, but they were probably no more numerous than the Royalist cavalry regiments guarding the king's person. Moreover, they were being put to good use elsewhere, as described below.

Indeed, it was not until the end of the first week in September that a large field army with an appropriate ratio of cavalry to infantry began to assemble at Northampton in preparation for active military operations against Charles's forces 50 miles to the north. By this time, however, the king was stronger in both horse and foot than he had been in mid-August, but Essex nevertheless appears to have set his army in motion towards Nottingham on 13th September. On that night, Colonel Hollis's regiment was quartered at Spratton, on the road to Leicester and the north, but the following day it received orders to halt, presumably as a result of Essex receiving intelligence that the king's forces had left Nottingham for Derby.[14] Parliament's army then remained stationary for five days until it became clear that the king was not heading for Lancashire or back into Yorkshire but westwards towards Chester or Shrewsbury. Either town was large enough to serve as an army base, or, if well garrisoned, to cover the king's retreat into Wales if his recruiting operations in England failed. Moreover, moving to Chester or Shrewsbury would make it easier for the eight or so infantry regiments being raised for the king in Wales and the northwest of England to join the field army. As Chester was thought to be the more likely destination, the Parliamentary army advanced from Northampton through Rugby to Coventry, but when the king's forces left the Chester road at Uttoxeter and marched to Stafford, it was obvious that he was heading for Shrewsbury. Essex responded by moving his army to Worcester, a convenient location from which to keep a watch on the recruiting activities of the king's supporters in South Wales and Herefordshire. He may also have seen Worcester as a good location for opposing any attempt by the royal army to join the Marquis of Hertford in the south of England. However, by the time Essex arrived at Worcester on 20th September, that strategic initiative was to all intents and purposes dead. Portsmouth had surrendered, and Hertford was about to leave Sherborne with the few hundred troops he had left. Finally, Worcester was close to the route the king's army would probably take in the unlikely event of his advisers recommending a march on London.[15]

While the bulk of Parliament's field army was making its slow progress through the villages and small towns of the West Midlands towards Worcester, Essex sent two mounted regiments ahead to secure the west bank of the Severn below the city. The aim was to capture a convoy of packhorses carrying silver plate from Oxford University that was heading for Shrewsbury. There followed the first major encounter of the war between contingents of the two field armies. This took place at Powick Bridge, just south of Worcester, where a similar-sized body of Royalist horse commanded by Prince Rupert was resting on its way to provide an escort for the convoy. In a short but hard-fought engagement, Essex's men were routed and several of the more enterprising Parliamentary cavalry commanders killed, mortally wounded or taken prisoner. The convoy then made its way safely to Shrewsbury. Thus was the reputation of the king's cavalry established.[16]

The weakness of Worcester as a headquarters was that an army stationed there could not prevent Charles receiving reinforcements from North Wales and the northwest of England, where most of his new infantry regiments were being raised. Nevertheless, Essex decided to remain at Worcester rather than advance on Shrewsbury. He certainly had prior authority to take the offensive, but he preferred to persist with his efforts to persuade the king not to fight, something that Parliament was prepared to go along with in the interests of avoiding unnecessary bloodshed. The only mildly aggressive move Essex made was to send the Earl of Stamford with an infantry regiment and some horse to occupy Hereford with the objective of preventing troops reaching Charles from South Wales. Essex also took steps to ensure that Gloucester was in safe hands while quartering his remaining regiments in an arc of market towns to the north and east of Worcester to discourage raiding by Royalist cavalry. However, the Royalist high command feared a lightning raid by a small force of cavalry and dragoons to capture the king should he venture out of Shrewsbury. This explains why Rupert's cavalry regiments, which had moved westwards to Ludlow after Powick Bridge, presumably to protect the South Wales regiments as they marched towards Shrewsbury, was recalled in late September to escort Charles on a visit to Wrexham and Chester. However, it was an unnecessary precaution. Essex was not in active mode. He was still convinced that the king would be unable to raise a large enough army to risk it in battle, especially as his own army was growing all the time as new regiments of foot and horse arrived at Worcester from London, the southwest and the south.[17] This remained the lord general's view until mid-October, when the Royalist army suddenly took the offensive.[18]

However, Essex's 'softly, softly' approach towards the conduct of the war must be put in context. It applied only to the way in which the lord general behaved towards the king himself and the forces under his direct control. In other parts of England, Parliament's military commanders adopted a more aggressive strategy during July, August and September that was highly effective. As contingents of the field army were raised, so they were used to consolidate Parliament's control over disputed parts of the country and to deny them to the enemy. The two great arsenals, Hull and Portsmouth, had been secured, the first by shipping troops from London, the second by a successful siege carried out by the Hampshire trained bands backed by eight companies of foot and several troops of horse under the command of Sir William Waller, a colonel in the field army.[19] Subsequently, the Earl of Bedford with some cavalry from the main army had helped local forces to force the Marquis of Hertford out of Dorset and Somerset in the manner described above. Lord Say and Sele's regiment secured Oxford; a force of dragoons from London occupied Cambridge; John Hampden's regiment helped to suppress Royalist activity in Buckinghamshire; and the Earl of Stamford gained control of Leicester with the aid of some of Essex's cavalry.[20] However, the most impressive achievement of all was in Kent, where there was considerable support for the king's cause. In two forays during August, Colonel Sandys's regiment of horse seized all the important fortresses and towns in the county and imprisoned the Royalist leadership.[21]

The king's mounted troops tried to carry out similar types of operation, but with much less success. In Cheshire, Lincolnshire and Warwickshire, cavalry regiments from the field army provided some protection for recruiting operations carried out by local Royalists, but they were no help to the Earl of Derby against Manchester. Moreover, in September plundering by Royalist horse in Staffordshire and its environs upset the local landed gentry, who at first had been favourably inclined towards the king's cause.[22] Earlier, a force of cavalry under Lord Wilmot had failed to block the passage of a brigade of Essex's army marching to the defence of Coventry, allegedly because of the timidity of its commander.[23]

Nevertheless, the wisdom of the king's decision to move to Shrewsbury was clearly shown in the weeks that followed. At least three infantry regiments joined the Royalist army while it was quartered in and around the town. Recruits from the Welsh borderland also filled up the ranks of the foot regiments that Charles had brought with him, and by 12th October, when the army left Shrewsbury, five others were on the march to join it. At first the direction of the king's march suggested that he was advancing on Worcester. Some companies of foot were transported from Shrewsbury to Bridgnorth by boat, while the rest of the army took the overland route, but then the army divided. The king with most of the infantry passed around the north of Birmingham as if intending to make a second attempt to capture Coventry. However, Prince Rupert with the bulk of the cavalry took a route to the south of the town, which could be seen as culminating in a lunge towards Worcester. Lord Wharton, commander of the detachment of the Parliamentary army at Kidderminster, took one look at Rupert's men passing over Kinver Edge and fell back on army headquarters, leaving some cannon behind him.[24]

Not until the royal army reunited at Meriden Heath between Coventry and Birmingham on 19th October did Essex decide that it was time to leave Worcester. The direction of the king's march now suggested very strongly that he was aiming for the biggest prize of all, the capture of London. Moreover, Charles's army was now much stronger, as the troops that had been hurrying to join him, two or three infantry regiments from Lancashire and a similar number from South Wales, had duly arrived. Essex claimed that it was his intention to follow the Royalist army, not to intercept it, but for the first time the air of self-confidence that had pervaded the lord general's despatches to Parliament, as reported in London newspapers, was replaced by one of disquiet. Not only was he a day's march behind the king, his very large train of heavy artillery would delay him still further if Charles headed for the capital at full speed. Essex therefore urged Parliament to assemble as many troops as it could under the Earl of Warwick or some other commander and station them in a defensive position covering the city. If they could only delay the king for half a day, they would be able to trap his army between them. The effect of such news on the capital and on the Parliamentary leadership must have been devastating. Only the day before the Committee of Safety had written to Lord Fairfax, its general in the north, boasting of 'the good state of our affairs here'.[25]

The prospect of a pre-run of Waterloo in the Chilterns with Warwick as Wellington and Essex as Blücher is an intriguing one, but it was not to be. By accident, on the morning of Sunday, 23rd October, Essex's foremost cavalry unit blundered into the troops of the king's rearguard at Wormleighton and Kineton, two settlements in the open field country of south Warwickshire. The rest of the Royalist army was some miles ahead intent on capturing Banbury and Oxford, not on reaching London as fast as possible. Charles could have put off an encounter, but he and his advisers decided to turn back and engage the earl in battle near Edgehill, three miles to the southeast of Kineton. The 650-foot high escarpment was not only a fine defensive position if the enemy attacked first, it was also an excellent rendezvous for the Royalist army, which, after over a week of strenuous marching, was enjoying a Sabbath day's rest in scattered billets in villages along the borders of Warwickshire, Oxfordshire and Northamptonshire.[26] Essex too was eager for a fight, even though some of his artillery, several regiments of foot and as many as ten troops of horse were still threading their way through the difficult country that lay between Stratford and Kineton.

Notes

1 The most scholarly account is in Russell, *The Fall of the British Kingdoms*, 481–2, but see also Whitelock, *Memoirs*, 59.

2 Whitelock, *Memoirs*, 56–7; CSP Venetian 1642–3, 60; CJ II 593.

3 CJ II 586–7; CSP Domestic 1641–3, 327; Russell, 'Why did Charles I', 32–3.

4 Wanklyn and Young, 'A king in search of soldiers', 150–1.

5 HMC Appendix to the 5th Report, 14, 28, 117; CJ III 492.

6 For a full discussion, see below Chapter XXII.

7 Roy, 'Council of war', 162–7; BL Additional ms 27402, 8–10, 15.

8 Wanklyn, 'Royalist strategy', 69, 72–4.

9 See Chapters XXI, XXIV below.

10 Cavendish, *Duke of Newcastle*, 15–18.

11 Hopton, *Bellum Civile*, 14–18; HMC Portland ms I, 50; Calendar Clarendon State Papers ii, 146.

12 CJ II 669–70; HMC Appendix to the 7th Report, 440.

13 *Ibid.*, 343; Clarendon, *Great Rebellion* vi, 1.

14 HMC Appendix to the 5th Report, 91; CSP Domestic 1641–3, 391; TT E114 1, 15.

15 Hopton, *Bellum Civile*, 17–18; CSP Domestic 1641–3, 366.

16 *Ibid.*, 396; HMC Appendix to the 2nd Report, 36; Corbet, *Military Government*, 13.

17 TT E123 5; TT E240 9, 12, 16, 34, 41; TT E242 2; Rushworth, *Historical Collections* V, 19.

18 LJ V 357.

19 HMC Appendix to the 7th Report, 191; Adair, *Roundhead General*, 32; CJ II 654.

20 LJ V 386; CJ II 720; HMC Cowper ms, 320; Whitelock, *Memoirs*, 62–4; TT E240 9.

21 Everitt, *Community of Kent*, 111–15.

22 HMC Appendix to the 5th Report, 142.

23 LJ V 321; CSP Domestic 1641–3, 380.

24 TT E240 40, 46; TT E242 2; TT E124 4, 32; Devereux, *Earls of Essex*, 355; HMC Appendix to the 7th Report, 531; Wanklyn and Young, 'A king in search of soldiers', 150–1.

25 BL Additional ms 18978, 127.

26 TT E126 24; Ellis, *Letters*, 2nd series 3, 302.

chapter V

The battle of Edgehill

On the Sunday afternoon, the armies faced each other across a tract of arable and meadow just to the northwest of the Edgehill escarpment, with infantry in the centre and cavalry on the wings as was customary in open country. On the Royalist right wing was Prince Rupert with about 1,400 troopers drawn up in two lines, the second of which was commanded by Sir John Byron, the senior cavalry colonel. In the centre were five brigades of infantry, 10,000 strong, set out in checkerboard formation in the Swedish rather than the Dutch manner, but not interspersed with squadrons of cavalry. On the left wing Henry Wilmot headed a smaller force of about 1,100 troopers, also drawn up in two lines. There were no substantial reserves behind the main body of the army, only a single troop of gentlemen pensioners, Charles's bodyguard, and a company or so of infantry protecting the position where the artillery had been positioned.[1]

Essex concentrated most of his 2,000 or so horse on the left wing facing Prince Rupert. On the opposite wing he placed two regiments supported by dragoons. The twelve infantry regiments that had arrived in time he drew up in three very large brigades, each about 4,000 strong, the first in front and on the right, the second some way to its left and slightly to the rear, and the third in the centre but some distance away behind a shallow ridge on which he had placed his artillery. Between the infantry brigades was Essex's lifeguard of horse, commanded by Sir Phillip Stapleton. The whereabouts of the remainder of the cavalry, several hundred horse under Sir William Balfour's command, is unclear. They were supposed to have been on the right wing, but they appear to have been somewhere to the

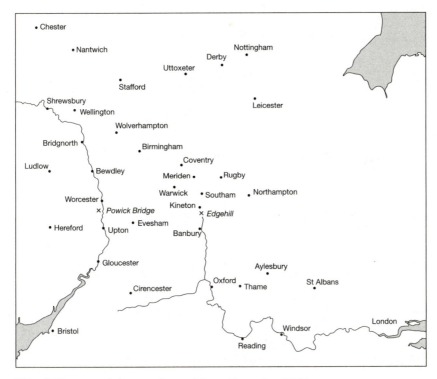

Map 1 The central theatre of war, July to November 1642

centre-rear when the battle began. They were possibly on their way to strengthen the left wing against Prince Rupert.[2]

The battle began with an attack by the whole of the Royalist cavalry. Essex's left wing was quickly overwhelmed by the first line of Rupert's horse, and as they fled they carried with them the second infantry brigade. The Royalist second line followed the first in disobedience to Rupert's orders, but this was not because Byron had lost control of his men. The troopers had been confused by a disruption in the first line as it charged caused by one of the enemy troops trying to change sides. On the Royalist left there was even less resistance, as Wilmot's men routed the cavalry and dragoons facing them and also Sir William Fairfax's infantry regiment. One commander, Sir Charles Lucas, apparently tried to stop his men before they lost formation, but they were swept away by a mob of defeated enemy horse and foot streaming in from the right before they could turn and attack Essex's remaining infantry.[3]

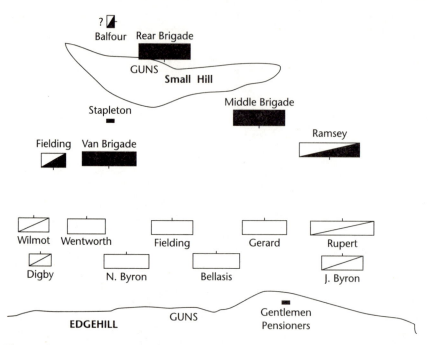

Figure 1 The battle of Edgehill, about 3p.m.

The infantry battle did not begin until almost all the cavalry had left the field. The Royalist brigades closed up to form a single line but did nothing to prevent Essex's third infantry brigade moving forward to take the place vacated by the second. Through the gap between the two Parliamentary brigades charged Sir William Balfour's squadron, which broke Fielding's brigade and possibly Bellasis's in the centre of the king's infantry formation. At about the same time, the two brigades on the Royalist left, Sir Nicholas Byron's and Henry Wentworth's, launched an attack on the remaining regiments of Essex's first brigade. However, this was discontinued after the intervention of Essex's lifeguard of horse, which may have charged Wentworth's brigade on its exposed flank, causing it to scurry back up the slopes of Edgehill, as it played no further part in the battle. The lifeguard then moved to the rear to protect the heavy artillery. After putting his men in order, Stapleton saw a body of what he took to be enemy horse riding towards him from the direction of the fighting. In fact, it was Balfour's squadrons, which, having inflicted some casualties on the Royalist artillery-

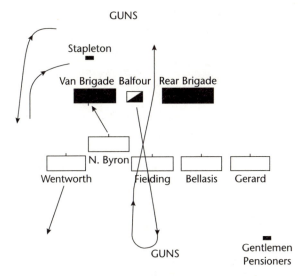

Figure 2 The battle of Edgehill, about 4p.m.

men, had ridden back through the gap they had created in the enemy infantry formation. Remarkably, they were not fired on by the musketeers of Sir Nicholas Byron's brigade, who took them to be their own cavalry reserves advancing to deliver a knockout blow against what was left of the enemy.[4]

With the centre of the Royalist line in disarray, the Earl of Essex decided to attack Sir Nicholas Byron's brigade. The three remaining regiments of the first brigade, supported by some regiments from the third, assaulted it from the front while Balfour's and Stapleton's cavalry attacked it in the flank and rear. After putting up a fierce fight, in which they sustained very heavy casualties, the Royalists retreated in great disorder, leaving the royal standard in enemy hands.[5] Having destroyed the left and centre of the enemy infantry formation, Essex drew up his remaining horse and foot as if to attack the Royalist right, where one or two brigades of infantry remained unbroken. However, by that time it was getting very dark. Moreover, the king's victorious cavalry were beginning to reappear on the battlefield. They had failed to make any impression on the Parliamentary rearguard as it entered Kineton at about 4.00 p.m., but they had managed to recapture the royal standard.[6] Both sides therefore withdrew for the night, Essex's army to the position that his third brigade had occupied at the start of the

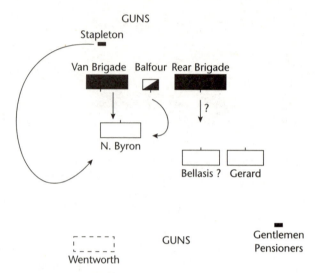

Figure 3 The battle of Edgehill, about 5p.m.

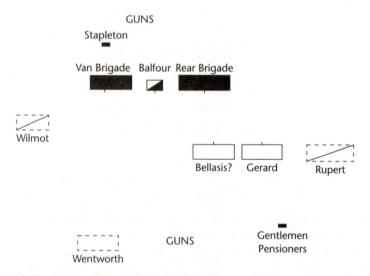

Figure 4 The battle of Edgehill, at nightfall

battle, the king's to the upper slopes of Edgehill. Neither side had won a clear victory, but Essex, reinforced by several fresh regiments of infantry and a number of troops of cavalry, looked to be in the better position to fight again on the morrow.[7]

Notes

1 Young, *Edgehill*, plate 9.

2 TT E126 1,24, 38; TT E242 2; James II, *Life*, 13. Essex's brigades were not tercios in the conventional European sense but appear to have been drawn up in linear or chequerboard formation. Otherwise it is impossible to see how Fairfax's regiment alone of the first brigade was routed.

3 TT E126,4; Carte, *Letters*, 10–11; TT E53 10.

4 Ludlow, *Memoirs*, 42; Bulstrode, *Memoirs*, 77–9; TT E124 26; TT E128 20; Carte, *Letters*, 10–11.

5 TT E124 26,32; TT E128 20.

6 TT E126 24, 39; Ludlow, *Memoirs*, 42–3.

7 *Ibid.*, 44–6; Rushworth, *Historical Collections* V, 35.

chapter VI

The first Thames valley campaign

The day after the battle the two armies faced one another for many hours, but fighting was not renewed. Both sides were in a state of shock induced by the bloody nature of the encounter, but they were also uncertain of the outcome. The Parliamentarians seem to have thought that they had won, as the enemy had retreated from the battlefield. Essex was advised to attack the king's forces, mainly by those who had missed the battle, but he thought better of it, probably because it would have meant advancing across open ground, thus inviting a charge by Charles's victorious cavalry. The king's military advisers, on the other hand, were not certain at first whether they had won or lost. They were not inclined to attack, as they knew that Essex's army had received substantial infantry reinforcements overnight, while their own strength in infantry had been severely depleted, as at least three of their five brigades had been routed. Thus neither side was confident enough to challenge the other to a second day's fighting. However, Royalist spirits lifted as the musketeers and pikemen belonging to the defeated brigades began returning to their colours. They soared when Essex's army retired towards Warwick in the late afternoon, whereupon Rupert unleashed his cavalry, causing heavy casualties among the enemy rearguard.

Essex's decision has been seen as leaving the way open for the king to continue his advance on London. However, the professionals on Essex's staff probably thought that the mauling the Royalist infantry had received meant that Charles's army would be incapable of resuming the offensive.

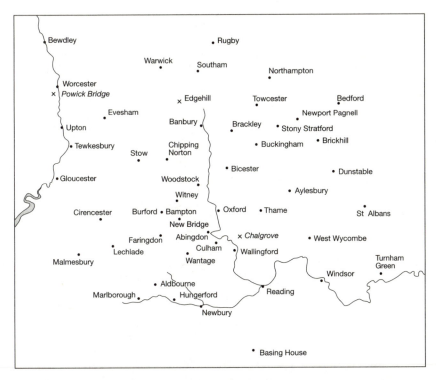

Map 2 The Thames valley theatre of war, 1642–45

They may therefore have expected the king to retreat towards Wales, a contingency that was apparently discussed by the Royalist council of war immediately after the battle. In such circumstances, Warwick would have been an excellent position from which to intercept the enemy army before it reached the Severn. There were only five bridges over the river between Shrewsbury and the estuary. Bridgnorth and Bewdley were some distance away. Moreover, to reach them, the king's troops would have to march across the front of Essex's army. Of the remainder, those at Worcester and Gloucester were in friendly hands, whereas the bridge at Upton could be seized or destroyed well before the king's army arrived by Parliamentary troops from Hereford or Worcester.[1]

When it became apparent that the king's army was on the move again, but making its way slowly towards Oxford rather than quickly towards the Severn crossings, Essex returned to Northampton, where his army rested from 31st October until the morning of 2nd November. However, he did

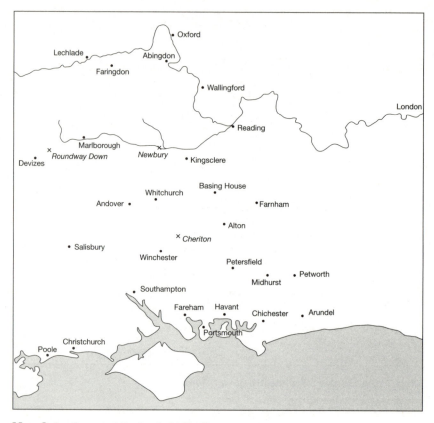

Map 3 South-central England, 1643–45

push forward a detachment to Aylesbury to guard one of the passes over the Chilterns. The considerations that lay behind a march across country that looked like a retreat are described in letters written from the army. Once it was clear that the king was not making for the safety of the Welsh hills, the lord general's preference would have been to pursue him, but the cavaliers had broken down all the bridges between Warwick and Oxford and so plundered the countryside that the Parliamentary army would have been starved of provisions if it had taken that route. Instead, Essex's plan was to place his army in such a position that it could quickly return to London if the Royalist army advanced in that direction, and Northampton, with its easy access to the present-day A5 road, was ideal for the purpose, whether the king took one of the routes across the Chilterns or approached the capital via the Thames valley. Thus, when news reached Northampton that the king's army was on the road from Oxford to Reading, Essex acted decisively. His army reached the capital on 8th November, well before the king's forces arrived in the London area.

The failure of the king's generals to make a rapid march on London before the enemy had time to recover from the shock of Edgehill has been seen as a fundamental mistake. However, contemporary sources differ concerning the timing of the meeting of the council of war that discussed the idea. James II in his autobiography, and Captain Pyne in his biographical sketch of Prince Rupert, allege that it took place on the day after the battle, when the two armies were still facing one another across the battlefield. The prince apparently suggested that he should lead a strike force of cavalry, dragoons and mounted musketeers across country and capture the MPs and Lords in a surprise attack on the Palace of Westminster, thus bringing the war to a speedy end. The suggestion was firmly rejected by the king's advisers, and rightly so given the circumstances. Essex was bound to respond, and indeed earlier in October he had made plans to use a 'flying army' if the king attempted to capture London by such a trick. And what would the rest of Essex's army have been doing in the meantime, reinforced as it had been by three regiments of foot and a regiment of cavalry, and with the king having few or no horse with which to defend his shattered infantry? Moreover, the evidence that such a discussion took place on the morning of 24th October is not at all convincing. Pyne himself had not been there, and James, only nine years of age at the time, is unlikely to have been personally present. However, the most telling counter argument is that Clarendon, who had been at Edgehill, does not mention it in his writings. If the discussion had taken place, it would have been completely out of character for him not to use it to add to the picture he was trying to build up of the prince as a hothead totally lacking in judgement.[2]

The more likely scenario is that Rupert proposed the surprise attack on 27th October, four days after the battle, when it stood less chance of ending in disaster. By that time Royalist confidence had risen yet again. Banbury had surrendered without a fight, and beyond it lay the undefended city of Oxford, large enough to offer some shelter for troops not selected for the assault on Parliament. However, the plan was still seriously flawed. Although the Royalists could have easily captured the Palace of Westminster, the Lords and the Commons would almost certainly have had plenty of time to escape to London before Rupert arrived. Capturing London was a completely different proposition. Admittedly the capital's defences were not in a good state of repair, but they would still have posed a formidable obstacle to an attacking force made up only of horse soldiers and musketeers. Without artillery, Rupert would have had no means of making a breach in the walls and, even if he had found a weak spot against which to make an assault, the defending force of London trained bands, well armed and well trained, would have found little difficulty in repelling it. An uprising by the king's supporters in the capital would have helped, but this would have had to take place without prior planning, and success in such circumstances could certainly not be guaranteed. Finally, although the Royalists were probably not aware of it, the opportunity to exploit the confusion and loss of confidence that followed Edgehill had passed. Before the end of October, the city had recovered its nerve and was busily raising a reserve army under the Earl of Warwick's command.

Instead of taking a gamble, the king opted for a more cautious strategy: a few days' pause at Oxford to put the city's defences into some sort of order and to replenish the ranks of his depleted infantry regiments with volunteers, followed by a measured march down the Thames valley. The justification was that it would give time for moderates in Parliament to respond to the king's request for serious peace negotiations. However, this was not to be. The first approach was made when the army reached Reading on 4th November, but Parliament's representatives did not come into the royal presence until the army reached Colnbrook, between Slough and Staines, a week later. As they talked only of a truce, Charles came to the conclusion that the Parliamentary leadership was merely playing for time, especially when news arrived that the Earl of Essex, his army and train of artillery were advancing westwards out of London towards Colnbrook. The response was swift. On the morning of 12th November, two brigades of foot attacked and destroyed an outlying detachment of the Parliamentary army quartered at Brentford, seven miles west of the capital. Afterwards the town was sacked. If the intention was to show Parliament the importance of taking negotiations seriously, the effect was the exact opposite. In London the king was adjudged to be guilty of dishonourable conduct in breaking the truce, while what had happened at Brentford was seen as evidence of how Charles's army would behave if it did manage to enter the capital.[3]

The day after the 'battle of Brentford' the king's troops encountered Parliament's field army, reinforced by the London trained bands, at Turnham Green, a mile nearer the capital. The force that Essex commanded was probably twice the size of the king's army and very much stronger in infantry and artillery, but the claim that it was also drawn up in a strong defensive position is probably incorrect. The Parliamentary army was described by one of those present as being deployed on the edge of Hounslow Heath in the conventional manner, with infantry in the centre, cavalry on both wings and a reserve to the rear. Only John Gwynne's account mentioned enclosures, whereas a letter from the Committee of Safety describing the Turnham Green episode placed the king's army behind hedges and Parliament's on the open common land. Another Royalist account, this time written immediately after the event, also describes the king's army as being 'in a close' but with the Parliamentary cavalry drawn up on a small piece of common that was not large enough for the king's cavalry to deploy in a similar manner. Given their lack of infantry and their inability to make best use of their horse, 'the greatest pillar of the army', the king's council of war 'very wisely' saw a direct assault on Essex's position as too risky.[4]

The alternative strategy of outflanking Essex's position by sending a brigade across the Thames to attack the city of London from the south was similarly rejected. Crossing the river was not the problem, as Essex had withdrawn the troops defending Kingston Bridge, but by splitting the army the king's council of war might encourage him to attack the troops left on the Middlesex bank. Moreover, even if the brigades on the Surrey bank had managed to capture Southwark, crossing the Thames into the city proper via London Bridge would have been impossible without a major collapse in the morale of the forces defending it.

Essex too had the option of launching an attack on the enemy army, but he chose not to do so and as a consequence was roundly condemned by civilians like Whitelock. The most he was prepared to do was to send a brigade around the north of the Royalist position, thus posing a threat to their escape route, but this entailed dividing his forces and he subsequently countermanded the order. Essex was not keen on taking risks, and rightly so as he could have lost the war in an afternoon. Moreover, in the Netherlands, where he and most of the professional soldiers on both sides had gained their experience, an army in the situation in which the king's army found itself would undoubtedly have withdrawn, giving the Parliamentarians a victory without having to strike a blow. Essex may also have feared that if he did attack, his cavalry would be as roughly handled as they had been at Edgehill, even though Rupert's men were not armed with carbines in the Dutch manner, and thus not best equipped to play a defensive role. Finally, the constricted nature of the battlefield at Turnham Green meant that the outcome of any attack would be doubtful.

Towards evening, the king's army duly retreated through Brentford, passing to the Surrey bank of the Thames at Kingston and breaking the bridge down as it went. This caused some consternation among the Parliamentarians, who thought that Charles might be heading for Kent or Portsmouth rather than retreating up the Thames valley. The anxiety persisted for some time, as the Royalist army remained in the Kingston area for a number of days. In the interim, a large body of mounted volunteers assembled at Southwark. Their task was presumably to delay the king's progress, thus giving Essex's army time to catch up.[5] However, it was not Charles's intention to march south. The reason his army took its time in leaving the immediate environs of London was probably because the king's generals hoped that Essex would be tempted to cross the Thames, and that this would provide them with the opportunity to fight a battle on a piece of open ground where the Royalist cavalry could destroy his army. But Essex refused to be tempted, despite instructions from the House of Commons that he was 'not to omit any opportunity in pursuing the king'. He seized the bridges across the Thames above Kingston as far as Maidenhead but made no attempt to cross the river. In fact he ordered the bridges to be destroyed, much to the surprise of a Royalist force charged with the same mission a day or so later. The king's supporters blamed his extreme caution on rebellion among his troops, but Essex's objective was to bring the campaigning season to an end in such a way as to ensure that the king's army no longer posed an immediate threat to London. Once this had been achieved, he intended to go into winter quarters in the Windsor/Maidenhead area, covering the western approaches to the capital. By late November the king's army had indeed gone into winter quarters at Oxford, Charles's base for the rest of the war, and in the small towns and villages surrounding it, but a brigade of infantry and some cavalry were left in garrison at Reading. The town was presumably seen as a possible starting point for another advance on London in the spring. Essex responded by quartering troops around the eastern fringes of Reading at Twyford, Wokingham and Henley, and stationing a large force at Aylesbury, 20 miles to the north, guarding one of the principal routes across the Chilterns in case the king had some thought of approaching London from that direction.[6]

The Earl of Essex also redeployed the forces he had left in the Severn valley area for their and its greater security. The two regiments still in garrison at Worcester were withdrawn to Gloucester, and then to Bristol, whose loyalty to the cause was causing great concern to local Parliamentarians. They were replaced at Gloucester by the Earl of Stamford's regiment, which had been in garrison at Hereford, although Stamford himself had by that time been appointed commander of Parliament's forces in the southwest of England. He left for Exeter early in January, taking one of the Worcester regiments with him, leaving Bristol in the charge of Colonel Thomas Essex. An important consequence of this relocation was that the king, having recovered Herefordshire and Worcestershire, issued a number of commissions to raise new regiments, most particularly in the latter county, which had contributed no more than a troop of horse to the field army for the 1642 campaign. Garrisons were also established in the two county towns. Thus, with the middle stretch of the Severn secured for the Royalist cause, the only gap in the land bridge between Oxford and the Welsh borders was the Cotswolds, where the Gloucestershire Parliamentarians were in the process of fortifying Cirencester.[7]

Notes

1   Clarendon, *Great Rebellion* vi, 79n; Whitelock, *Memoirs*, 64; TT E242 2; Ellis, *Letters*, 3rd series 4, 216.

2   Young, *Edgehill*, 279–80; Warburton, *Memoirs* I, 465–6.

3   Whitelock, *Memoirs*, 65; Clarendon, *Great Rebellion* vi, 129–36, 140–2.

4   Gwynne, *Military Memoirs*, 47; HMC Portland ms III, 100–1; Davies, 'Essex's army', 41–3.

5   Whitelock, *Memoirs*, 66; Ludlow, *Memoirs*, 46–8; CJ II 849, 851.

6   HMC Portland ms III, 100–1; Warwick, *Memoirs*, 257; Young, *Edgehill*, 181–2; TT E127 35; TT E242 35,37; Warburton, *Memoirs* II, 68–9.

7   HMC Portland ms I, 67, III 102; Corbet, *Military Government*, 14–15; TT E91 4.

Summary of Part II

The balance of military assets available to both sides at the start of the Civil War had been heavily weighted in favour of Charles I's opponents. Volunteers to fill the ranks of Parliament's army flocked in from London and its environs. There were sufficient weapons with which to arm them and there was no shortage of officers, both professionals and eager members of the gentry and aristocracy. Other military supplies were readily to hand, left over from the war against the Scots two years earlier or collected together more recently to put down the rebellion in Ireland. In July, August and early September the Parliamentary leadership made very good use of infantry and mounted units as they were formed. Kent and East Anglia were secured; the Marquis of Hertford frustrated in his attempt to secure central-southern England; and the king's commanders driven from the Thames valley and from Midlands towns such as Banbury, Warwick, Leicester and Coventry.

The king's army, on the other hand, came together slowly, as Sir Edward Nicholas, one of the secretaries of state, bewailed in a letter written to the Marquis of Ormonde on 31st August. However, Essex was unable to take advantage of the Royalists' period of extreme weakness. His army was not ready to take the field until the second week in September, by which time the king had managed to assemble a more substantial force at Nottingham and equip it with resources shipped over from the Continent or taken from the magazines of the county trained bands.[1] Nevertheless, muskets remained in short supply, and this probably helps to explain why the last infantry regiments to join the army performed the least effectively at Edgehill.[2]

Charles's initial lack of success lulled Essex and many others into a false sense of security. As the Parliamentary army continued to grow in size, it became widely believed that Charles would not dare risk his in a full-scale battle, as in the Second Bishops' War two years earlier. However, Essex did little to increase the pressure. As the king's army moved westwards from Nottingham, he merely shadowed its line of march. When it fixed its quarters at Shrewsbury, he occupied Worcester while deploying his infantry regiments in the towns of the lower Severn and Wye valleys in such a way as to prevent Charles receiving reinforcements from South Wales. Essex's big mistake was not to use his horse in a more active role, but he was probably deterred by the severe setback that his advance guard of cavalry and dragoons had suffered at Powick Bridge on 23rd September. A lack of accurate intelligence, caused by his consequent failure to use his cavalry for reconnaissance, largely explains not only why Essex was taken by surprise when Charles's army took the offensive in mid-October but also why he initially mistook the direction of its march. Thus the strategic initiative passed to the king. The fact that the first battle of the Great Civil War occurred when it did was because the king wished it.

After Edgehill, the strategic initiative still lay with the Royalist army. Charles has been described as having 'muffed his only chance of ending the war quickly' by not accepting Prince Rupert's advice on the day after the battle to seize Westminster with a force of mounted troops,[3] but this is a facile and ill-informed comment. Despite the clear statement in James II's memoirs, the balance of evidence is overwhelmingly in favour of the discussions having taken place in the king's council of war three days later. By that time, the Parliamentary leadership and its supporters in London had recovered their morale and begun to organize the abundant sources of men and munitions that they had to hand for the city's defence.

The agreed strategy of advancing down the Thames valley towards London was less of a gamble, but a gamble nevertheless. Its only chance of success would have been if either Essex had attacked the Royalist army as it advanced, which would have been out of character, or if moderates in the House of Commons and the House of Lords had achieved a majority in favour of peace, equally unlikely once it became apparent that Essex had managed to save the bulk of his army and would reach London before the king did. When the two armies did face one another again at Turnham Green in mid-November, the Royalist commanders agreed that they were not strong enough to attack and retreated back up the Thames valley. Even so, it can be argued in retrospect that the advance on London had been worth the effort. Casualties had been few, and the capture and garrisoning of Reading, in addition to giving the king a base from which to attack London in the spring, had immediate logistical benefits, in that it gave the Royalists control of the rich farmland of central Berkshire, where regiments could be quartered for the winter, thus reducing the pressure on the area around Oxford for supplies of food and fodder. However, the Royalist cause in a wider sense may have suffered on balance. Clarendon in particular viewed it as a humiliation. In his opinion, the field army should have ended its 1642 campaign with the capture of Oxford. The spring of 1643 would have been a better time for an attack on London, by which time the army would have received large reinforcements from other parts of England and Wales. By advancing on London too precipitately, then withdrawing without a fight, the weakness of the king's forces had been exposed, and the supporters of Parliament in consequence much encouraged.[4]

Notes

1   Wanklyn and Young, 'A king in search of soldiers', 150–1.

2   Bodleian Carte ms III, 474; Bulstrode, *Memoirs*, 77.

3   Kenyon, *Civil Wars*, 60.

4   Clarendon, *Great Rebellion* vi, 125, 142.

PART III

Parliament's offensive

chapter VII

Consolidation

I n the autumn of 1642, after the flight of the Marquis of Hertford and the return to Essex's army of the brigades commanded by the Earl of Bedford and Sir William Waller, there was a distinct power vacuum in the counties to the south of the Thames. However, once the Royalist advance on London had been turned back at Turnham Green, local loyalists sought to fill the vacuum, often with the aid of troops from the two field armies. Some of the king's supporters among the Surrey country gentlemen occupied Farnham Castle on the Hampshire border in late November, but Waller, sent back into south-central England with a small force of horse and dragoons, captured it in less than a day and then returned to the army. No sooner had he left than Lord Grandison's regiment of horse, which had fought with Wilmot at Edgehill, briefly occupied Basingstoke, whereupon the Marquis of Winchester seized the opportunity to put his principal residence, Basing Castle, two miles from the town, into a state of defence.[1] Further to the west, it was the supporters of Parliament who seized the initiative. Bristol was secured by the Earl of Stamford and garrisoned with troops from the field army, while Marlborough became the prime focus for activity in north Wiltshire. When Royalist cavalry patrols appeared on the surrounding hills in the last week of November, the inhabitants asked the lord general for military assistance. Essex sent them two Scottish officers, who set about fortifying the town and training the civilian population in the use of arms. Concerned with the enormous scale of their task and the closeness of the enemy, they begged for troops from the field army, but Essex dithered until it was too late. On 5th December, a scratch force of Royalist musketeers, cavalry and dragoons drawn from billets south of the Thames under the

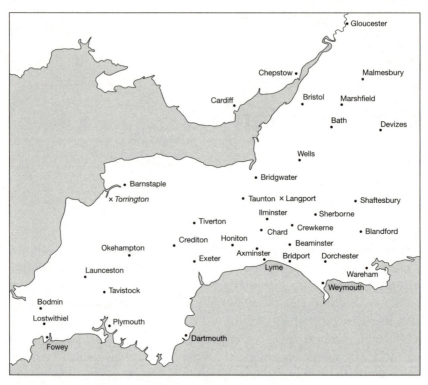

Map 4 The southwest of England and South Wales, 1642–46

command of Lord Wilmot sacked the town and marched many of its male inhabitants away into captivity. Finally, there was Royalist activity close to the south coast. Chichester declared for the king on 14th November, followed by Winchester three weeks later as troops from Oxford rode through the city on their way to support recruiting operations in west Sussex. Parliament's suspicions were raised that the king, known to be short of arms and ammunition, was about to try to recapture Portsmouth, which at the time was probably defended only by some of the Hampshire trained bands. Essex therefore sent Waller back into south-central England with over 2,000 horse and dragoons to clear the area of the enemy.[2]

Waller's first objective was the relief of Marlborough. Crossing the Thames at Henley he quickly reached Newbury, but there he heard that he was too late to save the town. His dragoons caught part of Wilmot's force at Wantage on its return march towards Oxford but inflicted few casualties, the operation being impeded by the atrocious weather. Waller's regiments then returned to Newbury. There they remained for a few days until they received orders to march into west Sussex, where they were to help local forces to recapture Chichester. When Waller's brigade arrived at Andover, one of his companies of dragoons was attacked in its quarters by cavalry from Winchester. Despite what was later claimed in newspaper reports, this was almost certainly a complete surprise. Winchester was on his itinerary, but he does not seem to have been aware that two of the regiments that had sacked Marlborough had taken up quarters there. Waller's men drove the Royalists back into the city, but their commander, probably unaware of the size of the force he was facing, decided to make a stand, not to retire into Sussex, despite having no infantry with which to defend the walls. Waller quickly carried the city by assault and the castle surrendered on terms. As a result, 500 or so troops of the king's field army passed into captivity, although Grandison himself managed to escape. After plundering the city and the cathedral, Waller's force moved on to Chichester, which surrendered after a two-week siege. Among the captives were at least two companies of dragoons and a number of Scottish officers sent from the Thames valley to recruit and train local volunteers. The city and cathedral suffered in the same way as Winchester had done the previous month, but Waller's own achievement had been the more impressive. He had conducted the siege using primarily the county trained bands, most of his regular regiments having returned to the field army before it was properly under way.[3]

It is impossible to say whether or not the king had a deliberate plan to occupy Hampshire and west Sussex and attack Portsmouth using troops from the field army. Such evidence as exists strongly implies that Grandison's men found themselves at Winchester by accident because of a miscarriage of orders. However, their presence so far from the perimeter of garrisons around Oxford suggests that they were part of a wider scheme of some kind. But, whatever the reason, the Parliamentary leadership's firm belief that there was such a strategy gave Waller the opportunity to refurbish the reputation he had won at Portsmouth, which had been badly tarnished at Edgehill.[4] After the capture in less than six weeks of Farnham, Winchester and Chichester Londoners hailed Waller as a new William the Conqueror. On 11th February, the two Houses of Parliament recognized the skills he had shown in handling large bodies of men and in commanding mixed forces of regular and trained band soldiers by promoting him from colonel of horse to major-general of Shropshire, Worcestershire, Gloucestershire,

Wiltshire and Somerset. His headquarters was to be at Bristol, the second largest city in England, which also had a substantial armaments industry.[5]

The timing of Waller's commission is witness to the deterioration of the military situation for the Parliamentarians in the Cotswolds and the lower Severn valley since 1st January 1643. The town of Cirencester, key to the central Cotswolds, had fallen to Prince Rupert and with it a thousand or so soldiers and large quantities of military supplies. Its capture was of even greater significance in strategic terms, as it completed Royalist control over the last section of the vital artery between Oxford and Royalist-controlled areas to the north and west, the so-called King's Road, along which passed recruits for the field army as well as arms and ammunition. To the Parliamentarians the loss of Cirencester, and the subsequent establishment of small garrisons there and at Malmesbury, posed a threat not only to communications between London and Bristol and Gloucester but also to the safety of the two cities. Such fears were exacerbated by Rupert's attempt immediately afterwards to persuade the governors, Edmund Massey and Thomas Essex, to change sides. Both were professional soldiers who had displayed no real evidence of religious enthusiasm, and who may simply have opted for the Parliamentary cause because it paid better.[6]

In assembling a brigade to defend his new command, Waller received some assistance from the Earl of Essex, namely his own regiment of horse, Sir Arthur Haselrig's troop, which was to form the nucleus of a regiment of heavy cavalry, and some dragoons, but no infantry. This niggardliness was not because the lord general disliked Sir William. Rather it reflected the fact that Waller was not the first but the last of a series of supplicants for troops from the field army to support military operations in the regions, whose activities are described later in this chapter.

Sir William set out from Farnham on 2nd March, arriving at Bristol a fortnight later. The five-week delay between the issuing of the commission and the start of the campaign is typical of Waller. Although a bold tactician, he was often a cautious strategist, rarely beginning a campaign or a new operation without making thorough preparations, including discovering the location of enemy forces. However, to non-professionals, this looked like time wasting, and the London press roundly criticized him in late February for his slowness and his failure to undertake any type of military operation. On this occasion, however, Waller had every reason to be cautious. After the capture of Cirencester, Rupert's flying army of cavalry and dragoons had rampaged across the chalk downs of Hampshire and Wiltshire. In the process they mauled a contingent of Waller's brigade at Alton in Hampshire in late February, causing him to recall his advance guard, which had already reached Winchester. Not surprisingly, when the march to Bristol began again a week later, Waller often moved his troops at night. His brigade also took a route well to the south of Rupert's area of operations, and as it passed through Winchester, Romsey, Salisbury, Sherborne, Wells and Bath it sacked churches and cathedrals, cozened local Royalists into surrendering their arms, and picked up the nuclei of two infantry regiments commanded by Somerset landowners. However, his *modus operandi* gave some cause for concern. He was criticized for not keeping the Committee of Safety, and by implication the lord general, informed of his movements so that they could be taken into account when formulating strategy.[7] Sir William's reply does not survive.

Having arrived at Bristol, Waller began to put together an army from the variety of units he had either brought with him or found already within the bounds of his command. He also continued to observe the movements of the enemy, and he spent a week at Gloucester assessing the military situation in the Severn valley and the opportunities it offered. At the beginning of the fourth week in March he finally took the offensive, but by that time he knew that Rupert's cavalry and dragoons were operating in the Aylesbury area: that is, too far away to pose an immediate threat to his plans.

One result of Waller's step-by-step approach was that he managed to alienate Colonel Nathaniel Fiennes, whose own march from the Windsor area to Bristol with several troops of horse and a regiment of dragoons had preceded his own by over a month. Once there Fiennes had deposed the governor, Thomas Essex, who was thought to be too friendly with fellow professionals fighting for the enemy, arrested some of his officers, uncovered a civilian plot to surrender the city to Prince Rupert, and began making provision for its defence. Later he and Waller were to be on different sides of a religious divide, but at the time dissatisfaction with Sir William probably stemmed from the fact that he had not been given an independent command as a reward for his success in securing Bristol. Admittedly he was now the city's governor, but as such he was subordinate to Waller and at his every beck and call. Within days of arriving, for example, Sir William demanded that Fiennes's troop should become part of the Western Association's marching army, not just a component of the Bristol garrison. This made good military sense given that the troop had fought in Balfour's squadrons at Edgehill, but Fiennes was upset at what he saw as an affront, particularly when Waller did not bother to reply to his letter of complaint. When Fiennes had an account of his own successes published in London in April, he used the opportunity to damn Waller with faint praise. While giving him full credit for operations against the Royalists from 25th March onwards, he reminded his readers of the general's lengthy stay at Farnham followed by a leisurely and circuitous march through southern England. As a result, Fiennes had been left on his own to face Prince Rupert, whose cavalry and dragoons had watched Bristol from the surrounding hills for two days and a night in early March waiting for Royalist sympathizers to open the gates.[8]

During the winter months, the territory immediately to the north of Oxford attracted less attention from the forces of either side than that to the south or the west. Local forces tried to force the Royalists out of Banbury in late December but were thwarted by the garrison commander, the Earl of Northampton. However, the earl's attempts to push into Northamptonshire were similarly thwarted by cavalry operating from the county town. Initially he had more success in Warwickshire, establishing a garrison in his own house at Compton Wynyates and a military presence at Stratford-upon-Avon. He also had some hopes of capturing Warwick Castle, which was held by a single company of foot. In March, however, a brigade of soldiers from the London area led by Lord Brooke chased the Royalists from Stratford and re-provisioned Warwick. Lord Brooke's orders were to establish a regional command in the central part of the Midlands by clearing Warwickshire of enemy troops and then expelling the weak Royalist garrisons holding Stafford and Lichfield in cooperation with forces from Cheshire and Derbyshire. However, Brooke was killed during the successful siege of Lichfield, and his composite army was defeated a few days later by a similarly constituted assemblage of Royalists from Banbury and the East Midlands led by the Earl of Northampton at Hopton Heath near Stafford. Here the Royalist commander met the same fate as Lord Brooke, and the two armies disaggregated.[9]

To the east and southeast of Oxford the Chilterns acted as a formidable defensive barrier behind which Essex's army could rest and recuperate. Rupert made serious attempts to capture Aylesbury, Parliament's only outpost to the west of the hills, in early November and again in mid-March, but Essex was able to rush in reinforcements to prevent this happening. The Buckinghamshire regiments in Essex's army attempted to lift the threat in late January by attacking two Royalist regiments quartered at Brill to keep an eye on Aylesbury, but they failed. Reading, however, although hemmed in by Parliamentary outposts, attracted little attention. Military operations against it during the winter were limited to probing attacks, which achieved nothing. What appears to have been a more serious attempt timed to coincide with the attack on Brill fell apart before it reached the town's defences.[10]

Beyond the central Midlands and south-central England other regional commands were beginning to take shape. The importance of Wales and the borderland to the king's ability to wage war was recognized by the appointment of Lord Capel as lieutenant-general of North Wales, Cheshire and Shropshire in February 1643. He was sent to Shrewsbury in the spring with orders to secure the region by fortifying the principal towns and raising several regiments of foot and horse, which were to provide assistance to adjacent regions as required, but North Wales and the borderland's greater significance in the king's grand strategy did not emerge until the very end of the year as a result of developments in Scotland and Ireland.[11] However, the seeds of the other two major Royalist regional commands had been sown before the battle of Edgehill with varying degrees of success. By the middle of October, the Earl of Newcastle was firmly in control of Cumberland, Westmorland, Northumberland and Durham and had raised a small army able to undertake offensive operations. In November he was invited by the Yorkshire Royalists to move into their county, where forces from Hull under Sir John Hotham the younger had broken a local truce and where Lord Fairfax and his son Sir Thomas were endeavouring to raise an army for Parliament in the West Riding.

Having established garrisons to safeguard the four most northerly counties of England, Newcastle and his army marched into Yorkshire. After a scrappy engagement at the crossing of the Tees on 1st December they occupied York, where the king's supporters in the county had taken refuge. However, the Yorkshire Parliamentarians continued to hover around the city, and there was an inconclusive engagement at Tadcaster in December, after which they retreated to their respective parts of the county. Newcastle established garrisons at Pontefract and Wakefield to guard York against attack from the West Riding. He then felt strong enough to lead a brigade into Nottinghamshire in obedience to the king's command to assist the sheriff of the county in occupying and fortifying Nottingham and Newark. By that time, the earl had received a more extensive commission from Charles covering Yorkshire, Nottinghamshire and Derbyshire.[12]

In the case of the county town, the local Parliamentarians got there first. Although they were few in number, Nottingham was an excellent defensive site and Newcastle dared not launch an assault. However, the Royalists had complete success at Newark. The earl began to fortify the town and, when he returned northwards, he left behind as governor a formidable Scottish professional soldier, Sir John Henderson, who rapidly put it and its castle into a good state of defence. Newark was to be a key Royalist stronghold for the rest of the war. Its strategic significance was threefold. It guarded an important crossing over the River Trent; it provided a gateway for attacking south Lincolnshire and the Fenlands, where there was considerable support for the Royalist cause; and, being 60 miles nearer to Oxford than York, it opened up the possibility of another 'King's Road' across the East Midlands to Banbury.[13]

The force that Newcastle led across the Tees was the progenitor of the king's Northern army, which by June 1643 rivalled the Oxford army in size. By the end of the year it dominated a tract of country stretching from southern Derbyshire to the Scottish border, but from the beginning of hostilities the northern command's prime purpose was to support the king's field army in its operations in the south of England, first with arms and ammunition and then with troops. Newcastle sent his first convoy of arms and ammunition to the king at Nottingham in August, escorted by his own troop of horse. Without it Charles could not have fought the Edgehill and Thames valley campaigns. In a letter written on 29th November he reminded Newcastle of his promise to join him with his army, a strategic plan confirmed in more general terms in a letter written by Sir Marmaduke Langdale in the same month. The significance of the northern command to the king's overall strategy became more immediate and more critical at the beginning of the new year.[14] On 22nd January, Queen Henrietta Maria landed at Bridlington with a large consignment of arms and ammunition purchased abroad. These were for the field army, the original intention being that they should be landed in Kent. However, the failure of the king's supporters to gain control of a port anywhere in southeast England had ensured that they could reach Oxford only by way of the northern command. Given the resource problem that the king faced, which is discussed in Chapter VIII, it was vital that these supplies arrived before the beginning of the 1643 campaigning season. However, between Oxford and Yorkshire lay a belt of territory controlled by Parliament's supporters, and Newcastle was not prepared to force his way through with Lord Fairfax following close behind. It was therefore up to the king to provide troops to escort the queen and her arms and ammunition to Oxford.[15]

If the establishment of Newcastle's command was a deliberate act on the king's part, the other very substantial Royalist regional army that came into being during the course of 1643 did so almost by accident. The Marquis of Hertford had been sent into Wiltshire and Somerset at about the same time as Newcastle had gone to the north, but he had encountered much stronger opposition from the supporters of Parliament. By the end of September 1642, he had left his command in the circumstances described in Chapter IV. His decision to send the few horse he had raised into Cornwall rather than anywhere else had been taken on grounds of expediency, not as a result of careful deliberation beforehand, but the consequences were to be immense. The military competence displayed by Sir Ralph Hopton, Sir John Berkeley and their companions helped the Cornish loyalists to overcome powerful local opposition and to establish a small Western army by the time of the first Thames valley campaign. Its strategic objective, like that of Newcastle's army, was to assist the field army against the Earl of Essex, and by the end of 1642 Hopton had duly secured Cornwall, invaded Devonshire and threatened Exeter. However, by mid-February the Earl of Stamford had reinforced the western Parliamentarians, and the Cornish were back across the Tamar. The wider perspective was even bleaker. Even if Hopton did manage to overcome regional opposition, it would be unsafe for him to leave the enclosed country that ended at the border between Devon and Dorset. The nucleus of the Western army was five infantry regiments. Hopton had been unable to recruit much more than a regiment of horse, and without cavalry support the Western army would be destroyed on the open chalk downs that lay between Lyme and Oxford.[16]

The contention that it was the objective of the king's advisers to build up the strength of the field army during the winter in preparation for the spring campaign is further supported by an analysis of its regimental history during the winter months. Although a few company and troop commanders such as Richard Bagot, Henry Hastings and Gervase Holles left for the regions with commissions as colonels to raise regiments of horse and foot, it is by no means certain that they all took their men with them, while Lord Capel left for Shrewsbury in March with no more than a single troop of horse. Moreover, the field army was strengthened by new arrivals. Just before the start of the new year, the Marquis of Hertford crossed the Severn and entered the Cotswolds with about 2,000 men, mostly infantry that had been raised in Caernarvonshire, Powys and the counties of southwest Wales. They joined Prince Rupert for operations against Cirencester soon afterwards. Lord Herbert was also raising further regiments in Glamorgan and Monmouthshire that were intended to be in the Oxford area by the spring.[17]

Support for the idea that the king intended to begin the 1643 campaigning season early is provided by the orders given to Sir Thomas Aston. In late January he and his small regiment of cavalry returned to Cheshire from Oxford to secure the city and county against a force that had just set out from London under Sir William Brereton. However, he was to take no longer than six weeks. Aston managed to lose the battle of Middlewich in mid-March, and with it a newly raised infantry regiment. His own regiment then returned to Oxford, probably with more troop commanders than it had set out, but Brereton was able quickly to build up a force strong enough to pen the remaining Cheshire Royalists up in Chester and its environs for most of the rest of the war. In this he received assistance from the Lancashire Parliamentarians, who overran almost the whole of that county after routing the Earl of Derby's troops at Whalley in April.[18]

A programme for concentrating forces in the Thames valley and adjacent areas in time for the spring campaign is not so clearly discernible in the resolutions of the Earl of Essex and the Committee of Safety. The three regiments of infantry left in garrison in the counties bordering Wales never rejoined his army. The Earl of Stamford's remained in garrison at Gloucester. Although it lost many men at Cirencester in February, its commander, Lieutenant-Colonel Edward Massey, used the remainder very effectively in operations in that county and beyond until he became major-general of the West of England in May 1645. Of the two regiments originally at Worcester, one remained in garrison at Bristol until the Royalists captured the city in July 1643; the other marched into the southwest of England under Stamford's command in January 1643. After the surrender of Exeter in August the London Greycoats, as they were popularly called, were permitted to march back into Parliament's quarters, by that time a hundred miles to the east. Whether the regiment disintegrated completely *en route* or was broken up and incorporated into Essex's or Waller's army is not known.[19]

More significant was the drain of troops towards the west, as opposed to the southwest, of England. The brigades of Nathaniel Fiennes and Sir William Waller left Essex's army for Bristol in February, never to return. They quickly became the core of the army under Waller's command, which had grown to a force of 5,000 or so men by the summer. This mushroom growth had two unfortunate consequences. First, Waller's successes against easy opposition in the spring of 1643 caused criticism to grow of Essex's conduct of the field army's operations. This bred resentment in Essex's mind and ambition in Waller's, with the result that each blamed the other when he did not receive the military support he expected. Second, Waller began to act as if he had a completely independent command, the dire consequences of which are discussed in Chapters VIII and IX.[20]

On the other hand, the regional army that the two Fairfaxes had established in Yorkshire by the end of 1642 was made up almost entirely of locally raised troops. This had not been the original intention. Two regiments with Yorkshire colonels were raised in London for service in their home county but were drafted into Essex's army for the Edgehill campaign. One, Sir William Fairfax's, may have been shipped to Hull during the winter, but this is by no means certain. It was routed by Wilmot's cavalry at Edgehill and may only have shared a name with the regiment that fought under Lord Fairfax in the north in 1643. However, the second regiment, that commanded at Edgehill by Sir William Constable, had fought well and remained part of Essex's army until absorbed into other foot regiments in the spring of 1645. However, Lord Willoughby of Parham's cavalry regiment, also raised for service in the north, although sucked into the Edgehill campaign by necessity, was fighting in Lincolnshire by January 1643. It returned to the north with a troop raised in Nottinghamshire in the summer of 1642 by Henry Ireton, Oliver Cromwell's future son-in-law and confidant.[21] At about the same time, Cromwell himself set out for Huntingdonshire with his troop of horse, which had arrived late for Edgehill but then probably run away along with the rest. He had a commission to raise a cavalry regiment, which he intended to be significantly different in composition and in commitment.[22]

This leakage of experienced units from Parliament's field army was offset by reinforcements from East Anglia. In February 1643, Lord Grey of Wark was commissioned as major-general of Norfolk, Suffolk, Essex, Cambridgeshire and Hertfordshire, the so-called Eastern Association, with orders to raise a regional defence force, which was to reinforce the field army on a temporary basis as required. His commission has not survived, but this aspect of its intended role is implicit in documents issued by Grey to his county committees. In April he joined the Earl of Essex in the Thames valley with a brigade of about 6,000 foot and horse. It played some part in the ensuing campaign, but by the middle of July what was left of it was back in the Association preparing to defend East Anglia against attack from the north. The experience had not been a happy one for either Lord Grey or his troops.[23] In just over two months the brigade had probably lost half its strength through disease and desertion. Grey himself was despondent, having been obstructed in his efforts to raise and maintain an army by the county committees serving under him. He had also had to endure the mockery of the Oxford newspaper *Mercurius Aulicus*, which compared his men to Falstaff's band in Shakespeare's *Henry IV*. Soon afterwards Lord Grey was dismissed, having refused to go on a mission to Scotland on the grounds that it would cause his regiments to disband.

Oliver Cromwell took no part in the Thames valley expedition. He remained in the Association, raising his regiment of horse and acting as Grey's second-in-command. His role was a defensive one similar to that performed by Waller in the south of England in the winter of 1642, that is putting down Royalist uprisings and defending the Eastern Association against possible threats from Newark after Ballard had suffered a disaster when he tried to capture the town in February. Lowestoft and Crowland were subdued in quick succession boosting Oliver's self-confidence no end. He also imposed Parliament's authority on such potential nests of Royalism as Cambridge, Peterborough and Stamford. However, more significant in the short run for Parliament's field army was the ongoing contribution of London. Two regiments of the city's trained bands joined Essex for the Thames valley campaign, as did six new regiments of regular infantry raised in the city by the Earl of Warwick during the threat to the capital in October and November 1642.[24]

Notes

1 CJ II 854, 860, 863; TT E130 13; TT E242 37; HMC Appendix to the 7th Report, 444.

2 Petrie, *Letters of Charles I*, 108; BL additional ms 27402, 8–10; TT E83 11; TT E127 21; HMC Appendix to the 5th Report, 61; HMC Portland ms I, 73; Rushworth, *Historical Collections* V, 82–3.

3 BL Additional ms 27402, 11–13; TT E84 22; TT E244 14; Adair, *Roundhead General*, 43–7.

4 At the start of the battle, one of the troops belonging to his regiment had deserted to the enemy. Soon afterwards, the rest fled the field like the rest of Parliament's left wing, taking Sir William with them.

5 TT E127 21; TT E128 28; Firth and Rait, *Acts and Ordinances* I, 79; Lynch, *For King and Parliament*, 122–32.

6 TT E90 11; Somers, *Tracts* IV, 510–11; Corbet, *Military Government*, 19–20, 22; Reid, *All the King's Armies*, 32.

7 TT E90 28; TT E91 5; Warburton, *Memoirs* II, 141.

8 TT E94 12; TT E97 6.

9 Warburton, *Memoirs* I, 504–5; *ibid.*, II, 116; Whitelock, *Memoirs*, 69; HMC Appendix to the 9th Report II, 434.

10 Whitelock, *Memoirs*, 64; TT E94 2; Adair, *Hampden*, 209–10.

11 HMC Beaufort ms, 38–9.

12 Cavendish, *Duke of Newcastle*, 20–1; BL Harleian ms 6988, 130; Slingsby, *Diary*, 84–7.

13 Hutchinson, *Memoirs*, 110–24; Young, *Newark*, 17; Cavendish, *Duke of Newcastle*, 28.

14 BL Harleian ms 6988, 127–8, 130; Sunderland, *Lord Langdale*, 64–5.

15 Dugdale, *Diary*, 47; Clarendon, *Great Rebellion* vii, 31.

16 Hopton, *Bellum Civile*, 25–30; TT E100 6.

17 Young, *Edgehill*, 215, 221; Reid, *All the King's Armies*, 19.

18 TT E246 3; Malbon, *Memoirs*, 34–42; BL Additional ms 36913, 112–22, 145–55.

19 TT E91 4, 25; HMC Appendix to the 5th Report, 63; HMC Portland ms I, 103–13; HMC Portland ms III, 67, 71.

20 Whitelock, *Memoirs*, 70; Adair, *Roundhead General*, 69; see also Chapter VIII.

21 TT E244 16; CJ II 893; Hutchinson, *Memoirs*, 118; Bodleian Tanner ms 64, 138.

22 Ashley, *The Greatness of Oliver Cromwell*, 108–12.

23 TT E96 16.

24 *Mercurius Aulicus*, 188; HMC Portland ms I, 704; LJ VI 86, 145; Davies, 'Essex's army', 39.

The second Thames valley campaign

The strategy devised by the Royalists for the 1643 campaigning season has been the subject of a debate that has rumbled on for years among those who write about seventeenth-century English history. Parliament's strategy, on the other hand, has attracted little attention other than as part of the backdrop against which political squabbles were played out at Westminster and in the city of London.

Forcing the king to abandon the war and to return to Westminster remained Parliament's war aim. The peace talks that took place at Oxford in late March and early April, if anything, strengthened that determination, as Charles's negotiators had reacted unsympathetically towards terms that were little different from those that had been on the table before the war began. The key strategic objective for 1643 was therefore to defeat the king's field army in battle before he could strengthen it by drawing on support from the regions. This meant that when the peace talks ended the Earl of Essex must immediately go on the offensive in the vital Thames valley theatre of war. A victory there would bring the war to a speedy close or, at the very least, remove the direct threat to London by forcing Charles back into the Welsh Marches or even the north of England.

To achieve its objective, the two Houses took measures during the winter to maintain, and indeed strengthen, Essex's army by, for example, adding to it the new regiments raised by the Earl of Warwick. However, Parliament had to listen to its paymasters in London, who distrusted the commitment to outright victory of the professional officers serving under

Essex, some of whom appeared to be encouraging his natural caution. Professionals, being mercenaries, had a vested interest in the war continuing and were of uncertain loyalty, having no ideological commitment to the cause. As a result, they were carefully watched, and if they showed signs of being too familiar with the enemy, they were removed from their commands, as happened in the case of Colonel Thomas Essex, the first governor of Bristol. There were also concerns that too much money would be absorbed by pay if the earl responded to a manpower crisis in the field army by raising additional regiments. Under-strength regiments were accordingly broken up, their officers discharged or given commands in the regions, and the rank and file allocated to other colonels.[1] Nevertheless, with reinforcements from East Anglia and London, the body of infantry under Essex's direct or indirect control for the Thames valley campaign in 1643 was considerably larger than the one he had commanded at Edgehill. However, cavalry was a major headache. In April 1643, the earl's army was even more heavily outnumbered than it had been at Edgehill, partly because of the king's success in raising new regiments of horse, partly because so many mounted troops had been despatched to other parts of the country during the winter.[2] There was also a big question mark over the quality of the horse that remained, many of whom had run away at Edgehill.

Problems with his cavalry restricted the lord general's options. In enclosed country he could use them with confidence, knowing that the horse, even if they became separated from the foot, could defend themselves against Rupert's regiments, provided that they were accompanied by dragoons. In open country, however, he dared not risk them straying too far from his pikemen and musketeers. Vigorous offensive operations were therefore out of the question, as he explained in a letter written to the Speaker of the House of Commons towards the end of the campaign:

this army being recruited with neither horses, arms, nor saddles, it is impossible . . . to fight with them (the Royalists) but when and where they list; we being forced when we move to march with the whole army, which can be but slowly. . . .[3]

Essex's ideal scenario would have been a battle in which the king's forces attacked Parliament's field army in unfavourable circumstances and suffered such heavy casualties that they could no longer campaign on equal terms. Yet the king also had every reason for being cautious because of his army's deficiencies in foot soldiers. Stalemate therefore looked as likely an outcome of the second Thames valley campaign as the first, provided that the king's commanders were not as unduly rash or that logistical factors, like shortage of gunpowder, did not force the Royalists to sue for peace.

The role of Parliament's regional commands was first to prevent reinforcements being sent to the king but also to give assistance to the Earl of Essex in the Thames valley if ordered to do so. The Eastern Association under Lord Grey of Wark was to fulfil its obligations, but some of the others were in no position to provide assistance. The central Midlands command went into abeyance on the death of Lord Brooke. It was not revived until mid-June, by which time the Thames valley campaign was to all intents and purposes over.[4] Two of the other regional commanders, the Earl of Stamford in the far west and Lord Fairfax in Yorkshire, were too far away and too hard-pressed by the enemy to spare any resources. A greater East Midlands command, which included counties as far south as Bedfordshire and Buckinghamshire, was the responsibility of Lord Grey of Groby, eldest son of Lord Stamford. He did what he could but was never able to impose his authority on an area that was too extensive and heavily dominated by particularist interests. As a result, his writ ran strongly only in Leicestershire, where the Grey family estates were concentrated. The committees in the other seven counties tended to run their own affairs, particularly if there was a strong local commander like Sir John Gell in Derbyshire.[5] Beyond the fringes of Grey's command, there were other powerful personalities, like Lord Willoughby of Parham in Lincolnshire and Sir William Brereton in Cheshire, but both were faced by a determined enemy in their own localities, the Newark garrison and Lord Capel, respectively. Finally, there was Sir William Waller. His primary tasks were to preserve Bristol and Gloucester against capture and to prevent reinforcements from South Wales under Lord Herbert reaching Oxford.[6] Once these objectives had been achieved, Essex intended that Waller's forces should play as direct a role in the Thames valley campaign as Lord Grey of Wark's.

Before the lord general began his spring offensive, Waller opened his campaign in the lower Severn valley in spectacular fashion. Gloucester had been threatened for some time by the brigade of infantry raised by Lord Herbert in Monmouthshire and Glamorgan. Consisting almost exclusively of raw recruits officered by gentry with little military experience, it had overrun the Forest of Dean, dispersing a similarly inexperienced force of Gloucestershire Parliamentarians. It had then taken up a reasonably secure defensive position at Highnam on the Welsh bank of the Severn only two miles from Gloucester, but having little in the way of artillery and no experience of siege warfare, all it could do was pull faces at Massey and try to prevent his obtaining supplies from the countryside to the west of Severn. A smaller force of infantry and dragoons stationed at Cirencester since its capture in early February was intended to perform the same function on the east bank of the river. Neither body was thought to be under any threat until Waller's arrival at Bristol on 15th March. This was not known in Oxford until the 20th, but it set alarm bells ringing. Three regiments were immediately sent to Cirencester under Lord Grandison's command, where they arrived on the 22nd. On that day Waller attacked Malmesbury, which surrendered within 24 hours. He then threatened Cirencester but decided that it was too strong to attack. Grandison's orders are not known, but he was probably told merely to watch Waller's movements until Rupert appeared with reinforcements, the prince having returned to Oxford from Aylesbury on the day that news arrived that Waller's force had reached Bristol. On 25th March Rupert and his force duly arrived at Cirencester, but by then it was too late. Waller had sprung yet another surprise.

Crossing the River Severn at Framilode, seven miles below Gloucester, via a bridge of boats Sir William surrounded Highnam on March 24th with the assistance of soldiers from the Gloucester garrison. Early the following morning he persuaded the Royalists to surrender. Grandison learned what was happening but could do nothing about it. His force was larger than the one with which he had faced Waller at Winchester in December, but still too small to be effective. More importantly, it was too far away to intervene, as it was a ride of 50 miles from Cirencester to Highnam via Upton-on-Severn, the nearest bridge over the river controlled by the Royalists. Even if Rupert's flying army had arrived at Cirencester a day earlier instead of spending the night at Lechlade, he would still have been too late to save Herbert's force.[7]

Prince Rupert made no attempt to confront Waller, who by the evening of the 25th was safe within the walls of Gloucester. Instead he rode back to Oxford, recapturing Malmesbury on the way and installing a new garrison there. Lord Clarendon exaggerated the significance of the Highnam episode, but its importance should not be underestimated. The king lost 1,500 foot soldiers intended for the Oxford army, which was short of infantry, and Waller's reputation received a further boost.[8] On the other hand, however impressive his tactics, all Sir William's successes up to that point had been either against raw recruits, as at Farnham, Chichester and Highnam, or against a heavily outnumbered enemy, as at Portsmouth and Winchester. The quality of his troops had yet to be tested in a situation where the odds were even or stacked against them. Also, he had not fought a set-piece battle, where other skills of generalship were required.

However, the withdrawal of Rupert did not signify that the king was prepared to allow Sir William Waller to control the lower Severn valley, even temporarily. Instead he sent Prince Maurice, Rupert's younger brother, with some cavalry and dragoons to join Grandison at Cirencester. For the next fortnight, Maurice and Waller chased each other around the Forest of Dean and the vale of Tewkesbury, with Maurice, on the whole, having the better of the scraps. On one occasion he nearly trapped Waller's army between the forest and the River Severn; on another he beat up Waller's rearguard at Ripple, near Tewkesbury. Waller, on the other hand, managed to destroy a small force of Royalist infantry at Tewkesbury when Maurice was caught on the wrong side of the Severn. But just as the prince seemed to be getting the upper hand, he and his brigade were ordered to return to Oxford to reinforce the field army for a confrontation with the Earl of Essex. The lord general had left Windsor on 13th April, immediately after the peace negotiations came to an end, and was setting siege to Reading.[9]

Although at the beginning of the year the king had intended to take the field in late March, he was not able to do so because of a lack of military resources, most particularly gunpowder and match. This was seen as only a short-term problem, as the supplies the queen had brought from the Continent included hundreds of barrels of gunpowder. All that was needed was for them to be safely conveyed to Oxford. However, Newcastle persuaded her that he dared not leave the north of England until the Fairfaxes had been driven from Yorkshire. Prince Rupert was therefore ordered to assemble a force of cavalry, infantry and dragoons, which duly left for the north at the end of March. He sacked Birmingham on 3rd April and then set siege to Lichfield. Once Lichfield had fallen, his intention was to attack Derby or Nantwich, the headquarters of Sir William Brereton and Sir John Gell, respectively. This uncharacteristically leisurely progress was almost certainly because neither he nor the council of war believed that there was any urgency about bringing the gunpowder to Oxford. The queen herself was not ready, and even when the peace negotiations came to an end, Essex was thought unlikely on past experience to make any move that would directly threaten the Royalist headquarters. Moreover, the attack on Reading was not unexpected. Given its garrison of 3,000 foot the earl would not dare bypass it whether he decided to advance on Oxford via the north bank of the Thames or the south. However, it had an experienced governor in Sir Arthur Aston, who had put the town into a good state of defence during the winter.[10] It was therefore deemed capable of withstanding a lengthy siege, thus giving the convoy from the north time to arrive. After this the king's field army could take the offensive, forcing the lord general either to fight or to retreat.

A letter written to Rupert immediately after Essex's army had surrounded Reading showed that the king and his advisers were not particularly worried about the turn of events. All the prince was ordered to do was abandon his operations against Lichfield and join the queen without delay. However, when Essex showed signs of preparing to take the town by assault, panic set in and Rupert was recalled, although by that time he had managed to capture the city. The lord general then rolled out the second stage of his strategy: Sir William Waller was ordered to bring all the forces he could muster to join the field army. This was particularly important as Waller's army was strong in cavalry, with possibly as many as 1,500 horse to Essex's 2,500. Together they would probably have outnumbered the Royalists on the battlefield. Oliver Cromwell and the Parliamentary commanders in the East Midlands, on the other hand, were not required to come south but to combine their forces to stop the queen's convoy leaving the Trent valley.[11]

On 26th April the king, reinforced by both Rupert and Maurice, advanced on Reading along the south bank of the Thames. In order to approach the town they needed to cross the bridge at Caversham, which was heavily defended by Essex's troops. Attempts to capture the bridge were met with very heavy fire, which the Royalists could not match, and casualties began to mount. The king's army then withdrew out of range to discuss the options, but early the following day Reading surrendered on generous terms, namely that the garrison, minus its arms and ammunition, could march to the king's quarters. Colonel Richard Fielding the acting governor, Sir Arthur Aston having been struck dumb by a falling roof tile some days before, was condemned to death by court martial for surrendering the town unnecessarily, but he was reprieved at the last moment. In the meantime, the king's infantry were set to work constructing a fortified camp at Culham, near Abingdon, covering the southern approaches to Oxford.

Essex did not follow up his success before Reading with an immediate advance on Oxford. Disease, probably typhus, was killing off his soldiers;

those who survived refused to march without pay; and as a result the strategic initiative was lost. Contemporaries and historians alike blame the lord general's habitual caution, but he had every reason to be cautious.[12] An approach to Oxford via the open field country to the north of the Thames beyond the Chilterns would enable the king to take full advantage of his superiority in cavalry. An advance through Berkshire, hugging the south bank of the Thames, was a more practicable proposition, as it would pass for the most part through enclosed country with plenty of woodland, but it would eventually entail an attack on the king's infantry brigades behind their new fortifications at Culham. Finally, whichever route Essex chose, his communications with Reading would be endangered by enemy units operating out of the Royalist garrisons at Wallingford and Abingdon, which could operate on either bank of the Thames.

The only way to smoke the Royalist infantry out of their lair at Culham would have been for Sir William Waller to attack Oxford from the west. This is what the amateur strategists in London expected, with one paper taking military speculation into the realms of fantasy by reporting that Waller had tricked his way into Oxford claiming to be Prince Maurice and captured the king's ministers. The king's commanders were also expecting Waller to move towards Oxford. On 26th April, the governor of Banbury was urged to keep a good watch out for his approach, as he frequently marched by night. However, Sir William, ignoring Essex's commands, was well the other side of the Severn terrorising the Royalists of Herefordshire, having occupied the county town in the face of limited opposition on the day that Reading fell. Even so, Waller's movements continued to be a cause of concern to the Royalist council of war. Prince Maurice was sent back into the Severn valley early in May, probably with the intention of protecting Worcester against attack by Waller but possibly to distract him from advancing on Oxford.[13]

Although Essex complained about Waller's failure to obey orders during the siege of Reading, subsequently he may have seen some advantage in it: the surrender of the town was his triumph alone. It had also worsened the king's resource problems, most of his remaining gunpowder having been either expended in the attempt to cross Caversham Bridge or captured when Reading surrendered. Rumours were circulating among Royalist commanders in the regions that Charles was planning to leave Oxford for a less exposed headquarters. This was indeed discussed at a council of war held immediately after the loss of Reading but was rejected on Rupert's advice.

However, by the middle of May, the military pendulum was beginning to swing back again towards the king. Essex's inactivity encouraged the king to risk sending the Marquis of Hertford into Wiltshire on a recruiting expedition escorted by a brigade of old and new horse, that is cavalry that had fought at Edgehill or been raised subsequently, but what really made the difference was the arrival at Oxford of a convoy from the north carrying 1,500 muskets, 300 barrels of gunpowder and other military supplies. Escorted by two regiments of foot and cavalry from the East Midlands garrisons commanded by Colonel Hastings, the governor of Ashby-de-la-Zouch, it had made its way very rapidly from York to Newark and so to Woodstock without encountering any opposition from the local Parliamentarians. Distracted, it seems, by problems of security in their own counties, the Roundhead leaders of the East Midlands and the Fenland counties could not combine their forces until 9th May, by which time the convoy was well on its way.[14] What is surprising is that Essex himself did nothing. Possibly he did not know that the convoy had left Newark: the intelligence network managed by his spymaster Sir Samuel Luke did not stretch that far north at the time. However, the most likely reason is that he considered interception too risky given the Royalist superiority in cavalry and the open nature of the landscape for 40 miles to the north of Oxford. Essex was therefore completely reliant on the provincial commanders. Not surprisingly, he was incensed by what he saw as their negligence, but Waller's name was not mentioned. The route taken by the convoy meant that Sir William was too far to the west to have interfered with its progress.[15]

Although the arrival of the munitions convoy restored Royalist confidence, the council of war did not feel totally secure. The infantry therefore remained at Culham, but the cavalry were employed further afield. Lord Wentworth and Sir John Byron quartered themselves in north Buckinghamshire, threatening communications between London and the northwest, but Prince Maurice was sent from the Severn valley to join the Marquis of Hertford in Wiltshire because of rumours that Waller would soon be heading in that direction. This was indeed the Earl of Essex's intention. Sir William's new orders were to march south, disrupt Hertford's recruiting operation and then proceed into the far southwest of England, where Stamford, the regional commander, had lost an important battle at Stratton in the northeast of Cornwall on 16th May. However, Stratton was only important in a regional context. It did not make the journey of the Royalist Western army to join the king that much easier, as much of Stamford's cavalry had escaped. To cross the chalk downs of Dorset and Wiltshire in safety it would need help, and the most obvious source of help was the force commanded by Prince Maurice and the Marquis of Hertford.[16]

Essex's plans for Waller's army were both prudent and practicable. If Sir William had carried them out with his customary verve, he could have kept the two Royalist forces apart and possibly destroyed them both. However, he had other ideas. After journeying to Bath on 22nd May to reassure local commanders that he would soon return, Waller moved to the opposite end of his command in the belief that he could capture the city of Worcester as easily as he had captured Hereford in the preceding month. He justified this to local commanders in Somerset and Dorset on the grounds that its capture would allow him to remove the garrison at Tewkesbury, allegedly 1,000 strong, and add it to his marching army. But Sir William was being economical with the truth. He stood a chance of capturing Worcester, but he would have been quite incapable of garrisoning it without using the troops at Tewkesbury, which were no more than a single newly raised regiment of foot and a few horse. However, the attack on Worcester at the end of May failed utterly. Waller duly set out for Somerset a few days afterwards, but too late to prevent the two corps of what can now be described as the Royalist army of the west uniting at Chard on 4th June and occupying most of the county, including the two principal towns, Taunton and Bridgwater.[17]

Early in June, goaded by radicals in London and the House of Commons but with no additional resources, Essex reluctantly resumed his offensive in the Thames valley. Avoiding the obvious route to Oxford along the riverside, he moved his army north through the Chilterns and then east, occupying the town of Thame and thus threatening the north side of Oxford. This alarmed the Royalist council of war, which ordered the camp at Culham to be abandoned and the king's infantry to be stationed along the line of the river Cherwell. Probing attacks to test the strength of the defences of the bridge at Wheatley, the most direct route to the city, between 6th and 8th June caused some concern. A week or so later, there appears to have been an unsuccessful attempt to cross the Cherwell at the village of Islip, after which Essex's offensive fizzled out in the face of Royalist counterattacks.[18] Prince Rupert, having learned of the exact dispositions of Parliament's field army from a deserter, Colonel Urry, directed two substantial raids against Essex's outposts. When a scratch force of Parliamentary cavalry tried to inter-cept him on his return from the first raid at Chalgrove, just to the east of Oxford, there was a fierce fight, but the Royalists won convincingly yet again.

Among those mortally wounded in the engagement was John Hampden, one of the leaders of the House of Commons and a possible replacement for Essex as general. The second raid on West Wycombe, deep in the Chilterns, was almost unopposed. These setbacks convinced Essex that he could do nothing further without additional resources, and he invited a party of MPs and peers to inspect his army and report back to the two Houses on its disastrous condition. For the present, all he could do was defend the territory he held.[19]

In early July the earl and his army abandoned Thame and moved to the north of Aylesbury, the intention being to protect the Ouse valley against plunder and to block any attempt by the king's field army to march into the Eastern Association. Once there he would also be better placed to intercept a second, even larger convoy of arms and ammunition that Henrietta Maria herself was threatening to lead from Newark to Oxford. Her march south had been delayed for several weeks by the successful rendezvous of a large force of cavalry and dragoons from Hull, the East Midlands and East Anglia at Nottingham at the end of May. It was only after quarrels between the leaders, and the return of the Lincolnshire and Derbyshire forces to their respective counties, that she was able to set out on 3rd July. Essex had responded to a call from Cromwell and Lord Grey of Groby that they needed an experienced commander to lead them by sending Sir John Meldrum to Nottingham, but Meldrum found that the forces that remained were too weak to attack her. He nevertheless shadowed the queen's convoy as far as Dunsmore Heath outside Coventry in the hope that more troops would join him, but Essex could not send assistance without first fighting a battle with Rupert, whose cavalry lay across his line of march to Coventry from north Buckinghamshire. Another possible source of assistance against the queen was Sir William Brereton, but he was too tied up in Cheshire after suffering two minor reverses at the hands of the local Royalists in June and early July. Waller also was too preoccupied in administering the killer blow to the king's Western army at Devizes to provide any help. As a result, the second convoy arrived without incident in the Banbury area on 13th July, having travelled the length of Roundhead-controlled Warwickshire.[20]

Realizing a few days earlier that he was powerless to do anything to prevent the convoy's arrival, Essex seemingly gave way to despair. Blaming his inactivity on a massive lack of resources, he suggested to Parliament that his and the king's army should come together and fight it out in a trial by ordeal, the result of which would be a clear sign of God's wishes for the future political and religious structure of England and Wales. This strange recommendation was taken at the time as evidence of lack of moral fibre, but it may have been a final desperate attempt to force Parliament to send him money and supplies, without which the war could easily be lost simply through the mouldering away of his army. If the latter was the case, Essex must be commended for his realism. Unlike many of his critics, he knew that if he lost his army, for whatever reason, Parliament's cause was also lost. On the other hand, the suggestion may merely have been an extension of his military logic into the realms of theology. He was not in a position to bring the war to an end by forcing the king to surrender, as he had hoped in the autumn of 1642 and the spring of 1643. The only other way of achieving a quick end to the war was by arranging that a decisive battle take place, which, given Parliament's overall superiority in numbers, had a fair chance of ending in victory if the contending forces comprised all those in arms for the king or for king and Parliament. Not surprisingly, both sides rejected the proposal, but in due course Essex did receive the supplies he needed when realism began to sink in with the loss of Bristol and the siege of Gloucester.[21] However, from June 1643 until the spring of 1644 Parliament's strategy was reactive rather than proactive, and at times vitiated by rivalries at Westminster and in the field.

Finally, it is necessary to assess the king's strategic plans for the 1643 campaign, necessarily put on hold by Essex's advance up the Thames valley and his own shortage of gunpowder, and at the same time to nail once and for all what is probably the most longstanding myth in seventeenth-century studies, the so-called threefold advance on London. As first described by S.R. Gardiner, it involved the king using the Oxford army to keep the Earl of Essex in check in the Thames valley while his armies in Cornwall and Yorkshire pushed forward on the flanks to smother the enemy between them.[22] Subsequently, other historians have proposed a more complex strategic plan: the Northern and Western armies were to cut the Thames below London while the king's forces marched down the Thames valley for a final confrontation with Essex.[23] Despite a total demolition of the hypothesis in a paper published twenty years ago, the threefold attack continues to haunt the textbooks, such is the respect in which Gardiner's narrative skills are held.[24] However, both versions are fictions based on sources that are fragile and in some cases totally irrelevant. Indeed, the strongest piece of evidence reinforces the view that the king's grand strategy devised in the aftermath of the first Thames valley campaign, or even earlier, was not a threefold advance on London but to assemble all his armies at Oxford before carrying out a direct attack on the capital.

The weaknesses of the case for the threefold attack are self-evident. In the first place, it makes no military sense. If the king's intention had been to attack London from three different directions, Essex, operating on interior lines, could have thrown the bulk of his forces against one prong and then against another as opportunity offered. In other words, Parliament's field army, even though numerically weaker than the forces the king was sending against the capital, could destroy each of the three prongs of the attack in turn through achieving local superiority.

Second, the two documentary sources that Gardiner cites are worthless. The first is a letter of advice written in November 1642 from the Netherlands, probably by George Goring, the former governor of Portsmouth, during the first Thames valley campaign, which merely recommended sending forces into Kent. The strategic aim, given the date, was not so much to surround London as to capture a port through which the queen could ship the arms and ammunition she had collected on the Continent, which were landed in the north of England early in the following year.[25]

The second is a letter written by the Venetian ambassador in January 1643 describing an interview with a man called Herne, who claimed to be a royal emissary. However, the words Herne used as recorded by the ambassador were not as Gardiner described them. Herne stated very clearly that the Northern and Western armies were *not* to advance directly on London via East Anglia and the south-coast counties. Instead, they were to march to Oxford for a rendezvous with the main field army. Then the king would divide his forces in such a way as to block the Thames above and below the capital while the Royalist cavalry scoured the countryside, cutting London off from its sources of food and fuel and reducing the citizens to such straits that they would overthrow the enemy leadership by force.[26]

The more elaborate versions of Gardiner's hypothesis depend exclusively on reports of captured Royalist correspondence printed in the London newspapers in early June 1643, but such reports are of questionable value as evidence of the king's strategic plans. In the first place, it is impossible to ascertain whether the letters contained direct or indirect evidence of decisions taken by the Royalist council of war, as they are not reproduced in full or, indeed, quoted. Second, since the original letters do not survive, there must be some doubt as to their provenance. During the Great Civil War newspaper editors on both sides were quite capable of dressing up vague rumours as fact in order to curdle the blood of their readers. Third, the editors themselves had doubts about the reliability of the information they were putting before the public. One, for example, described the northern prong of the trident, by which forces under the queen's command were to advance into Suffolk and Essex, as 'not likely'. However, there is a possibility that the reports in the journals were based on material found among the papers of one of the participants in Sir Nicholas Crispe's plot, a scheme to bring about a Royalist uprising in London, which was uncovered at precisely the time they were printed.[27]

But did an advance by the provincial armies into Kent, Sussex and East Anglia not play any part in the king's strategic plans for the first half of 1643? In the case of the northern prong of the trident, the answer must be no. It was not a practical proposition until after the Earl of Newcastle's commanders had inflicted a severe defeat on Lord Fairfax's army at Adwalton Moor at the end of June, and it is not mentioned in the memoirs of Sir Phillip Warwick, who twice journeyed from Oxford to Yorkshire in 1643 with messages from the king to the earl concerning strategy. Moreover, the king's wish from November 1642 to August 1643 was for Newcastle to join him at Oxford. As for the southern prong, Clarendon stated that before the Marquis of Hertford left Oxford there was some excited talk (but not an agreed strategy) of raising a new army which 'should never join with the king's' army but capture Portsmouth and then advance into Sussex and Kent.[28] Nevertheless, a plan to attack London from two directions was to emerge briefly later in the year when the strategic initiative had fully passed to the king, and again possibly in the early spring of 1644.[29]

Notes

1 TT E90 12; Hexter, *King Pym*, 109–10; CJ II 884, 976. Lord Brooke made similar remarks about the superiority of volunteers over professionals in a speech to his regiments in February 1643 (TT E90 27).

2 See Chapter VII.

3 LJ VI 127.

4 *Ibid.*, VI 89.

5 Beats, 'East Midland Association', 166–72.

6 The southern part of Waller's command caused him much less concern at the start of the second Thames valley campaign, as the Earl of Stamford was

successfully containing the Cornish army from his base at Exeter. However, Waller was to keep an eye on attempts by the king's supporters to raise troops in Wiltshire and Dorset. There had been a flurry of activity around Sherborne in March and April, and rumours persisted that the Marquis of Hertford would return to his command when the moment was right. (BL additional ms 18983, 1; Wanklyn, 'Royalist strategy', 60).

7 Corbet, *Military Government*, 26–9; Bodleian Firth ms C6, 152; Adair, *Roundhead General*, 62; BL Harleian ms 6852, 258–62; Clarendon, *Great Rebellion* vii, 290–2.

8 See above Chapter VII.

9 Corbet, *Military Government*, 31–5; BL Harleian ms 6802, 48; *ibid.*, Harleian ms 6852, 258–61; *ibid.*, Additional ms 18978, 137.

10 HMC Portland ms I, 98; Warburton, *Memoirs* I, 497; *ibid.*, II, 144, 155–6, 159–60; Slingsby, *Diary*, 95; Clarendon, *Great Rebellion* vii, 30.

11 Warburton, *Memoirs* II, 165–7; BL Additional ms 18983, 3–4; LJ VI 16–17.

12 *Ibid.*, 43; *Mercurius Aulicus*, 224; Gwynne, *Military Memoirs*, 50–1; Warburton, *Memoirs* II, 176, 177–9.

13 Corbet, *Military Government*, 35–7; Warburton, *Memoirs* I, 505; TT E94 29.

14 Bodleian Tanner ms 62, 76; HMC Portland ms I, 713; Wilts CRO 413/444B 3; Green, *Letters*, 197–8; *Mercurius Aulicus*, 256, 261; Abbott, *Writings and Letters*, 228–30.

15 Luke, *Journals*; LJ VI 43; TT E102 8; *Mercurius Aulicus*, 256.

16 LJ VI 52–3; Warburton, *Memoirs* II, 195n; Bodleian Dugdale ms 19, 13.

17 TT E105 10, 27; BL Additional ms 18979, 137; HMC Portland I, 209–10; Hopton, *Bellum Civile*, 44–7.

18 Bodleian Tanner ms 62, 136; Rushworth, *Historical Collections* V, 290; TT E71 7.

19 LJ VI 11; Warburton, *Memoirs* II, 202–3; *Mercurius Aulicus*, 321–2, 330.

20 Bodleian Tanner ms 62, 134, 149, 159, 170; *ibid.*, Firth ms C6, 176; TT E60 8–9; TT E61 1, 9; TT E71 7; Abbott, *Writings and Letters*, 234–7; Malbon, *Memoirs*, 62, 64; HMC Appendix to the 9th Report II, 388; Warburton, *Memoirs* II, 225.

21 LJ VI 127, 144, 160; Devereux, *Earls of Essex*, 367–8.

22 Gardiner, *Great Civil War* I, 231.

23 E.g. Thomas-Stanford, *Sussex in the Great Civil War*, 71.

24 Wanklyn, 'Royalist strategy'. It is referred to in a number of books that have been written during the last decade, including two recent textbooks (Hirst, *England in Conflict*, 214; Smith, *Modern British Isles*, 140). At about the same time as the essay was published, Coward attacked the threefold assault from

two different, but somewhat incompatible, directions. The passage can be read in several ways, but what he appears to believe is that what the Parliamentarians thought they saw in the summer of 1643 was in fact an illusion, and that although there may have been such a plan, the king's armies were never in a position to implement it (Stuart Century, 208).

25 Gardiner, *Great Civil War* II (1886 edn), 78 citing Rushworth, *Historical Collections* V, 70; TT E127 21.

26 CSP Venetian 1642–43, 231.

27 TT E110 8, 24.

28 Clarendon, *Great Rebellion* vii, 84 note 4.

29 See Chapters VII, XII.

Summary of Part III

Parliament's generals should have forced the king's forces out of the Thames valley area in the spring of 1643, as military resources were once more heavily weighted in their favour. During the winter months the king had raised a number of new cavalry regiments in the Oxford area but had been joined by only a single infantry brigade from the regions, about 1,000 strong. Another, larger contingent had been destroyed near Gloucester in March, whereas conditions in Yorkshire and in the far southwest made it impossible for other bodies of foot to make their way to Oxford. To make matters worse, gunpowder was in exceedingly short supply in the Thames valley theatre of war. However, there were large quantities of powder in the north of England following the safe arrival of a convoy from the Continent in January, which ships from the navy had failed to intercept. Initially, the king's advisers were not unduly worried about the shortage of munitions. They trusted that the Earl of Essex's lethargy would give them time to bring gunpowder to Oxford before the start of the new campaigning season.

The supporters of Parliament had been more successful during the winter months in raising forces, some of which were capable of being deployed in the Thames valley theatre of war, thus making it possible for the Earl of Essex to take the offensive in the spring. Although this success had been achieved only at the expense of depriving the field army of cavalry and dragoons, most would return by late April with two new army corps, one of which had been raised in East Anglia by Lord Grey of Wark. The other, under Sir William Waller, was stationed in the Gloucester area. Moreover, although the field army itself was temporarily weaker in mounted troops, it had been strengthened by the addition of at least six new infantry regiments raised in London during the winter months.

Essex's siege of Reading and its speedy surrender took the king's advisers by surprise, and serious discussions took place concerning the advisability of abandoning Oxford. However, a combination of bad luck and poor operational practice meant that Parliament's lord general was not able to put further immediate pressure on the king. Disease broke out among his troops, and the city of London failed to provide sufficient pay and military equipment for his army to resume the campaign. Moreover, although the East Anglian brigade arrived in the Thames valley in mid-April, other regional commanders were less obliging. Those in the East Midlands and the Fenlands failed to rendezvous in time to prevent a convoy of arms and ammunition reaching Oxford from Newark in mid-May, while Waller ignored orders to advance towards Reading to cooperate with the main field army and began campaigning on his own initiative in the Welsh borders. This was particularly galling as Waller was strong in cavalry and dragoons.

The lord general therefore remained at Reading for six weeks after its capture, while his army's military capability declined as the supply situation worsened and his regiments faded away under the twin impacts of disease and desertion. Taking the offensive depended on Waller, who was now ordered to deal with a major new Royalist recruiting operation in Wiltshire and Dorset led by the Marquis of Hertford. Thereafter, he was to leave for Devonshire to deal with the king's Cornish army, but to send back the mounted troops he had borrowed from the field army.[1] However, Waller ignored his orders for a second time by attempting to capture Worcester. As a result, Hertford's force was able to combine with the Cornish army marching westwards, thus making it impossible for Sir William to return any of Essex's troops.

The lord general's consequent shortage of cavalry made military operations in the open country to the east of Oxford extremely difficult. As a result, when forced in early June to renew the offensive against Oxford by pressure from London and Westminster, Essex made little progress. The poor weather and lack of supplies of all sorts made matters worse, and Rupert's cavalry showed its superiority once again in an engagement at Chalgrove. After a fortnight Essex gave up, ordering his troops into north Buckinghamshire to defend the Ouse valley against cavalry raids and to prevent a second convoy of arms and ammunition reaching Oxford from the north. Thus, apart from the capture of Reading, which had improved London's security, the Thames valley campaign had been a humiliation in which an initial superiority in resources had been allowed to ebb away in circumstances that were largely beyond the lord general's control.

Note

1   Warburton, *Memoirs II*, 196.

PART IV

A king's game

chapter IX

The battle of Roundway Down and the capture of Bristol

On the very day that the queen's convoy arrived in the Oxford area, Parliament's hopes in the west of England were dashed by the comprehensive defeat of Sir William Waller's army at the battle of Roundway Down. The root cause was that every strategic decision that he had made since Prince Maurice left the Severn valley in mid-April had been a mistake. First, by disobeying Essex's orders to join him in besieging Reading, he must bear some responsibility for the ease with which the first convoy from the north reached Oxford. His strength in horse and dragoons, although not as great as it was to be in July, would have enabled the lord general to put together a flying army operating out of Aylesbury, Coventry or Northampton to block its advance. Second, his failure to concentrate his forces in the southern part of his command in late May, despite Essex's orders and the pleas of the local Parliamentarians, had allowed the western Royalists to unite to form an army similar in strength to his own. Thus he had made his task of preventing it joining the king's field army much more difficult. Finally, when on the verge of destroying the Western army, he failed to plan with his usual thoroughness against the possibility of a rescue expedition from Oxford, relying instead on the Earl of Essex to prevent such a thing happening.

There were further signs of weaknesses in Waller's generalship. Throughout the campaign in Somerset and Wiltshire in June and July, he behaved towards other Parliamentarians with a disregard amounting almost to arrogance. He expected more of his Somerset forces than they could possibly perform against the two corps of the king's new army converging on the county from the east and the west; he shamelessly plundered Bristol, his most important garrison, of troops to recruit his field army; and when he left the region, all he left behind were half a regiment of infantry at Bristol and wounded soldiers at Gloucester, which were a burden, not a reinforcement, for Massey's garrison.[1] Possibly Waller's single-mindedness stemmed from having insufficient resources to carry out all the tasks allotted to him, a constant theme in the letters he wrote to his political masters in June and July. On the other hand, his religious zeal, its flames fanned into spiritual exaltation by the string of successes he had enjoyed from Farnham Castle onwards, may have convinced him that he was the instrument of God's will and not bound by the need to plan for every eventuality or to handle his fellow Parliamentarians with tact and consideration. His state of mind is apparent in the letter he wrote to the Speaker of the House of Commons the day before Roundway Down, which contained the clause:

we have such experience of God that we doubt not to give you a good account of Sir Ralph Hopton.[2]

He had also apparently foreseen his victory well in advance, as the Royalists found a wagon full of leg irons in his baggage train after the battle, but in retrospect Waller blamed himself for his rashness:

So sure was I of victory that I wrote to Parliament to bid them be at rest, for that I would shortly send them an account of the numbers taken and the numbers slain.[3]

This is not to suggest that Waller had lost touch with reality. In his campaign in Somerset and Wiltshire against the forces of Hopton and Hertford he displayed all his accustomed tactical skills. He blunted the momentum of the Royalist advance in a major skirmish at Chewton Mendip on 9th June and in a pitched battle at Lansdown just to the north of Bath on 3rd July. When, immediately afterwards, a carelessly placed tobacco pipe not only destroyed much of the Royalists' remaining gunpowder but also seriously wounded Sir Ralph Hopton, he seized his opportunity. As the king's Western army, which before Lansdown had seemed to be advancing into the Cotswolds, moved sideways into Wiltshire, he used his cavalry to harry their march and delay their progress. After some days the Royalists found a precarious shelter in the town of Devizes, which the local Parliamentarians had partially fortified prior to Sir William's arrival in the West Country and then abandoned. The infantry regiments prepared to withstand a siege, while the cavalry set out a day or so afterwards for Oxford in search of assistance. Waller in the meantime had successfully ambushed a munitions convoy heading for Devizes escorted by the Earl of Crawford's brigade of horse. Sir William was now confident of his biggest triumph to date.[4]

Uncharacteristically, however, Waller failed to post scouts in the surrounding villages and nearby market towns to warn of the approach of a relieving force, even though he was well aware that the enemy was confident in 'that great strength they expect from Oxford'. As a result, he may not have received warning of the approach of three brigades of enemy cavalry led by Lord Wilmot, until they were a mere two miles away. Before they arrived, however, he did have time to draw up his army on the downs above the town in the conventional manner with infantry in the centre and cavalry on the wings. The Royalist brigades, led by Sir John Byron, Crawford and Wilmot himself, swept away both wings of Waller's horse either at the first charge or with some difficulty depending on which source one reads. Waller's regiments of foot held out for an hour or so against attempts by the Royalist horse to break up their formation, but when Hopton's infantry marched out of Devizes to attack them in the rear they surrendered or fled. It is perhaps surprising that the troops in Devizes kept out of the battle for so long, but this can be put down to Sir William's reputation. Despite Hopton's advice to the contrary, the opinion of the officers in the town was that their troops should remain behind the barricades. The gunfire in the hills above them might be the latest of Waller's cunning tricks.[5]

Immediately after the battle Waller appears to have been in a positive frame of mind, believing that much of his army had escaped. He fell back on Bristol, expecting the stragglers to arrive over the next few days. In a letter sent to London, one of his colonels claimed that no more than fifty horse and 200 common soldiers had been lost. Similarly optimistic noises were made in a letter from Captain Edward Harley to his father written on 15th July, and by Sir William himself in communications with the Earl of Essex. However, at a rendezvous held outside the city on the afternoon of the following day he managed to assemble only between 300 and 400 infantry and less than 600 cavalry.[6] That so many foot soldiers escaped is surprising; possibly the survivors had been on the way to join Waller at Devizes but failed to arrive in time for the battle. On the other hand, the small number of horse is extremely surprising. Admittedly a number had been killed falling over a precipice as they fled from the battlefield, but in accounts of the battle the victorious Royalists claimed to have captured or killed only 1,400 of the 5,000 or so soldiers under Waller's command. One possibility is that the Parliamentary horse had rallied in considerable numbers but deserted when they heard rumours of Sir William's next move, which was to leave the west of England altogether.[7]

At a council of war held after the review, it was agreed that horse would be of little use to a garrison that was likely to be besieged, but that the infantry were essential to the defence of the city. Sir William was therefore to preserve what was left of his cavalry either by joining the Earl of Essex in Buckinghamshire or by retreating to London. He would then exert all his efforts to organize a relief expedition.[8] On the following night, Waller and his men rode from Bristol to Gloucester, where they rested briefly before making off in a northeasterly direction.[9]

As the ghost of Parliament's army of the west retreated through the south Midlands, Sir William's mood darkened. By the time he met the lord general in Buckinghamshire, probably on 24th July, he was talking of resigning his commission, which Essex probably did little to discourage. However, when he arrived in London, Waller was greeted like a conquering hero, as Roundway Down was not seen as his fault. The press, elaborating on a letter he had written straight after the battle and on rumours from the Bristol area picked up by Sir Samuel Luke's spies, were blaming the lord general for not coming to his aid. Waller strengthened his case by claiming that between the battles of Lansdown and Roundway Down he had written to Essex asking him to keep a watch on the enemy forces at Oxford and, if they tried to assist Hertford and Hopton, to send his cavalry after them or else distract them by threatening to attack the city. However, he had done nothing.[10] The media furore that followed led Essex to demand an official inquiry as to whether he or Waller was responsible for the destruction of Waller's army. At the time, the lord general's political position was too weak for the proposal to win much support in Parliament, and he was forced to agree to a compromise by which his own forces were to be recruited but Sir William would be allowed to raise a new army in London to operate independently of his command. However, later in the year, the lord general reopened the debate by publishing his own account of the fighting in the south of England and the Midlands between the siege of Reading and the end of July. Although somewhat one-sided, it is nevertheless a highly convincing indictment of Waller's generalship, as much of the argument is substantiated by other sources.

Essex began by pointing out that Sir William had brought down trouble on his own head by disobeying the order he had sent him in late May to march into Somerset to prevent the two halves of the king's Western army from uniting. He then acknowledged that he had received a letter from Sir William asking him to keep an eye on the cavaliers at Oxford, but only two days before Roundway Down and at a time when his army was 30 miles to the northeast of the Royalist headquarters watching the movements of Prince Rupert and the queen's convoy. He was therefore on the wrong side of the city to observe reinforcements leaving Oxford in a southwesterly direction. He duly sent a reply to Waller's request for help on the day before Roundway Down to the effect that Sir William should exercise extreme caution and avoid fighting a battle if there was any chance of forces from Oxford being involved. Finally, and most importantly, Essex pointed out that the length of time Waller's letter allowed for any type of military operation on his part was far too short. Sir John Byron's cavalry brigade left Oxford on the morning of Wednesday, 12th July. Essex learned something about it later in the day from Sir Samuel Luke, and the battle took place on the following afternoon. Admittedly Wilmot's brigade may have left a day or so earlier. On the Monday it was described as being ready to leave 'to complete the business of the west . . . immediately', but the very full reports supplied to Sir Samuel Luke by his informants in the city on the Monday and the Tuesday make no mention of its departure.[11] There is some mileage in the argument that the lord general should have considered moving some of his regiments of cavalry and dragoons closer to the Oxford perimeter to deter such a breakout. However, given the concentration of enemy forces around Oxford itself and 20 miles to the north in the Brackley area, a body of Parliamentary cavalry riding in a southwesterly direction would have been in extreme danger of being cut off and destroyed, particularly as the Royalists were expecting Essex to make just such a move, not to assist Waller but to threaten the queen's convoy.[12]

On receiving certain news of Sir William's defeat on 17th July, Essex's thoughts were for the safety of Bristol and Gloucester, as he learned on the same day that several brigades of infantry and some cavalry belonging to the king's field army were about to leave the Oxford area for the west under Prince Rupert's command. Despite the appalling state of his own army, Essex wrote to Waller suggesting a rendezvous to plan a relief expedition or some kind of diversion. By the time the two met, the lord general had been reinforced by some troops of cavalry commanded by Lord Grey of Groby and Oliver Cromwell, and also possibly by some horse from London. To his great surprise, however, he found Sir William's army much smaller than he had been led to believe by letters and verbal messages.[13] In such circumstances the relief of Bristol was impossible, especially as cavalry from the Earl of Newcastle's army had reached the borders of Northamptonshire, and Cromwell's men were anxious not to be involved in lengthy military operations at such a distance from the Eastern Association. They were therefore allowed to depart, and two days later they captured Burghley House, near Stamford. The lord general, thoroughly dispirited once again, fell back first to Aylesbury, and then to Beaconsfield. On 6th August he was at Uxbridge covering the western approaches to London. By that time, Bristol had been in Royalist hands for a week.[14]

Rupert's new offensive was initially intended to capture Gloucester, probably because it was assumed that Waller would remain in Bristol to defend the principal garrison under his command. However, when the prince's forces reached Hampton Road (probably Hampnett on the Fosse Way) only 10 miles from Gloucester on 20th July, a letter from Worcester informed them that the remnant of Waller's forces had arrived at Gloucester the day before, and that it was 2,000 strong. As a result, Rupert decided to attack Bristol instead, with precautions being taken to ensure that the siege operations were not disturbed by a relief expedition mounted from Gloucester.[15] When on the following day he learned that Sir William had left Gloucester and was heading in a northeasterly direction, he did not revert to the original plan. If Waller was going in search of assistance from the Earl of Essex, any relief expedition that might result would arrive too late. Rupert intended to take Bristol by storm, not to starve it into surrender. This was not exactly what the king wanted, but he was willing to endorse his nephew's decision. In a letter written on 20th July, he emphasized that he was more interested in destroying what was left of Waller's army than in capturing towns, but that whatever Rupert's intentions haste was essential. He was worried about the concentration of Parliamentary forces in north Buckinghamshire, which might be tempted to attack Oxford if Rupert was away for long.[16]

In retrospect, the decision to storm Bristol was probably the most serious strategic error that the king made in the summer of 1643 if his aim was to end the war quickly by either a decisive victory or a negotiated peace.

The motives for attacking Bristol were sound, but only in the context of a long war. Although the second city of the kingdom in terms of population, it was too small to provide an important and immediate recruit to the field army if it fell. Moreover, the garrison was known to be weak, most particularly in cavalry, and so unlikely to pose a danger to Royalist operations in other parts of southern England if it was simply ignored. Control of Bristol was therefore irrelevant to any short-term offensive strategy the king might have had in mind, but if his intention was to wait until 1644 before making a full-scale assault on the capital, capturing Bristol would be of considerable benefit to the Royalist cause. It had important metalworking industries, which could be turned over to producing muskets and pikes, and its ships could provide the nucleus for a Royalist navy.[17]

Rupert's contingent of the king's field army and Hopton and Hertford's Western army sat down before Bristol on 23rd July. The garrison surrendered three days later, after the Royalists had successfully stormed its outer defences and captured one of the city gates. The haul of military supplies was outstanding: one account claimed about '80 pieces of ordnance, many hundred barrels of powder, and 6,000 arms' with other ammunition, and another 1,700 barrels of gunpowder. However, the human cost had been very high, with many officers and possibly as many as 500 pikemen, musketeers and dragoons killed.

The strategic alternatives available to the king and his council after the capture of Bristol were therefore limited. Casualties had been such that a march on London followed by an assault on the city's defences was totally out of the question. The only other outright offensive operation that was possible at the time was a thrust into the east of England. Such a proposal is mentioned in Prince Rupert's diary, but no details are given. However, it is likely to have involved an invasion of the area around the Wash, where the king could recruit his depleted infantry regiments by tapping into the measure of popular support he enjoyed there, as evidenced by the uprisings that had recently taken place in and around Crowland, Stamford and Kings Lynn. Such a move would also have disrupted the Eastern Association, but this is unlikely to have featured as strongly in the Royalists' list of priorities as it would have done later in the war after its new commander, the Earl of Manchester, had carried out the administrative reforms, which produced the army that won the battle of Marston Moor.

Manpower for an expedition into East Anglia would have been a problem, given the casualties suffered by the infantry brigades during the storming of Bristol. It was also possible that the Cornish infantry, which had suffered very severely in the assault, might refuse to march further east. However, presumably the advance towards the Wash would have been undertaken in cooperation with forces from Newark, and it is difficult to see how the Earl of Newcastle could not have been drawn into a campaign that crossed the boundaries of his own command and at a time when he had overrun most of Lincolnshire. However, having trounced the Fairfaxes at Adwalton Moor in late June, he was committed to capturing Hull. In this he was egged on by the queen and threatened by the Yorkshire gentry, who would not march south if the garrison of Hull, which now sheltered the remnants of Fairfax's cavalry, was not eliminated first. There was also another element of uncertainty. Although an advance into East Anglia was likely to force Essex to take the field at a time when his army was particularly weak and demoralized, this was not a guarantee that he would seek a direct confrontation with the king's field army. Essex might instead advance on Oxford, which would be in great danger if he was reinforced by city of London trained band regiments at a time when the king's forces were approaching Norwich, 80 miles away. Rupert's proposal was therefore probably dismissed very quickly on the same grounds as the raid on Westminster had been after Edgehill – it was too risky. This may explain why the East Anglian project is not mentioned in any of the other accounts of the strategic discussions that took place in early August 1643. It may also explain why Rupert distanced himself from the next operation undertaken by the king's field army. Despite his triumph at Bristol, his advice had been ignored. He therefore returned to Oxford.

The council of war's first decision was that the Western army should march back into the southwest of England under the command of Prince Maurice. It was to assist local forces in capturing the remaining Parliamentary garrisons there, and then to return strengthened by new recruits and new regiments. Clarendon, who was present, wrote that it would be able to complete its task 'very speedily'. *Mercurius Aulicus* also implied that Maurice's campaign would take little time, but if it was reporting what had been said in the council of war, this could only have been intended to win the support of those on the council who favoured an advance on London as a way of pushing Parliament into renewed peace negotiations. By no stretch of the imagination could the western campaign have been a speedy operation with four major fortified towns to be captured: Plymouth, Exeter, Barnstaple and Dartmouth, Weymouth having surrendered to a force under the Earl of Caernarvon's command while the strategic discussions were taking place.[18]

If all had gone well, the Western army might have been ready to rejoin the king for an advance on London by mid-November, and the weather would not have prevented a long march eastwards that late in the year. Severe snowfalls did not begin in the south of England until the second week in January. Three of the enemy garrisons did indeed surrender reasonably quickly: Barnstaple on 2nd September, Exeter on 7th September, and Dartmouth on 5th October, but Prince Maurice fell seriously ill during the operations against Dartmouth, delaying the attack on Plymouth by a fortnight. If Plymouth had been attacked a month earlier, when it was allegedly in a very demoralized state, it might have capitulated quickly, but in the interval 500 troops had arrived from London under the command of a professional soldier, Colonel James Wardlow, who replaced the mayor as military governor. Various attempts by the Royalists to storm the outer ring of forts met with mixed success during November and early December, but the town was in no mood to surrender, and the Western army went into winter quarters in the Tamar valley just after Christmas, where it remained for the next two and a half months.[19]

Sir Ralph, now Lord Hopton and Rupert's deputy governor at Bristol, bewailed the delay that had occurred in army operations in late July and early August 1643, but he did not explain why.[20] The likelihood, given Hopton's record as a member of the moderate group around Clarendon, is that he favoured a quick operation to put pressure on the enemy to negotiate, such as another advance down the Thames valley. This might have yielded dividends at a time when there were serious divisions at Westminster and in the city between the supporters of Essex and Waller. Moreover, even though it could never have been anything more than a bluff, it might possibly have exacerbated the impasse between the two Houses concerning negotiations with the king. A majority in the House of Lords favoured talks, and there was considerable support in the House of Commons, but the terms the peers were proposing were quite unacceptable to a powerful minority in the Lower House and to the radical group that controlled the city of London. Essex, despite his grievances, would not side with the majority in the Lords, having probably decided that it was he who would be the sacrificial victim on the altar of peace. The most likely outcome of a stronger 'push for peace' would not have been serious negotiations but a coup against the House of Lords, but the king would not have been strong enough to take any military advantage of it. His field army and the Western army combined would have been too weak in infantry to attack Essex's army drawn up in a defensive position.[21]

In the event, the decision was taken that the next objective of the king's field army should be to complete the conquest of the lower Severn valley by capturing Gloucester, an undertaking that was to be managed by the Royalist lord general, the Earl of Forth. However, it was not until 10th August that Welsh and Herefordshire forces under Sir William Vavasour's command began to construct entrenchments on the western side of the city, while the field army regiments that had suffered the least casualties in the storming of Bristol, aided by infantry the queen had brought from the north and by troops from Worcester, hemmed the city in on the east. Possibly Hopton thought that a quicker move against Gloucester would have caused it to surrender without a fight, but this seems unlikely given the fortitude shown by the garrison and the civilian population of the city during the siege that followed.[22]

Notes

1 Bodleian Tanner ms 23, 197; TT E64 12.

2 Bodleian Tanner ms 23, 128, 164–5; HMC Portland ms I, 710–14; CJ III 113.

3 *Mercurius Aulicus*, 371; Adair, *Waller*, 93.

4 Hopton, *Bellum Civile*, 55–6; HMC Portland ms III, 112–13.

5 Hopton, *Bellum Civile*, 56–8; Bodleian Tanner ms 23, 164; Young, 'Roundway Down', 130–1.

6 TT E71 7; HMC Portland ms III, 113; Washbourne, *Bibliotheca Gloucestrensis*, 202–3.

7 *Mercurius Aulicus*, 371; Young, 'Roundway Down', 131.

8 TT E64 12.

9 BL Additional ms 18980, 87, 93; TT E61 25; TT E249 30; TT E71 7.

10 TT E61 1, 9; Devereux, *Earls of Essex*, 374; TT E 71 7; Luke, *Journals*, 120.

11 TT E67 36; LJ III 166; TT E71 7.

12 Luke, *Journals*, 114–15; Dugdale, *Diary*, 52; BL Harleian ms 6852, 130; Warburton, *Memoirs* II, 225–7.

13 Luke, *Journals*, 118–19; BL Additional ms 18980, 93; TT E71 7.

14 Holmes, *Eastern Association*, 91; Snow, *Essex the Rebel*, 379–81; Bodleian Tanner ms 23, 232.

15 BL Additional ms 18980, 86; *Rupert's Marches*, 733; Warburton, *Memoirs* II, 238.

16 BL Additional ms 18980, 87, 93; Warburton *Memoirs* II, 243; Petrie, *Charles I, Rupert and the Civil War*, 110–11.

17 Edwards, *Dealing in Death*, 31–2; Warburton, *Memoirs* II, 263.

18 Warburton, *Memoirs* II, 264n; *Mercurius Aulicus*, 403, 427; Wilts CRO 413/444A, 23; Holmes, *Eastern Association*, 92–5; Warwick, *Memoirs*, 268; Clarendon, *Great Rebellion* vii, 152. See also Chapter XII for a discussion of Newcastle's priorities.

19 Andriette, *Devon and Exeter*, 97–101, 208.

20 Hopton, *Bellum Civile*, 60; Warburton, *Memoirs* II, 281–2.

21 Gardiner, *Great Civil War* I, 185; HMC Appendix to the 5th Report, 98–100; Hexter, *King Pym*, 143–6.

22 Warburton, *Memoirs* II, 243, 263.

chapter X

The Gloucester and Newbury campaign

As they reflected upon the war in their memoirs, Charles I's former generals and civilian advisers were largely in agreement that the siege of Gloucester had been a fundamental strategic mistake.[1] However, as has been explained in Chapter IX, all the alternatives were problematic. Also, there were important benefits that would have resulted from the city's capture. In the first place it was to be invested, not stormed, so casualties would be much lower than had been the case at Bristol. Moreover, the siege would provide a breathing space during which the regiments mauled at the storming of Bristol could be recruited. Third, its capture would complete the conquest of the lower Severn valley, thus allowing all the resources of that part of the country and of much of South Wales to be used to supply and reinforce the field army. Admittedly, the expected short duration of the siege would not give time for the armies of the north and the west to complete their operations against Hull and the Parliamentary garrisons in Devonshire, thus permitting them to play a full part in national strategy. However, the capture of Gloucester might encourage the regional commands to speed up their operations while possibly undermining the morale of their opponents. Only in retrospect was setting siege to Gloucester seen as bait to lure the Earl of Essex's army into a battle in open country, where it could be intercepted and destroyed. There is little doubt therefore that the king was genuine in the words he addressed to the representatives of the city before the siege started to the effect that they had no prospect of relief: 'Waller is extinct and Essex cannot come'.[2] However, against all expectations,

Parliament managed to assemble a well-equipped and well-motivated army to go to the relief of Gloucester.

What is remarkable about the expedition to Gloucester is the speed with which its various components were assembled. As late as 6th August, Essex had threatened that his army would quickly disintegrate through lack of pay at a time when it seemed that all available resources would go towards the raising of a new army for Sir William Waller. However, less than three weeks later it was Essex's army that was on the march, having been supplied with recruits, military supplies, two weeks' pay and a whole new infantry brigade. This was partly in gratitude for the stand that Essex had taken against the House of Lords' proposal to reopen negotiations with the king after the loss of Bristol, but also because it began to sink in that William the Conqueror had lost an army by fighting a battle he could have avoided.[3]

Essex's speed is even more remarkable in that the decision to relieve Gloucester does not seem to have been taken until 16th August, the day after three leading members of the House of Commons visited Essex at his headquarters at Kingston to discuss the various options. A letter written by Essex on the 13th makes no mention of an expedition of any sort. On the 14th, the Lower House resolved merely that something should be done to strengthen the garrison of Plymouth and that the field army should soon depart on a new campaign.[4] The discussion at Kingston apparently weighed up the respective merits of attacking Oxford and relieving either Exeter or Gloucester, and it came to the conclusion that relieving Gloucester was the only practicable proposition. Possibly the lateness of the decision reflects doubts as to whether Gloucester could be saved. Between the surrender of Bristol and the start of the siege, both the committee at Gloucester and the governor, Edward Massey, had written to Westminster in heroic but pessimistic language describing the enfeebled condition of the garrison and the disloyalty of the townspeople. Moreover, if support was not sent, and the city was forced to surrender, 'we will be acquitted before God and man that we have done our duty'. A draft reply promised £2,000 'if it can get there', and also soldiers and ammunition, but the message may not have been received before the Royalist besiegers arrived at the gates.[5] The former governor of Bristol, Nathaniel Fiennes, thought that Gloucester would not be able to hold out for long, and Massey's letter in particular could be read as a justification for surrendering quickly, but as the days and weeks passed Sir Samuel Luke's informants in the Royalist camp continued to send comforting news about the slow progress of the siege operations. Nevertheless, it was not until the relief expedition was well on its way that messengers arrived from the city itself carrying good news about the morale of both the garrison and the townspeople.[6]

The army that Essex led to the relief of Gloucester was a composite force. He had been promised impressed men, but as Parliament did not finally accept the new expedient until a week before he set out, few are likely to have arrived at Kingston before his departure. However, the ranks of his regiments filled up as former soldiers returned to their colours, motivated by the seriousness of the situation and the certainty of pay. A personal appeal by Parliament's unofficial leader, John Pym, and fears that if Gloucester fell London would be the king's next target, persuaded the city authorities to allow five trained band regiments to join the expedition. The city brigade, comprising the red and blue regiments and the red, blue and orange auxiliaries, was almost certainly larger in size than the combined strength of the regular infantry regiments belonging to Essex's army. The trained bands were also very well trained, even if they had no direct experience of the battlefield.[7] Lord Grey of Groby and his regiment of horse joined the lord general during his march north, but not Oliver Cromwell, who was quartered in south Lincolnshire with the Eastern Association horse to resist any attempt by the Earl of Newcastle's forces to move south. Also in Essex's army was a regiment of horse under Colonel Harvey from London, another from Hampshire under Colonel Norton, and several unregimented troops, as well as Sir William Springate's regiment of Kentish foot.[8] In total, the army consisted of over 10,000 infantry and between 3,000 and 4,000 cavalry. Around Gloucester Charles probably had about twice as many cavalry, but his infantry was not much more than half the size of Essex's. In mid-September, however, he received substantial reinforcements from Bristol, and the Prince of Wales's regiment of foot, 800 strong, arrived from Shropshire, but neither these nor the infantry that Sir William Vavasour had brought from the southern Welsh borderland to the siege of Gloucester had seen much in the way of active service. However, most of the king's cavalry were of the highest quality.[9]

For the first ten days of his march to Gloucester, the most opposition that Essex faced was a small number of probing attacks by a body of Royalist cavalry, a brigade or so strong, under Wilmot's command, which were easily repulsed. From the start, the line of advance showed clearly that Oxford was not his destination, but not until the beginning of September did it become apparent that the lord general was heading directly for Gloucester.

As his march had taken him as far north as Banbury, it was possible that he intended to visit Coventry first in order to reassure the local Parliamentarians, who had written to the House of Commons in a highly demoralized tone the previous month, and to pick up reinforcements from the Midlands garrisons.[10] Nevertheless, it is amazing that the Royalist council of war did not consider abandoning the siege of Gloucester and seeking to fight a battle with Essex's army in the Cotswolds, where the king's cavalry could be used to best effect, until it was far too late.[11] We can only assume that Charles and his military advisers thought that the earl's army would move from the Banbury area towards Gloucester in as leisurely a manner as it had from Kingston-on-Thames to south Northamptonshire. In fact, Essex doubled his army's rate of march. Passing through Chipping Norton it reached Stow-in-the-Wold on 4th September, less than 20 miles from Gloucester. The following night it was less than 10 miles away approaching the city from the southeast, having fought off a determined attempt by Prince Rupert's cavalry to cut off and destroy the red regiment of the London trained bands, which failed because of a lack of the firepower that only infantry and dragoons could supply. The reasons for Essex's unprecedented speed are understandable. All the reinforcements and resources he had been promised had arrived. He had also received intelligence from Gloucester itself to the effect that ammunition was running very low.[12]

At about midday on 5th September, the infantry besieging Gloucester hurriedly left their billets and climbed the Cotswolds escarpment to join Rupert. The king's army missed Essex's army by about five miles, but it stood in battle order on Birdlip Hill for two days and nights barring its most direct route back to London.[13] However, having made his way safely to Gloucester and presented Massey with military supplies and pay for his soldiers, the lord general moved north to Tewkesbury. He also sent a party to occupy the bridge at Upton to safeguard the Gloucester garrison's efforts to collect food and fodder from the villages on the west bank of the Severn. The king's forces responded by moving first to Winchcombe and then to the Evesham area so as to block any attempt by the Parliamentary army to follow the route up the Avon valley to Warwick taken by Waller's cavalry six weeks earlier. Evesham also provided easy access to the Cotswold plateau. An army quartered there was thus well placed to follow the Parliamentarians if they chose a more southerly route. Essex's troops tried to persuade the Royalists to move even further north by constructing a bridge of boats across the Severn at Tewkesbury, thus threatening to attack Worcester from the west. However, the lord general had no intention of marching in a north-easterly direction towards the safety of that part of the Midlands controlled by Parliament's supporters. On 15th September his whole army, desperately short of provisions, suddenly headed off in the general direction of London, reaching Cirencester that night, 20 miles to the southeast of Tewkesbury.[14] That the Royalists were left a day's march behind was an accident rather than the result of Essex's tactical brilliance. The king's commanders, apart from Rupert, at first greeted the intelligence with disbelief and did not order a pursuit until late in the evening, whereas Essex had made more progress than he had intended. His plan had been to quarter for the night at Cheltenham, but, hearing that there was a Royalist food convoy at Cirencester guarded by newly raised troops, he pushed his vanguard into the Cotswolds, catching the escort in their beds at two o'clock in the morning.[15]

Duly refreshed by the convoy's contents, Essex's men set off for home along a route that would take them over the Wiltshire downs to the valley of the River Kennet and so via Newbury to Reading. However, taking a more direct route, the king's army gradually caught them up. A skirmish on the downs at Aldbourne between Swindon and Hungerford on 18th September, in which Rupert's cavalry tried to cut off a small infantry brigade and the artillery train that had become detached from the rest of Essex's army, failed, but it was sufficient to disrupt the lord general's plans. He had intended to join the London to Bath road at Hungerford and head down it at full speed towards the safety of the Thames valley garrisons, but this was now too dangerous. Further attacks by the king's cavalry in the open country between Hungerford and Newbury, this time supported by infantry, could easily result in a bigger version of Roundway Down, with first the Parliamentary horse being destroyed and then the foot being surrounded and forced to surrender. Instead, Essex ordered all his regiments to cross to the south bank of the Kennet at Hungerford, thus putting the river between them and their pursuers, but the penalty was that the army had to struggle eastwards along country lanes, which further delayed its progress. He probably hoped to be able to rejoin the London road at Newbury, and almost immediately afterwards gain the protection of the enclosed country that ran along the north bank of the river as far as Reading. However, Rupert's cavalry and dragoons reached the town just before his advance guard. They not only secured the bridge over the Kennet and the supplies that had been collected locally to feed Parliament's army, they also pushed patrols into the chalk downs to the south of the town directly in the path of Essex's troops.[16] The only way the lord general could now bring his men safely back to base was to fight his way through.

Notes

1 Wilts CRO 413/444A 22–3; Hopton, *Bellum Civile*, 60; Bodleian Clarendon ms 1738, 5; Warwick, *Memoirs*, 290, but not Lord Clarendon, who defended the siege on the grounds that it was the only possible option for the field army given the losses it had suffered at Bristol (*Great Rebellion* vii, 239).

2 Corbet, *Military Government*, 44–5.

3 Bodleian Tanner ms 62, 232; TT E70 10.

4 CJ III 204; LJ VI 192; Bodleian Tanner ms 62, 254.

5 *Ibid.*, Tanner ms 62, 197, 209.

6 Luke, *Journals* II, 142, 145; Corbet, *Military Government*, 54; Bodleian Tanner ms 62, 298; TT E255 1.

7 LJ VI 192; TT E69 15; Bodleian Tanner ms 62, 309.

8 Bodleian Tanner ms 62, 309; TT E69 15; TT E70 10.

9 Hopton, *Bellum Civile*, 60–1; HMC Beaufort ms, 39; Warburton, *Memoirs* II, 281–2.

10 Bodleian Tanner ms 62, 279–81.

11 Even then there was no great sense of urgency. The king wrote to Rupert on the morning of 5th September, when Essex was over the Cotswolds and in the Severn valley, that reinforcements had arrived from Bristol, some 1,600 foot and 400 horse, and that as a result the army could be in a condition to march the following day (Warburton, *Memoirs* II, 286–7).

12 TT E69 15; TT E70 10; Bodleian Tanner ms 62, 298, 309.

13 TT E69 15; *Mercurius Aulicus*, 503; *Rupert's Marches*, 734.

14 TT E69 2; TT E70 10.

15 Bodleian Clarendon ms 1738, 5; Wilts CRO 413/444A 25–6; TT E70 10.

16 TT E69 2, 15; TT E70 10.

chapter XI

The first battle of Newbury

The options available to the Earl of Essex on the morning of 20th September 1643 were extremely limited. Retreat was out of the question. So also was pushing down the road from the villages of Enbourne and Hamstead Marshall, where his army had spent the night, towards the bridge at Newbury, as almost the entire Royalist army was drawn up on the Green, a piece of flat open ground to the west of the town through which the road passed.[1] The only alternative route to Reading and safety entailed a circuitous march around the south of Newbury, first through enclosed country and up a steep slope to the plateau of Wash Common, an area of open chalk downland stretching along both sides of the Newbury to Andover road, and then through enclosures again, and finally across the much larger Greenham Common before enclosed country was reached once more near Aldermaston, only six miles from Reading. Crossing the commons would be perilous given the king's army's strength in cavalry, but the London brigade in particular had shown coolness in repelling cavalry attacks on the way to Gloucester, while at Aldbourne Chase infantry and cavalry had combined successfully against Royalist horse in open country. Moreover, as the Royalists were massed in and around Newbury, the operation might be well under way before they properly understood the direction of the Parliamentary army's line of march. The vanguard of the army therefore set out just as day was dawning.[2]

Essex's first objective was to secure the western boundary of Wash Common. This task he allotted to several of his infantry brigades and his own regiment of foot. Once this had been achieved, the right wing of his cavalry was to move through them and draw up on the common itself,

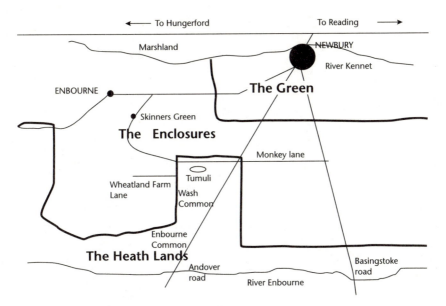

Figure 5 The first battle of Newbury: the landscape

forming a flank guard for the infantry that was to form the main body of the army. Meanwhile, the train of artillery escorted by more infantry would be climbing from Enbourne up the steep incline of Skinners Green Lane to the northeast corner of the common. When it arrived, the main body would begin its advance due east towards Reading. Protecting their rear would be the remainder of the cavalry and one or two infantry brigades. However, the rearguard's first function was to create as much sound and fury in the Kennet valley as possible while the rest of the army was assembling on the common, the objective being to make the enemy think that the chief threat was still to the bridge at Newbury and the fighting on the downs merely a feint.[3]

The king's generals were alerted soon after the push towards Wash Common began when the small force stationed overnight on the downs reported enemy infantry on Round Hill, a position on the western edge of the plateau essential for the defence of Skinners Green Lane, the only route by which Essex's heavy artillery could reach the common. Mistaking this for an attempt to establish an artillery platform overlooking the Green prior to an assault on the bridge at Newbury, Prince Rupert, who was on the spot, ordered a scratch force of infantry and cavalry to attack Round

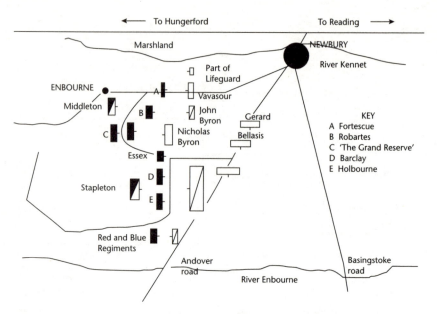

Figure 6 The first battle of Newbury, about 10a.m.

Hill. When this ground to a halt, Sir Nicholas Byron's brigade, supported by two regiments of horse, was told to go to their support. At about the same time, Rupert grasped the essentials of Essex's plan and began moving cavalry brigades and light artillery up the Andover road onto Wash Common, leaving Sir John Byron to continue the attack on Round Hill. Byron's force made some progress but was unable to capture the hill after Essex pushed Lord Robartes' brigade forward from the reserve to reinforce the position.[4] By the end of the morning, the front overlooking the Kennet valley had stabilized. Nothing of military significance occurred there or in the valley for the rest of the day other than the consumption of prodigious quantities of gunpowder.

To the south, other infantry brigades had reached their allotted positions on the western edge of Wash Common unopposed two hours or so after daybreak. However, two London regiments, which moved forward onto the southern part of the common, were subjected to probing attacks by the first cavalry regiments that Rupert managed to get there. These they repelled with little difficulty.[5] By mid-morning, most of the king's horse had arrived on the common and, when Essex's cavalry regiments under Sir Phillip Stapleton's command attempted to deploy there via Wheatlands Farm Lane, they were

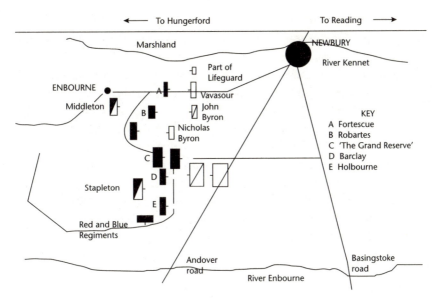

Figure 7 The first battle of Newbury, about 4p.m.

pushed back into the enclosures, suffering heavy casualties in the process. Concentrated musket fire from the infantry brigades prevented the Royalist cavalry pursuing them any further, but Stapleton's horse took no further part in the battle.[6]

For the rest of the day, fighting was concentrated at the top end of Wash Common, close to where Skinners Green Lane entered it, although further south the two London regiments, after some adventures, were pushed back off the common into the enclosures during the early afternoon. The struggle at Skinners Lane End drew in more and more troops as the day progressed. Initially, Essex's own regiment had taken up a defensive position some way into the Common, probably making use of the protection afforded by a line of tumuli. Soon after midday, Prince Rupert mounted an infantry attack on the regiment that had replaced them, which he drove back into the enclosures, capturing several light artillery pieces in the process. However, Essex brought up infantry reinforcements, which recovered some of the lost ground. Three hours later Rupert launched a second attack, but he found some of his foot regiments less than enthusiastic because of the heavy fire that was coming from the hedges on the edge of the common and from Essex's artillery train, which had at last arrived at Skinners

Lane End. The cavalry brigades on Wash Common were therefore ordered to do the job instead. As a result, they suffered very heavy casualties without managing to push the enemy back down the lane.[7]

As darkness fell, Essex's men saw Royalist heavy cannon arriving from Newbury and being positioned so that they could direct concentrated fire against Skinners Lane End, presumably in preparation for a renewed assault on the morrow. When day dawned, however, they were delighted to discover that the Royalists had retreated back down the hill into Newbury, having expended almost all the gunpowder they had with them that was suitable for infantry use. The Parliamentary army therefore resumed its march eastwards, reaching Aldermaston at the far end of Greenham Common by mid-afternoon, where an attack on the rearguard led by Rupert himself was repulsed with little difficulty.[8]

Notes

1   TT E69 10; TT E250 14; Ogilby, *Britannia*, plate 81.

2   TT E69 15; TT E70 10.

3   Essex does not appear to have written an official account of the battle, but his intentions can be inferred from some of the principal sources on the Parliamentary side, most particularly TT E 70 10 and Codrington, *Life and Death of Essex*, 32.

4   BL Additional ms 18980, 120; Bodleian Clarendon ms 1738, 5; TT E69 10.

5   TT E69 15.

6   TT E70 10; TT E268 3; *Mercurius Aulicus*, 528.

7   TT E68 5, 7; TT E69 12; TT E70 10; HMC Ormonde ms II ns, 383; Gwynne, *Military Memoirs*, 53; Wilts CRO 413/444A 38–41; *ibid.* 413/444B 4–5; Walsingham, *Hector Britannicus*, 89–90. Rupert estimated that his own regiment lost 300 troopers at the first battle of Newbury.

8   TT E69 2, 10, 15; TT E70 10.

chapter XII

Maintaining the strategic initiative

Despite Clarendon's hints to the contrary, failure to destroy the Earl of Essex's army at Newbury was not followed by paralysis, as the king's council of war tore itself apart in a storm of argument and recrimination.[1] Before the end of September, a new multi-faceted strategy was in place for the winter months. Its implementation was entrusted to commanders whose reputations had not been damaged by the siege of Gloucester and the Newbury campaign. The first was Prince Rupert. He had distanced himself from the siege, and his cavalry brigades had stopped Essex's army in its tracks on Wash Common. The second was Lord Hopton, who had not taken part in the campaign but had done all he could to supply the king's army with recruits. The third was Sir John, now Lord Byron, whose inspirational leadership at brigade level at Roundway Down and Newbury had restored a reputation clouded by what had happened to the second line of cavalry at Edgehill. Finally, there was Sir William Vavasour, whose Welsh borderland troops had loyally assisted in the campaign but had not been required to perform any prodigies of valour.

Dispersal was the keynote of the new Royalist strategic initiatives. By moving resources out of the Thames valley into the regions, the council of war intended to help the regional commanders to expel the enemy from their parts of the country. This having been achieved, the regions in their turn would then be able to supply the main field army with large quantities of arms, ammunition and most particularly foot soldiers for an advance on London in the spring of 1644. A strategy of decentralization also meant that the forces remaining in the Thames valley area could be more easily paid and fed, which ought to have a beneficial effect on both morale and desertion rate. Controlling territory in central Berkshire and north Hampshire from which supplies could be obtained also helps to explain the decision to reoccupy Reading, to put a garrison into Donnington Castle near Newbury, and to reinforce the Marquis of Winchester's garrison at Basing House.[2] However, at the start there was an overlap with the previous policy of centralizing resources, as the king had not totally given up hope that Newcastle's army would march south before the winter set in.

The understanding between the king and Newcastle was that, if the siege of Hull succeeded or if it had to be abandoned for any reason, the earl would advance with his army into the Eastern Association, his aim being to reach the Thames estuary and cut the capital off from its sources of food and fuel by instituting a blockade. As Newcastle's and the royal army were to operate independently of one another, the result would have been a twofold advance on London. Charles's instructions to this effect no longer exist, but Sir Thomas Fairfax saw them among Newcastle's papers when they were captured in 1644, and their contents can be inferred from a letter sent by Queen Henrietta Maria to the earl in mid-August and by Sir Phillip Warwick's report of his conversations with Newcastle in September. Preparations for such an operation can also be seen in the new commission issued to Newcastle on 19th August covering the four principal Fenland counties. Four weeks later, Sir Charles Lucas was appointed general, under Newcastle's command, of the trained bands of the eastern counties as far south as Essex. A political softening up began at about the same time. In a letter written on 24th August, the king asked the earl to recommend Royalists in the north of England who deserved to be rewarded when the war was over. This was possibly aimed at undermining the determination of the Yorkshire gentlemen that Newcastle should not march south until their county had been totally cleared of the enemy. It also gave the earl additional powers of patronage. On 14th September, such powers were further extended to cover the right to confer knighthoods, an honour normally given only to generals fighting overseas campaigns. Finally, Newcastle himself was created a marquis as a reward for his past victories and as an encouragement for the future. The patent was not entered into the official records until 26th October, but the king's decision to honour him was probably common knowledge over two months earlier, as the queen had addressed him as marquis in a letter she had written to him on 13th August.[3]

However, such inducements had no effect. Although Newcastle's siege operations had made little progress, the new marquis remained utterly committed to the capture of Hull.

However, this was not quite the end of the story insofar as the northern army invading East Anglia was concerned. Soon after the battle of Newbury, possibly after receiving intelligence from Sir Phillip Warwick that the siege of Hull was not being pursued with much vigour, Prince Rupert wrote to the earl suggesting a joint operation against the rebels in the Fenlands. The letter no longer exists, but it provides the context to an untypical communication from Newcastle to Rupert written at Cottington outside Hull on 3rd October. Two letters sent by the earl to Rupert dated 7th August and 29th August are no more than short messages of fulsome congratulation on the prince's victories written in Newcastle's normal courtly style in which flowery verbosity fights with flattery for predominance. The third letter began in a similar manner by congratulating Rupert on his great victory at Newbury, a compliment that was probably not intended to be ironic but merely a reflection of the tone of a letter that Newcastle had just received from the queen reporting briefly on the battle. He then came quickly to the point: a move south was quite out of the question because of the alliance recently concluded between the Parliamentary leadership and the dominant party in Scotland:

We are daily threatened here with the Scots coming in, and certainly, if it were not for this army, I think they would; and should [it] move from hence, I assure your Highness there would be a great army raised here besides . . . I am not in despair in time of Hull.[4]

This drew a line under any joint operation of the king's Northern and Southern armies until the Scots had been defeated. It should also be noticed that the letter was written over a week before the defeat of Newcastle's Lincolnshire cavalry by Sir Thomas Fairfax and Oliver Cromwell at the battle of Winceby, which is supposed to have permanently blunted the northern prong of the threefold attack on London.[5]

The effect of Newcastle's letter was soon apparent. On 26th October, Rupert was appointed lieutenant-general of all the eastern counties from Lincolnshire southwards. By that time, the prince's forces had been active for some time on the borders of the Eastern Association, showing that the presence of the marquis's troops was not essential for a more limited operation, which probably involved pushing down the Ouse valley through Bedford into the Fenlands. Nevertheless, this was not the sole purpose of Rupert's plan. The other was to cut the important trunk roads, which today are known as the A1, the A5 and the A6, which linked London with Yorkshire, the Midlands and Lancashire, respectively. If successful, the operation would have severely limited the movement of troops, arms and provisions from London into the provinces, and of foodstuffs from the provinces into London. It would also have increased the area from which the king's army drew its sustenance.[6]

The first signs of Royalist interest in the valley of the upper Ouse occur in the reports of Sir Samuel Luke's spies concerning gossip they overheard in Oxford from 24th September onwards.[7] Ten days later, a mixed force of cavalry, infantry and dragoons led by Sir Lewis Dyve moved into Bedfordshire, capturing some of the county committee at Ampthill the following day. On the 6th, the Royalists moved northwards to the small town of Newport Pagnell on the far side of Watling Street, where Buckinghamshire, Bedfordshire and Northamptonshire joined, and set about fortifying it. Ten days later, Dyve's troops briefly occupied Bedford on the A6, which, surprisingly for a county town on the edge of the war zone, was unfortified. They also sent out raiding forces up to and possibly beyond the eastern boundary of the county, and they marched all around the enemy-held town of Northampton gathering up cattle.[8]

This operation brought a speedy end to the Earl of Essex's plan to lay siege to Reading again before winter set in. Instead, he sent forces northwards under Phillip Skippon, his major-general of foot, with the object of evicting the Royalists from Newport Pagnell. He himself with the rest of the field army moved to St Albans, another unfortified county town, which his troops began to put into a state of defence. This had the advantage over Kingston or Windsor of being only a day's march away from Newport Pagnell and Bedford if the Royalist threat increased. It also served as a reassurance to Oliver Cromwell, who was considering moving part of the Earl of Manchester's Eastern Association forces out of north Lincolnshire to defend Huntingdon and Cambridgeshire.[9]

For the Royalists, however, a major operation in the Ouse valley could not progress any further without more resources. Dyve appears to have had only a small commanded force of musketeers only 700 strong and no artillery. With the pressure removed from Reading, a third of its garrison was therefore ordered to march to Newport Pagnell, but the king's council of war was slower to take action than Essex, and Rupert's strategic plans for the Ouse valley began to unravel. The order for the troops to march was not despatched until 27th October, by which time Skippon had reached Dunstable. As a result, even though the Reading brigade took a route that passed dangerously close to the Parliamentary garrison at Aylesbury, they failed to arrive in time.

Despite the fact that he had almost completed the fortification of Newport Pagnell, Sir Lewis Dyve fled the town just after midnight on 28th October and marched across the front of the advancing enemy to Stony Stratford, where Watling Street crossed the River Ouse.[10] The Parliamentary officers, who quartered a brigade at Newport Pagnell for the next few months and then established a permanent garrison there, were amazed how readily the Royalists had given ground and reasoned that shortage of ammunition was the cause. However, faulty intelligence as to the enemy's movements exacerbated by the king's interference was the decisive factor. Dyve heard just before midnight that almost the whole of Essex's army was at Brickhill, only six miles to the south, and was marching fast towards him, whereupon he took the action that the king had authorized in a verbal instruction delivered some days before: if faced by overwhelming force, he should immediately abandon Newport.[11] Subsequently, Charles accused the messenger of garbling his words, but given the king's anxieties about the eastern approaches to Oxford in July such a command does not seem out of character. Rupert, who arrived in north Buckinghamshire on the same day as the retreat from Newport, blamed his uncle, not Sir Lewis, extracting from him a promise to be more careful to whom he entrusted his orders in future.[12] However, as an alternative to Newport, Rupert ordered a garrison to be established in Towcester, a small town situated on the A5 midway between Newport and Northampton.

Against the entry for 28th October in the itinerary of Rupert's marches is the bleak comment 'the mistake about Newport that spoiled it all', which suggests that Dyve's precipitate abandonment of the town brought an end to the project to invade the Association, but this was not the case. The Reading brigade, which arrived two days later, remained in the area until the middle of November, as did Prince Rupert himself, the allegation that he recaptured Cirencester early in the month being an error in Warburton's cataloguing of his correspondence.[13] However, doubts about the project began to be expressed. On 30th October, a letter from Oxford suggested that Rupert was facing criticism in the council of war, largely on the grounds that his strategy was too vague. The opposition was apparently overcome, as the magazine at Oxford was ordered to provide him with artillery early in November, but new orders had to be issued on the 10th of the month, and then nothing was despatched until the 13th. The reason for this may have been the need to keep as many resources in the south as possible. Sir William Waller had assembled a new army at Farnham out of regiments supplied by London and the South-Eastern Association, namely the counties of Kent, Surrey and Sussex, and was on the march westwards. Rupert also received intelligence that he might be overwhelmed if he continued to hover around Stony Stratford. Parliamentary troops were massing in the middle Ouse valley near Bedford, with Essex's army close enough to provide support if necessary.

These factors seem to have put paid to the prince's original plan, as he made no attempt to recapture Newport Pagnell, but he had thought up an alternative. Reading between the lines of a letter that Essex received from Skippon, now commanding at Newport Pagnell, the reports of Sir Samuel Luke's informants, and correspondence between Rupert and Sir Edward Nicholas, it involved a force of cavalry led by Sir Charles Lucas advancing up the Welland, not the Ouse, valley. This had the advantages of being too distant for Essex's army to intervene and of leading directly into the Lincolnshire fens, where there had been considerable support for the king's cause earlier in the year. However, by the end of November the Royalist council of war had abandoned completely any idea of attacking the Eastern Association. Lucas was preparing to ride north with 1,000 horse to support the Marquis of Newcastle's army against the Scots, Rupert was back in Oxford, and most of the troops and the artillery train had returned to the Thames valley.[14] The only voice in favour of the original project, ironically, was that of the Marquis of Newcastle. In a letter written on 10th December from Chesterfield, he claimed that he would be unable to put an army into the field against the Scots if Rupert did not 'fall into the Associated counties'.[15]

Nevertheless, a Royalist presence in the Ouse valley area was retained, presumably because the second objective of the operation could still be achieved, namely stopping traffic passing along the main roads between London and the north. Sir Arthur Aston, having fully recovered from the accident that he had received at the siege of Reading, was sent to Towcester to supervise the completion of the fortifications and to establish quarters for cavalry regiments in the surrounding villages. Not only was Watling Street now firmly blocked, but cavalry patrols could use the town as a base for operating all over south and central Northamptonshire, possibly as far east as the A6. The garrison at Towcester also had sufficient resources to maintain an out-garrison at Grafton Regis, blocking the Northampton to Newport Pagnell road. However, Towcester was too far away from the Royalist garrisons at Oxford and Banbury to be safe from surprise attack, and the colonels who had moved there to recruit their regiments were unable to do so because of the vigilance of the enemy garrisons at Northampton and Newport Pagnell. They also complained bitterly about the shortage of food, fodder and money in the Towcester area and a consequent rise in the desertion rate. However, such complaints about impoverished quarters sit oddly with other evidence: 500 head of cattle captured in the villages around Northampton in October and the large quantities of barley transported from Towcester to Oxford when the town was eventually abandoned. Probably of greater concern to the commanders in and around the town was the threat of surprise attack. The horse quarters were tested on several occasions, officers who dined away from their billets were taken prisoner, and Grafton Regis fell on 24th December after a three-day siege by forces from Newport Pagnell. Soon afterwards the governor of Tewkesbury, Colonel Cockeran, wrote to Rupert about a new cause of concern. Severe frosts began at New Year, with the result that the watercourses, which had been the strongest feature of Towcester's defences, were now easily passable by the enemy. In early January 1644, Rupert, searching around for something positive that the garrison could accomplish, suggested that the cavalry might attempt to gain entry to Northampton by posing as Sir William Brereton's troops marching south to support the Earl of Essex. Cockeran quickly pointed out several weaknesses in the plan, the most important of which were that his cavalry was too weak and unreliable and that, given the pressure that Brereton was under at the time from Lord Byron (which is discussed below), he would have had no military resources to lend to another theatre of war. With no more ideas, and his mind preoccupied with other matters, Rupert withdrew the Towcester garrison to Oxford on 19th January.[16]

The Royalists had lost little as a result of the Ouse valley campaign, as the Towcester garrison escaped unscathed and that at Grafton had been less than 200 strong. Moreover, it had taken the pressure off Reading in the critical weeks when Sir Jacob Astley was repairing the deficiencies in its defences that had become apparent during the siege in April. Finally, the Parliamentary leadership, worried about a revival of Royalist interest in the

Ouse valley, kept most of the Eastern Association cavalry there for the rest of the winter.

The Royalists similarly lost little through the failure of another winter initiative, the attempt to persuade Gloucester to surrender by a mixture of long-distance blockade and intrigue. This began in early December and was motivated by the same strategic considerations as the earlier siege. Sir William Vavasour's brigade was to recruit itself from South Wales and the borders and guard the west bank of the Severn, while the iron-master and courtier Sir John Wintour secured the Forest of Dean. Several brigades of cavalry, including regiments that had been involved in the Ouse valley, were to be quartered in the Cotswolds to cut off supplies coming from that direction. To prevent the enemy using the Severn estuary or the Avon and Severn valleys to provision Gloucester, garrisons were established at Newnham to the south of the city and at Evesham and Tewkesbury to the north.[17] Parallel to the military pressure on Gloucester ran the attempt to persuade Captain Backhouse, one of Massey's officers, to betray the city. When approached by a former comrade in arms, however, he immediately informed the governor, who decided to allow the intrigue to continue in the hope of trapping the enemy as they tried to enter the city. The Royalists became wary when Backhouse asked them to withdraw some of their troops as a sign of their commitment, and in mid-February the 'plot' was revealed for what it was. But pressure on the city continued for a further six weeks and even then the successful despatch to Gloucester of some supplies that had been accumulating at Warwick for months only became possible because of events elsewhere. A new threat to the West Country in early April caused the king to order all the Royalist forces in the lower Severn valley to march to a rendezvous in north Wiltshire, apart from those manning the principal garrisons. Thus the Gloucester initiative, like the operation in the Ouse valley, had done nothing to lessen the offensive capacity of the king's field army, although all that Sir William Vavasour could add to the king's army in the spring was a single regiment of foot, not the 5,000 infantry and 1,500 cavalry he had promised five months earlier.[18] However, the two most ambitious strategic initiatives begun in the autumn of 1643, although they initially achieved a considerable measure of success, ended in grave disappointment and in significant losses of infantry, the resource the king needed most for a successful attack on London.

The conclusion of the alliance between Parliament and the Scots in August 1643, the Solemn League and Covenant, coincided with a truce between the king and the Catholic rebels in Ireland. Both were to have a very significant impact on grand strategy in 1644, but it was the Royalists who were first to bring their new military resource into play. Almost immediately, the king was able to transport to the northwest and southwest theatres of war the bulk of the Protestant forces around Dublin and Cork, which were made up of men impressed in England the previous year and Irish loyalists. Most of the troops were pikemen and musketeers. Of the fifteen regiments known to have left Ireland between October 1643 and February 1644, only two were horse. The Munster contingent disembarked at Bristol and Minehead, where they were to join the Western army. The Leinster contingent was to sail to ports in North Wales as close as possible to Chester, where they were to combine with nearly 1,000 horse and a single regiment of infantry from Oxford under Lord Byron to form a new army. The commander was originally intended to be the Irish Marquis of Ormonde, general of the troops in Leinster, but he was replaced by Prince Rupert before he could arrive in England. In October, the army's purpose was seen as re-establishing Royalist control over Cheshire and Lancashire and thus deterring the Scottish army from using the more attractive west coast route to attack the heartland of Royalist England. This was not only shorter than the east coast route, it was mostly under the control of supporters of Parliament as far south as Coventry in the central Midlands. A few weeks later, when it became apparent that Scottish troops were massing in the Tweed valley on the eastern side of the country, the emphasis changed. Having secured Lancashire and Cheshire, the new Royalist army was to cross the Pennines to assist the Marquis of Newcastle. However, for the moment Byron's troops were confined by royal order to their own theatre of war. Newcastle was desperate for support against the Scots, as evidenced by the letter from Chesterfield quoted above, but the king warned him not to try to draw troops into Yorkshire from across the Pennines, as Byron was not his subordinate officer.[19]

The first regiments from the army in Munster began arriving in the West Country in mid-October, but because of a shortage of shipping and a partial blockade of the mouth of the Dee by ships from Liverpool, which was held for Parliament, the first Leinster contingent, about 2,000 strong, did not set sail from Dublin for another month. Also, it was forced to land at some distance from Chester because of the conquests of Sir William Brereton, the leader of the Cheshire Parliamentarians, who was gaining a reputation as Parliament's second William the Conqueror. His destruction of Sir Thomas Aston's scratch force of Oxford army cavalry and locally raised infantry has been briefly described elsewhere. Thereafter, having taken measures during the summer to keep trouble at a distance by helping colleagues in neighbouring counties to capture Warrington, Stafford, Wem and much of northeast Shropshire, he thwarted a major attempt by Lord Capel to recapture Wem in mid-October. Brereton followed this up by capturing the bridge over the Dee at Holt, 10 miles to the south of Chester, early in November and was rapidly overrunning the counties of northeast Wales when the troops from Ireland arrived. Like his namesake in the south, Sir William had benefited from the king's policy of concentrating resources in the Thames valley by winning easy victories against the weak Royalist forces left behind. The capture of Wem, for example, had taken place while Lord Capel's main infantry regiment, the Prince of Wales's, had been fighting in the Newbury campaign.[20]

However, despite capturing Wrexham and Ruthin, Brereton was unable to intercept Byron's brigade in its march from Oxford to Chester or to attack the first contingent from Ireland as it disembarked at Mostyn and Flint on 20th November. By the time the second arrived in mid-December, Byron was ready to take the offensive. Within a fortnight he had defeated the Cheshire forces, although not decisively, at Middlewich and had cleared the rest of the county of enemy troops, apart from those defending Nantwich, to which he lay siege. Byron and his officers had every confidence that the town would fall very quickly, after which their army would march into Lancashire, but help was at hand for the Parliamentarians. Sir Thomas Fairfax, who had spent November and December reducing enemy garrisons in Lincolnshire, assembled a relief expedition by combining his cavalry regiments with foot and horse from Lancashire, including those that had fled there from Cheshire. On 30th January 1644, he brought the Royalist army to battle on Acton Heath, just outside Nantwich. Byron, apparently unable to use his cavalry, saw over half of the infantry from Ireland surrender when they were attacked in the rear by the Nantwich garrison.[21]

However, Fairfax's victory, although achieved very much against the odds, was of tactical rather than strategic importance. Nantwich had been saved, but Byron's army had not been destroyed. The cavalry was intact, half the infantry had escaped from the battlefield, and a third contingent from Ireland, consisting mainly of Protestant volunteers under the command of Colonels Tillier and Broughton rather than native-born Englishmen, had just arrived in North Wales. Byron also took some comfort from the fact that those infantry who had surrendered would probably have proved unreliable in the long run, as many took up arms under Brereton claiming that they had been brought to England under false pretences to fight for the king. Moreover, Rupert arrived in his command three weeks after the battle of Nantwich to replace Lord Capel. He brought with him reinforcements from Bristol and quickly set about organizing his new command, which included North Wales, Shropshire and Worcestershire as well as Cheshire and Lancashire. Like Capel, he fixed his headquarters at Shrewsbury rather than Chester.

Finally, Fairfax did little to exploit his victory. His forces helped the Cheshire Parliamentarians to recover some of the minor strongholds they had lost, but within a few weeks he was back on the other side of the Pennines leaving Brereton on his own to recover the rest of the ground that he had lost in December. This took Brereton six months, and as a result his forces played little part in the momentous events that occurred in the northwest of England in the spring and early summer of 1644.[22]

However, if Byron had won the battle of Nantwich, the prospect of defending the north against a Scottish invasion would have been enormously enhanced. With an army approaching 10,000 strong, he and Rupert could easily have overrun Lancashire and then crossed the Pennines to assist Newcastle. The two Royalist armies would have been more than a match for the Scottish army in terms of quality and numbers, and as a result the northern campaign of 1644 would have taken on a very different shape. Nevertheless, despite the losses incurred at Nantwich, the marquis was convinced that an overwhelming victory in his theatre of war would bring hostilities in the country as a whole to a successful conclusion. He wrote to the king to that effect, adding that he would need substantial reinforcements if he was to succeed. However, the ability of the Royalist-controlled south and Midlands to provide the north with troops and other military resources would depend on what happened in the crucial area between the Thames valley and the English Channel, where the Western army was now to operate.[23]

Nine days after the battle of Newbury, Lord Hopton attended a meeting of the council of war at Oriel College, Oxford. There he received instructions to clear the counties of Wiltshire, Dorset and Hampshire of enemy troops and then to push forward as far as he could towards London. He was allotted a number of weak cavalry regiments, but insofar as infantry was concerned he would have to rely on west of England resources: new regiments raising in Somerset and Dorset, soldiers he himself could provide out of the garrison of Bristol, and whatever Prince Maurice could spare from Devon and Cornwall. Subsequently, he received two regiments shipped over from Munster totalling about 500 experienced infantry. Hopton's initial plan was a cautious one, namely to blockade Poole, to complete his control of the rest of Wiltshire and Dorset by capturing Wardour Castle and Lyme, and then to move forward into Hampshire. However, he was forced to take the offensive by Sir William Waller, who set out from Farnham at the beginning of November with his new army to reconquer the west. Waller's first destination, as in the spring, was to be Winchester, where Sir William Ogle had just carried out a Royalist coup, despite his misgivings about the backing he would receive from the ragbag of regiments under Hopton's command. Waller's army was also incomplete and a patchwork of different formations. His main strength was a large brigade of London trained bands, but none of the three regiments had seen action in the Newbury campaign. Nevertheless, he probably had between 5,000 and 6,000 men to Hopton's 3,000 to 4,000.

Hopton gathered his forces at Salisbury urged on by the king, who had personally ordered Ogle to carry out the coup, and so the race for Winchester began. Hopton sent ahead a regiment of infantry, which, supported by a brigade of horse from the Oxford army, occupied the city. Waller proceeded more cautiously, taking five days to reach Alresford. There he received reports that exaggerated the strength of Hopton's little army and informed him that a brigade from Reading was intent on cutting him off from Farnham. Not surprisingly, given his experience at Roundway Down, Waller halted, but instead of returning to Farnham he lay siege to Basing House. After an eight-day attempt to capture the place by storm, in which his infantry performed very poorly, he learned that Hopton was advancing to its relief, whereupon he retired under the guns of Farnham Castle. Hopton followed him and, having received reinforcements from Reading and Devonshire, offered battle on 27th November, but Waller declined, being by this time heavily outnumbered. The Royalists then withdrew, having apparently decided that Sir William could be ignored for the moment. This seems rather an uninspired decision. The boldest move would have been to bypass Farnham and cut Waller's communications with London, but Hopton probably reasoned that his hastily assembled force needed time to settle down before attempting so ambitious a move.[24]

After retreating from the area to the west of Farnham, where there was little food or fodder, the Royalist army marched back to Winchester. Hopton then divided it into four mixed brigades of cavalry and infantry, which he quartered in such a way as to protect north and central Hampshire against attack not only from Waller but also from the string of Parliamentary-held garrisons along the Channel coast, Chichester, Portsmouth, Southampton and Poole. The towns chosen as headquarters for the four brigades were Romsey and Alresford guarding the southern and eastern approaches to Winchester, Petersfield, 'an entrance into Sussex', and Alton, where the Reading brigade was stationed. According to Hopton, Alton was not intended to serve as anything other than a temporary base, because it was too close to Farnham for comfort. It was also too far from the other towns to receive rapid support if attacked. Finally, the wooded nature of the landscape surrounding it provided the ideal cover for one of Sir William's covert operations. Hopton's intention was apparently to move the Alton contingent to Midhurst in Sussex, where, 'by fortifying the pass (over the South Downs) to have had that winter a fair entrance through Sussex into Kent', but nothing came of it as Midhurst was occupied by enemy troops the night before the Reading brigade was due to march there.[25]

Historians, following some contemporary or near-contemporary sources, have tended to see the developments described above as evidence of an army going into winter quarters, but this is an oversimplification.[26] Hopton's comments concerning the Petersfield brigade and the occupation of Midhurst suggest that he was not closing down military operations for the winter but intended to probe the defences of southeast England in accordance with the king's instruction. His next move made this intention even clearer, but sources differ as to whether the idea was Hopton's or something forced on him by the king. Encouraged by some of the leading Royalists of west Sussex, the brigade at Petersfield was charged with capturing Arundel Castle, which was garrisoned by only a company or so of Parliamentary soldiers. The castle surrendered on 2nd December, and the Petersfield brigade was ordered to quarter there instead. To strengthen Arundel against attack, the Royalists tried to seize Bramber Castle commanding the river crossing over the Adur 10 miles to the east, but their efforts were frustrated by local forces belonging to Waller's South-Eastern Association.

The governor of Arundel, Colonel Joseph Bamfield, spent the next ten days provisioning the castle from the rich countryside of west Sussex. In other respects neither he nor Hopton did much to secure the area, apart from stationing small parties of horse at Uppark and at Cowdray House near Midhurst to keep a watch on the passes over the South Downs. The Royalist brigades were thus spread across an even larger tract of Hampshire and Sussex, some of which was quite difficult country making mutual support even more problematic (although Hopton was probably unaware that Waller had received some reinforcements since the confrontation at Farnham). Moreover, of the towns in which they were quartered, only Arundel was endowed with defences strong enough to give the brigade stationed there any chance of resisting an assault by Sir William's army. It is also a matter of some surprise that Hopton did not move the brigade at Alton to the Midhurst area, given that he now had a troop of cavalry in Cowdray House. Possibly the fact that Waller had done nothing for the past fortnight suggested that he had gone into winter quarters. However, Hopton should have been extremely wary, as on several occasions in the past year periods of inactivity on Waller's part had been followed by vigorous and very effective military operations. Admittedly, two weeks was a longer period of quiescence than usual, but Hopton was not to know that for several days after the Royalist retreat Sir William had been concentrating on strengthening the defences of Farnham. He had heard that the king was at Basing and feared that Charles and Hopton were about to combine their forces for a major attack on Farnham. Only when he realized that the king was on a private visit to the Marquis of Winchester did he begin to plan his next move.[27]

On the night of 12th December, the arrangements that Hopton had made for quartering his army began to unravel. A sortie by the Southampton garrison drove the Royalists out of Romsey, although Hopton exaggerated its significance in his account of the campaign, as Colonel Norton took large numbers of horses but few prisoners. Hopton then claimed that he warned the other brigades to be on their guard, but the following night 5,000 of Waller's troops descended on Alton via country roads and surrounded the town. The Royalist cavalry managed to escape, but after a short but fierce fight almost 900 veteran infantrymen were forced to surrender. Sir William's next move was to set siege to Arundel in accordance with instructions from Essex and the Committee of Safety, but in the six days between the two events Hopton was able to extract two of the three cavalry regiments from west Sussex and to send Colonel Bamfield some ammunition. The garrison held out for almost a fortnight, but Hopton's attempt to disrupt the siege operations failed. The king sent Lord Wilmot from Oxford with 1,000 horse to assist him, but what Hopton needed was infantry, and this could not be provided immediately. As at Farnham, the Royalist general drew up his army in battle formation outside the town, but Waller refused to be tempted, probably because the London brigade had marched home and been replaced by local trained bands of uncertain quality. Hopton therefore withdrew to quarters in and around Havant to await the arrival of two regiments from southern Ireland that had recently disembarked at Bristol. However, on 6th January Arundel unexpectedly surrendered, its water supply polluted by a dead ox that had fallen into one of the two castle wells, although the spread of typhus or something similar among the garrison soldiers was also a factor. As a result, another thousand Royalist soldiers, mostly infantry, were taken captive.

Hopton, by now heavily outnumbered as Wilmot's cavalry had been recalled to the Thames valley, received the king's orders to retire to Marlborough so that he could keep in touch with the field army and the Bristol garrison. He succeeded in persuading Charles to allow him to decide whether or not to obey the command on the grounds that if he retreated immediately Waller would recapture Winchester, thus allowing enemy cavalry to range all over the chalk downs of Wiltshire and Dorset. However, Sir William did not put him under immediate pressure. In a letter to the Speaker of the House of Commons written on 12th January, he stated that he was busy fortifying and provisioning Arundel Castle and had no intention of moving west until he had recruited his infantry. Moreover, the new brigade of London trained bands had not arrived. Then the weather intervened. A heavy fall of snow during the third week in January brought military operations in southeast England to a halt for well over a month.[28]

Thus Sir William Waller had fought a successful campaign in defence of the South-Eastern Association because Hopton had allowed him to play to his strengths. Hopton's excuse was that the king's personal strategic initiatives forced him to take the field before he was ready, and independent evidence in Sir William Ogle's memoirs tends to confirm this. Charles seems to have thought, on the evidence of the support he enjoyed in Kent and west Sussex, that conquering the counties of southeast England would be like pushing at an open door. However, after the losses his armies had sustained in the Gloucester and Newbury campaign, the king did not have the resources to provide an appropriate level of push. In such circumstances, it would have been best to wait for the spring before taking the offensive.

Once it became apparent in late November that Waller was not prepared to fight a battle, the most sensible move would have been to concentrate on putting Winchester into a state of defence. Then the rest of the Royalist army could have withdrawn into Wiltshire and Dorset, where it would have been able to recruit in safety but at the same time have been close enough to Winchester to form the nucleus of a relief expedition should Waller lay siege to the city. Attempting to set up a base in west Sussex was a bridge too far.

Notes

1 Clarendon, *Great Rebellion* vii, 238–9.

2 *Ibid.*; Warburton, *Memoirs* II, 314; Wilts CRO 413/444, 34–41; Carte, *Letters* I, 23–5.

3 Bodleian Fairfax ms 36, 12; Bodleian Dugdale ms 19, 26, 28, 36; Washbourne, *Bibliotheca Gloucestrensis*, 369–70.

4 Warburton, *Memoirs* II, 275, 309–10; BL Additional ms 18983, 157.

5 Young and Holmes, *English Civil Wars*, 157; Barratt, *Cavaliers*, 129.

6 Bodleian Dugdale ms 19, 36; Tibbutt, 'Sir Lewis Dyve', 45; BL TT 669.7 75; TT E73 8. See also Chapter XXIII below.

7 Luke, *Journals*, 155–8; TT E69 27; TT E74 10.

8 Tibbutt, 'Sir Lewis Dyve', 35; TT E70 15; TT E71 22; TT E74 4.

9 TT E73 8; TT E74 1. Manchester had replaced Lord Gray of Wark as major-general of the Eastern Association in August 1643 (Holmes, *Eastern Association*, 94).

10 LJ VI 249; BL Additional ms 18980, 132–4; Warburton, *Memoirs* II, 321–2; Bodleian Firth ms C6, 237–8, 243, 246.

11 HMC Portland ms I, 144; TT E74 10; *Rupert's Marches*, 735.

12 Warburton, *Memoirs* II, 322.

13 *Rupert's Marches*, 735; Warburton, *Memoirs* II, 324; Kitson, *Rupert*, 158–9.

14 BL Additional ms 18980, 136, 146, 148–9, 154; Roy, Ordnance Papers II, 305, 309–10, 496; HMC Portland ms I, 144, 148–9; Luke, Journals, 168.

15 BL Additional ms 18980, 158; HMC Portland ms I, 144.

16 BL Additional ms 18980, 136, 159, 168; *ibid.*, 18981, 1, 19; Walsingham, *Hector Britannicus*, 91–4; Bodleian Firth ms C6, 266–9, 278. 291; *ibid.*, Firth ms C7, 51; Dugdale, *Diary*, 59.

17 Corbet, *Military Government*, 68–75; Carte, *Letters* I, 37; BL Additional ms 18980, 131, Warburton, *Memoirs* II, 332.

18 Corbet, *Military Government*, 76–90; BL Harleian ms 6802, 62–4; Bodleian Firth ms C6, 232.

19 Carte, *Ormonde* I, 468–9; Bodleian Dugdale ms 19, 44, 48; Roy, Ordnance Papers II, 312; Toynbee, Stevens Papers, 23; BL additional ms 18981, 147, 151; Warburton, *Memoirs* II, 327–9.

20 Carte, *Ormonde*, 469–73; Malbon, *Memoirs*, 75–88; HMC Beaufort ms, 39; Roy, Ordnance Papers II, 293. See also above Chapter VII.

21 Malbon, *Memoirs*, 89–114; Carte, *Letters* I, 39; Warburton, *Memoirs* II, 312; Fairfax, *Short Memorial*, 434.

22 Carte, *Ormonde*, 472–3; *Rupert's Marches*, 735; HMC Portland ms I, 170–1; Fairfax, *Short Memorial*, 435–6; Malbon, *Memoirs*, 118–24, Warburton, *Memoirs* I, 507.

23 BL Additional ms 18981, 42, 104.

24 BL Additional ms 27402, 15–16; *ibid.*, Harleian ms 6804, 224; HMC Portland ms I 154–5; Hopton, *Bellum Civile*, 62–5.

25 Hopton, *Bellum Civile*, 68.

26 TT E 78.8; Bamfield, *Apologie*, 41–2; Young and Holmes, *English Civil Wars*, 160; Edgar, *Hopton*, 151; Reid, *All the King's Armies*, 164.

27 Hopton, *Bellum Civile*, 68–9; Bamfield, *Apologie*, 42–3; Colonel Edward Apsley's narrative in Thomas-Stanford, *Great Civil War in Sussex*, 82–3; Bodleian Tanner ms 62, 410, 490; TT E78 8; HMC Portland ms I, 164.

28 Hopton, *Bellum Civile*, 72–7; TT E79 9; Bodleian Tanner ms 62, 410, 508.

chapter XIII

The Hampshire campaign

In the winter campaign in Sussex and Hampshire, Lord Hopton's uninspired generalship had resulted in the death or capture of about 2,000 troops, mostly infantry, the military resource the king could least afford to lose. Surprisingly he was not dismissed, but on 1st February Prince Maurice was promoted over his head as lieutenant-general of the southern counties from Cornwall to Kent, with the same sweeping powers as those enjoyed by the Marquis of Newcastle in the north of England. This is almost certainly proof that Sir Samuel Luke's spies in Oxford had heard correctly when they reported that the king's council of war intended the two corps of the Western army to unite to undertake operations in the southeast of England in the spring. But Parliament was quicker off the mark. Its strategy for the southern theatre of war was for Essex, supported by city trained bands and a corps of the Eastern Association army, to relieve Gloucester and to keep the king's army on the defensive in the Thames valley and the Chilterns while Sir William Waller reconquered the west of England. On 4th March, orders were given for Waller to push westwards with an army of 5,000 foot and 3,500 horse and dragoons. The lord general was not yet ready to take the field, but over a third of the cavalry and one of the dragoon regiments assigned to the western expedition were from his army and commanded by his lieutenant-general, Sir William Balfour. The task of threatening Oxford, and thus deterring the king from sending forces to assist Hopton, therefore fell to the corps of the Eastern Association army under Oliver Cromwell, which had been overwintering in Bedfordshire and north Buckinghamshire. This is a useful reminder that the principal strategic function of that army other than defending the association itself was to act as a strategic reserve.

Although its victories beginning with Grantham and ending with Marston Moor all took place in the north of England, throughout 1643, 1644 and the first four months of 1645 troops from the Eastern Association were used as often in the south of England as they were in Yorkshire and Lincolnshire.[1]

The king's council of war learned that Waller was about to take the offensive from Sir Richard Grenville, one of his senior officers, who arrived at Oxford on 7th March bringing with him a record of 'their generals' meetings this last week . . . [to agree on] all this summer's service'. A day or so later, Hopton learned that Essex had sent troops to aid Waller. He therefore wrote to the king asking for reinforcements. By vigorous recruiting since the loss of Arundel he had managed to double the size of his army, but it was still only about 4,000 strong, less than half the intended size of the enemy army, and Prince Maurice could not give him any immediate assistance. Hopton suggested a rendezvous at Kingsclere, high on the Hampshire downs, from which the troops could respond rapidly to any threat as it materialized. The council of war immediately ordered 800 horse and 1,200 foot from the Reading and Oxford garrisons to march south by way of Newbury, but they were to head straight for Winchester. It had heard almost certainly from Sir Richard Grenville that, while the rest of the enemy army distracted the Royalists by threatening Basing House, Waller was to 'slip westwards' into Dorset and Devon. If Hopton's forces were based any further north than Winchester, it would be difficult for them to stop him.

The brigades from the field army duly arrived at Winchester on about 13th March under the command of the lord general, the Earl of Forth. In this way, the king's council of war ensured that Hopton would not be able to exercise independent command, thus preserving the principle enshrined in Prince Maurice's commission. However, Forth did not bring any senior infantry officers with him, and this may explain what went wrong on the Royalist right wing at the battle of Cheriton later in the month. Subsequently, two cavalry regiments from Faringdon joined Forth and Hopton, raising the size of their army to between 6,500 and 7,000 men. Nevertheless, the Royalist army still fell short of Waller's army in numbers, most particularly in infantry. Insofar as quality was concerned, there was little to choose between them. Both contained experienced troops and raw recruits.[2]

When Forth convened a council of war at Winchester, it rejected the plan proposed by the governor that the army should take up a position covering the city, to which it could retreat if defeated in battle. Instead,

guided by the advice of Lord Hopton, whose judgement was probably influenced by a determination to recover his martial reputation, the council
decided on an active rather than a passive defence. This is why the two
Sir Williams, who had joined forces in west Sussex, found their progress
along the road to Winchester challenged by the Royalist army drawn up on
Old Winchester hill, about 10 miles to the east of the city. They attempted
to sidestep the enemy position by sending Balfour's cavalry northwards
along a track towards Alresford so as to approach Winchester from a different direction. However, the Royalists won the race for the town, and Balfour
fell back to a position at the rear of the Parliamentary army, which took up
its quarters for the night of 27th March along the stretch of the Petersfield
to Winchester road between Bramdean and Cheriton. Forth's army meanwhile bivouacked four miles away on Tichbourne Down, a low ridge immediately to the south of Alresford.[3]

The following day, small parties of cavalry skirmished all over the countryside between Bramdean and Alresford, but by dusk the Royalists were
firmly in control of the high ground that lay between the two armies,
where Cheriton, Apple and Sutton Downs meet. This enabled them to look
down the Itchen valley to where the vanguard of the enemy army could
be seen 'in a low field enclosed with a very thick hedge and ditch and their
ordnance planted upon the rising of the hill behind them'. Forth therefore
ordered George Lisle, the commander of the Reading brigade, to occupy a
small wood somewhere on Cheriton Down with 1,000 musketeers supported
by a force of 500 cavalry.[4]

Both sets of generals were keener on out-manoeuvring the opposition
than fighting a pitched battle, but the action of subordinate officers turned
the cut and thrust that Waller and Hopton so much enjoyed into a major
confrontation. The fact that neither side was prepared for such an eventuality explains why the battle of Cheriton bears little resemblance to any
other Civil War encounter involving thousands of combatants. The day began
with the Royalists finding that during the night Sir William had moved a
brigade of infantry into Cheriton Wood, which overlooked Lisle's position.
With Forth's agreement, Hopton ordered the wood to be recaptured, a task
that his musketeers performed with considerable panache. This opened up
the right flank of Waller's whole army, and Hopton asked for reinforcements
to enable him to attack it in force. However, Forth refused on the grounds
that Waller's position was now so threatened that he would be forced to
retreat. Having put the wood into a state of defence, Hopton returned to

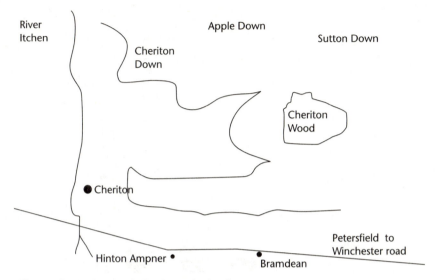

River
Itchen

Apple Down

Sutton Down

Cheriton
Down

Cheriton
Wood

● Cheriton

Petersfield to
Winchester road

Hinton Ampner ●

● Bramdean

Figure 8 The battle of Cheriton: the landscape

Cheriton Down only to discover that Royalist infantry on the other wing had exceeded their orders and were heavily involved in an attempt to capture Cheriton village. When they began to fall back in the face of superior numbers, Colonel Henry Bard went to their support on his own initiative. However, as his infantry regiment hurried towards the village across some open ground, it was pounced upon and quickly destroyed by a squadron of Parliamentary horse. A major cavalry engagement then followed in the stretch of country between the village of Cheriton and Cheriton Wood. The four Royalist cavalry brigades suffered heavy casualties from musket and cannon fire as they repeatedly charged home against prepared positions. In the process, they lost three of their four brigadiers and were eventually driven back onto Cheriton Down. In the meantime, Waller's infantry had pushed their way up the Itchen valley and were threatening to outflank the whole Royalist position on the west. Other regiments were also making progress on the opposite flank, where they reoccupied Cheriton Wood, which the Royalists seem to have abandoned in order to reinforce their right wing. To prevent their forces being surrounded, Forth and Hopton organized a retreat to Tichbourne Down, after which the army split. The horse made their way to Newbury over the downs, while the infantry and artillery marched safely through the woods to Basing House. Waller failed

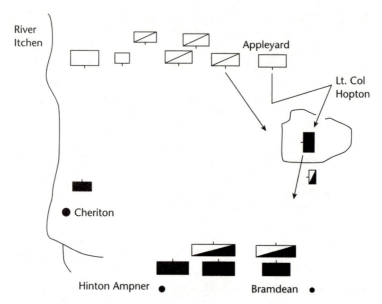

Figure 9 The battle of Cheriton, about 10a.m.

to order an immediate pursuit, probably because most of his cavalry were too exhausted.[5]

The battle of Cheriton was of very limited strategic significance for the Parliamentarians, as Waller and Balfour were quite unable to exploit their success. They sacked Winchester and launched cavalry raids against places as far away as Newbury and Salisbury, but there were no permanent gains from the Hampshire campaign, apart from the little town of Christ-church, which Hopton had garrisoned to cut communications between Southampton and Poole. Sir William Ogle successfully defended Winchester Castle and reoccupied the city once Waller's men had left, whereas a pro-posal from the Committee of Both Kingdoms, the allies' new 'war cabinet', that Sir William should attack Weymouth, thus securing the whole of the coast of Dorset for Parliament, was dismissed as too dangerous. The basic reason for the failure to exploit the victory at Cheriton was the resurgence of the king's forces. Surprisingly, the battle itself had not resulted in heavy Royalist losses. Compared with the winter campaign, the Parliamentarians took comparatively few prisoners, and the number of slain was not that large and was concentrated in the cavalry rather than the infantry regiments. Also, despite the initial panic, the process by which the Royalist troops across

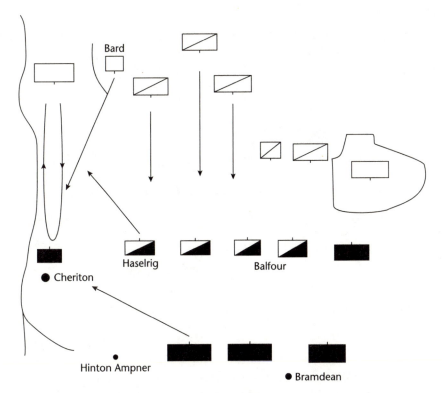

Figure 10 The battle of Cheriton, about midday

southern England coalesced into one body, which had caused admira-
tion on the Parliamentary side during the Newbury campaign, worked well
once again. When Charles called a rendezvous at Aldbourne Chase near
Hungerford on 10th April, he had at his command an army of about 10,000
men, almost equally divided between cavalry and infantry. To the anger of
their masters in London, Waller and Balfour, whose London brigade had
returned home, would not attack him. By 17th April they had retreated to
Farnham, whereas the king's forces advanced from Wiltshire into central
Berkshire, where they took up quarters for the rest of the month and the
first half of May while the commanders and politicians discussed strategy.
Waller blamed the Earl of Essex as he had done after Roundway Down, but
only in his memoirs, as the lord general had an even sounder defence than
in the summer of 1643. He had reinforced Sir William with several regiments of cavalry and dragoons, and the rest of his army would not be ready

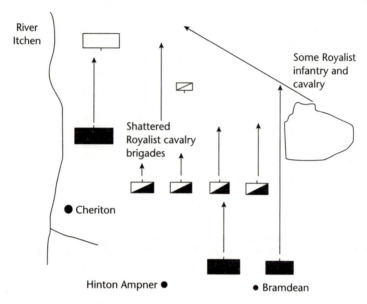

River
Itchen

Some Royalist
infantry and
cavalry

Shattered
Royalist cavalry
brigades

● Cheriton

Hinton Ampner ●

● Bramdean

Figure 11 The battle of Cheriton, about 5p.m.

to take the field until May, as Waller's forces had absorbed the bulk of the available resources for the Cheriton campaign. Moreover, the military situation had deteriorated elsewhere, and he needed to keep what troops he had to the north of London in case there was an attack on the Eastern Association, as the corps of Manchester's army that had quartered in the Ouse valley would probably be required to counter a possible attack on the Association from the north.[6]

The scare to the north of the Thames was caused by an unexpected Royalist recovery in the East Midlands in late March. Parliament's northern strategy for 1644 was an obvious one: to destroy the Marquis of Newcastle's army. The Royalist high command not surprisingly thought that the Scottish army, 20,000 strong, was intended to play the principal role on account of its size, and it instructed the marquis to take care that it did not try to sneak along the coast to join up with Lord Fairfax's forces in and around Hull. But if this was the allies' intention, it did not even get to the launching pad. Operations by the Scottish army in Northumberland and Durham in the first three months of the year were unspectacular and taken at a snail's pace, allegedly because its general, Alexander Lesley, Earl of Leven, dared not confront the much smaller Royalist army directly as he had only 2,000 cavalry to Newcastle's 3,000. Soon after the battle of Nantwich, the Committee of Both Kingdoms ordered Sir Thomas Fairfax to reinforce the Scots with the forces he had in Cheshire, but Sir Thomas preferred to recapture the west Yorkshire towns that had been lost after Adwalton Moor. He and his father, who was still at Hull with some Yorkshire infantry, then persuaded the committee that it would be better if they were to join forces to threaten York by attacking the army corps that Newcastle had stationed at Selby under Lord Bellasis. The committee intended the Fairfaxes to be supported by the second corps of the Eastern Association army, which had remained in Lincolnshire after the battle of Winceby besieging enemy garrisons. However, before marching further north, it wanted to secure its home territory completely by capturing the enemy garrison at Newark, which, in association with the small army of Colonel Henry Hastings, now Earl of Loughborough, based at Ashby-de-la-Zouch, was large enough to play havoc in central Lincolnshire and further afield during its absence. Operations against Newark began in mid-February under the command of Sir John Meldrum, whose besieging force consisted of troops from the Trent valley counties stiffened by Eastern Association infantry. By mid-March, with the king's army split between the Cotswolds and Hampshire and the Marquis of Newcastle fully preoccupied with containing the Scots, Newark's only hope of relief was from the Welsh borderland.

No sooner had Prince Rupert taken over his new command and summoned the remains of Byron's army to Shrewsbury than he was put under pressure to do something about Newark. However, it was not until mid-March that he was able to assemble an expeditionary force, by which time the garrison was on the verge of surrender. Marching via Lichfield and Ashby and picking up local forces as he advanced, he took Meldrum's force by surprise, chasing the cavalry away and forcing the infantry to surrender. In terms of its speedy organization and its success, Rupert's expedition to Newark is comparable to Sir Thomas Fairfax's relief of the siege of Nantwich seven weeks earlier. However, there were differences that made Rupert's achievement the greater: he captured large quantities of military supplies and the enemy general. Yet Rupert, like Fairfax, quickly quitted the scene of his triumph, leaving the king's supporters in the region to recover the major towns in Lincolnshire that they had lost after Winceby.

The Marquis of Newcastle was delighted at the blow given to the enemy threatening his rear and urged Rupert to remain in central England so that he could march north or south as occasion offered. The strategic argument was a telling one, but Rupert had commitments in the Thames valley, and from late April onwards he had to bend his mind to the developing crisis there, which threatened the whole Royalist position in the south.[7] As a result, the relief of Newark had as few strategic consequences as Waller and Balfour's victory at Cheriton, as the Royalist troops that remained were too weak to hold on to their gains. Within six weeks, the Eastern Association army had won back the ground lost in Lincolnshire, the Fairfaxes had crushed Bellasis's corps at Selby, and Newcastle, falling back southwards just ahead of the Scots, had thrown his infantry into York and sent his cavalry to find Prince Rupert. Indeed, the disaster at Selby was attributed by the governor to his cavalry remaining too long in Lincolnshire looking for easy pickings.[8]

One final point needs to be made about Cheriton before passing on – the consequences for the Parliamentarians if the battle had been lost. In a speech delivered at the Guildhall on 9th April, the Earl of Essex reminded his audience of the lucky escape their cause had had.[9] He did not go into details, but it is easy to guess what was in his mind. If the Royalists had managed to destroy the army led by Waller and Balfour, the king would have been in a very good position to take the offensive. Prince Maurice, known to be hurrying up from Devonshire, could provide his uncle with an extra 6,000 troops, mainly infantry, by the end of April. The king would then have had a force of well over 15,000 men ready to advance on London. As his own army would not be ready to take the field by then, the only thing standing in the Royalists' way would be the city trained bands, supported by the few infantry he had in arms and whatever troops had managed to escape from Cheriton. To defend the capital, the two Houses would have to draw in the Eastern Association army, already shaken by what had happened at Newark. This would leave Prince Rupert free to add another 6,000 men to his uncle's army, thus giving it an overwhelming numerical advantage in the south, including up to 15,000 foot. In such circumstances, the best that could be hoped for was a negotiated peace.

Notes

1   Bodleian Dugdale ms 19, 55; Luke, *Letterbook*, 629, 633, 635; CSP Domestic 1644, 54.

2   Bodleian Firth ms C6, 134, 142; Hopton, *Bellum Civile*, 77–80; Walker, *Historical Discourses*, 7.

3   BL Additional ms 27402, 94–5; HMC Portland ms III, 107; TT E40 1.

4   Adair, *Cheriton*, 195–7; Adair, *Roundhead General*, 162–3, 287; BL additional ms 27402, 95; Young and Holmes, *English Civil Wars*, 164; Hopton, *Bellum Civile*, 80, 101; Reid, *All the King's Armies*, 167; HMC Portland ms III, 108–9; Bodleian Wood Pamphlets 377 2, 3.

5   *Ibid.*; Hopton, *Bellum Civile*, 81–4; Slingsby, *Accounts*, 100–2; Birch, *Military Memoir*, 9–11; BL Additional ms 18779, 87; TT E40 1, 9, 12.

6   Clarendon, *Great Rebellion* viii, 17; Walker, *Historical Discourses*, 7; Wanklyn, 'Royalist strategy', 115; Bodleian Firth ms C7, 22, 27; CSP Domestic 1644, 71; BL Additional ms 27402, 96–7.

7   Kitson, *Rupert*, 166–72; BL Additional ms 18981, 99–100, 104; Bodleian Firth ms C6, 88, 93, 113, 135; Adair, *Cheriton*, 138–9.

8   HMC Ormonde ms II ns, 384–6.

9   TT E42 18.

Summary of Part IV

Victories won by the king's supporters in the north of England and in the southwest in late June and early July and the arrival of the second convoy of arms and ammunition from the north at Oxford in mid-July gave a significant but not decisive advantage to the Royalist cause in the crucial theatre of war. It enabled them to storm Bristol, the second largest city in England, but an advance on London with serious intent required the king to have sufficient infantry to fight the Earl of Essex's army in an entrenched position, or, if it withdrew into the city, to maintain a blockade or mount a successful assault. The defeat of Waller enabled the king to add some Welsh borderland regiments to his army for the siege of Gloucester, but the regiments that had arrived from the north as escorts for the munitions convoys did little more than offset the losses incurred at Bristol. Admittedly, Lord Hopton managed to raise large numbers of new recruits for the field army regiments in the Bristol area in August and September, but they would have received little training, which may explain the poor performance of some Royalist infantry brigades at the first battle of Newbury. Moreover, the Cornish regiments were so depleted by the fighting at Lansdowne and Bristol that they had been sent home to recruit. Essex, on the other hand, had huge infantry reserves in the shape of the city of London trained bands, and his shortage of cavalry was being resolved.

In operational terms, the king's management of the campaign in south-central England in August and September 1643 was no better than satisfactory. The siege of Gloucester was almost certainly the best course available for retaining the initiative after the storming of Bristol, but Charles's failure to abandon the siege when it became known that the Earl of Essex's army, reinforced by the London trained bands, was approaching the Cotswolds, very good cavalry country, via a route that did not permit an easy sidestep into the enclosed vales of Avon or Severn, is difficult to justify. Rupert claims in his diary to have advised such a move, but we have only his word for it.[1]

On the other hand, the Earl of Essex's management of the relief expedition to Gloucester cannot be faulted, and the first stage of his march back towards London was a very creditable exercise in outwitting the enemy. However, the king's superiority in cavalry took effect on the Wiltshire downs, slowing his progress sufficiently for the Royalists to intercept the Parliamentary field army at Newbury, just short of safety. Essex then, as at Edgehill, conducted the battle as well as the circumstances permitted, but he was only saved from destruction by the enemy withdrawal because they had run out of gunpowder for their pistols and muskets. This was thanks to an administrative hiccup rather than the complete exhaustion of the supplies brought into the Thames valley theatre of war from the north of England.

During the autumn and winter, the king's council of war attempted to maintain the strategic initiative in a more complex military situation and failed. Only in the case of the Ouse valley campaign can failure be attributed largely to lack of resources. Other initiatives failed for operational reasons rather than shortage of infantry, but their failure worsened the military prospects for the 1644 campaign by squandering that very resource. Hopton's attempted thrust into southeast England was badly conducted throughout, and as a result the king had lost well over 2,000 infantry, both veterans and new recruits, by the beginning of April 1644. Moreover, Lord Byron's operations in Cheshire in December and January had squandered many of the experienced musketeers and pikemen brought over from Ireland.

In regional and national terms, the victories won by Sir Thomas Fairfax at Nantwich and by Waller at Alton, Arundel and Cheriton were defensive in nature and were not followed by major acquisitions of territory, but they had effectively scuppered the king's attempts to increase his infantry strength. To make matters worse, both Waller in the southeast of England and the Earl of Manchester in the Eastern Association had managed to raise a considerable number of new cavalry regiments since August 1643. However, the king's field army's problem with gunpowder and other military supplies disappeared with the capture of a string of ports in southwest England, the most important of which were Bristol and Weymouth. From the autumn of 1643, there would be no shortages on gunpowder and arms in the south of England until the war's end.

Note

1   Wilts CRO 413/444A, 35.

PART V

The allies' counterattack

chapter XIV

The third Thames valley campaign

Despite Sir Edward Walker's contention that the defeat at Cheriton was a turning point that 'necessitated his Majesty . . . in the place of an offensive to make a defensive war', the 1644 campaigning season in the south had not opened all that badly for the king. Waller's expeditionary force was back at Farnham, and the country to the west of a line between Reading, Basingstoke and Winchester was once more firmly under Royalist control. The only disquieting factor was that Charles and his council of war would eventually have to contend with the armies of both Essex and Waller, whose combined strength would be considerably greater than that of the field army, even after it had absorbed Hopton's regiments. They might also have the support of a corps of the Eastern Association, as in the spring of 1643. In such circumstances, the king's field army would be very heavily outnumbered.

However, such calculations do not take into account the forces commanded by Prince Rupert and Prince Maurice. Admittedly, the army at Shrewsbury had received orders by 20th April to mount an expedition into the north of England to rescue the Marquis of Newcastle and his infantry, but Rupert was instructed to send 2,000 foot and a regiment of cavalry to Oxford before he left, and also to return by 1st June. With Maurice it was a different matter. He was expected to leave his winter quarters in the Tamar valley in late March and join his uncle, bringing with him about 4,000 infantry and 2,000 cavalry. This would make the Royalist forces in the Thames valley similar in strength to Essex's and Waller's armies combined. Moreover, with the Earl of Essex's regiments quartered around High Wycombe and Sir William Waller's well to the south of the river at Farnham, the chance of one or the other having to fight the very much larger royal army that lay between on its own was not inconsiderable. However, the rendezvous between Charles and Maurice did not occur until late July and in very different circumstances, namely on the outskirts of Exeter, not at Marlborough or Newbury. Instead, Maurice spent seven weeks besieging Lyme, a small 'fisher town' on the Devon/Dorset border, while his uncle's situation in the Thames valley became increasingly perilous.[1]

It is somewhat surprising that so little attention has been paid to the strategic significance of the siege of Lyme. When historians do mention it, they tend to accept Gardiner's analysis, but that is faulty on several counts. First, he stated that the siege began before the battle of Cheriton. Second, he claimed that it was prolonged unnecessarily because of the prince's pride and/or stubbornness, which caused him to neglect the most important strategic imperative: 'Maurice could not bear to leave his task unaccomplished, even to bring succour to his uncle in his hour of danger'. Finally, he implied that Maurice began the siege on his own initiative, not at the king's command. However, contemporary sources on both sides indicate very clearly that operations against Lyme did not begin until mid-April. Careful reading of the official Royalist account of the 1644 campaign written by Sir Edward Walker and a letter sent by Lord Digby, one of the secretaries of state, to Prince Rupert on 3rd April do indeed show that the siege was supposed to have started in late March, but that it had been postponed on the king's orders. Moreover, neither Walker's narrative nor the surviving correspondence between the council of war at Oxford and the generals in the field contains the slightest hint that laying siege to Lyme was Maurice's decision, which was subsequently accepted as a *fait accompli* by the king and the council of war.

But why, given that Lyme was not a major Parliamentary stronghold, did its capture become more important to the king than uniting his forces in the Thames valley? One reason was that the garrison had become much more active in raiding the towns and villages of east Devon and west Dorset. It could therefore have been argued that Lyme posed a threat to a new Association of the West comprising the counties of Cornwall, Devon, Somerset and Dorset. This project, which had begun to take shape during the winter, was much favoured by the king, who intended the Prince of Wales to travel to the West Country to act as its nominal commander. Its purpose was to provide resources for the Royalist cause to balance what Parliament was receiving from the Eastern Association. However, neutralizing Lyme scarcely warranted the attention of an entire army once its subsidiary garrisons at Axmouth, Hemyock and Studcombe House had been captured. Thereafter, it would have been a simple operation to surround the town with a ring of Royalist outposts, given its small size and remote location.

However, the Royalist high command may have learned from Sir Richard Grenville, Waller's former lieutenant-general of cavalry, that Lyme was intended to play a crucial role in Parliament's strategic plan for 1644 once Maurice and his army had left for the Thames valley theatre of war. Assisted by ships of the Parliamentary navy working out of Portsmouth, Sir William Waller could move cavalry and dragoons west from Southampton or Poole to disrupt Royalist control of the Associate Counties. Lyme was the only possible base for supplying such a force, and therefore more dangerous to the Royalist control of the west of England than Plymouth. This scenario is not mere speculation on our part; a number of pieces of circumstantial evidence point in that direction. For example, it is difficult to explain why Parliament reinforced the Lyme garrison with 500 infantry under Colonel Weare in February if the port was not intended to have a greater military significance than it had previously enjoyed. Also, there is no doubt that disrupting the Royalist Western Association before it could become effective was an important plank in Parliament's strategy from February to July 1644.[2]

As Maurice had received some sort of go-ahead from the king in mid-March to lay siege to Lyme, why did the siege not commence until a month later? The explanation lies in the strategic uncertainties that followed Waller's victory at Cheriton. Digby's letter to Rupert of 3rd April makes it clear that the prince was very worried that his brother would be marching into a trap. Waller's army was apparently on the rampage, and there was a fair chance that the infantry reinforcements needed so desperately if the king was to take the offensive in the Thames valley would be lost in a repeat of the Alton operation. However, Digby advised Rupert that his brother had been sent the strictest orders not to fight Waller on his own or to lay siege to Lyme. Instead, he was to stand on the defensive in a position where he could draw on the support of the garrison at Weymouth until the king's army could do something to assist him. Moreover, the troops about to besiege Lyme, 2,000 foot and 600 horse, can only have been the vanguard of Maurice's army. At the time, Digby wrote that the main body may still have been to the west of Exeter, as it did not leave winter quarters near Tavistock until 25th March. Its progress would also have been slow, as it was escorting the artillery train previously employed in operations against Plymouth.

However, when the mood of panic at Oxford lifted ten days or so after Cheriton, requiring Maurice to capture Lyme became an even more attractive proposition, provided that it did not take much time. The queen was about to leave Oxford for Exeter, seen as a safe place for her to spend the final weeks of her latest pregnancy. She would be even more secure with Maurice's army standing in the way of any attempt by Waller to launch a surprise attack on Exeter via the south coast ports. This was in the forefront of the king's mind, if not those of his generals. In the previous year, Henrietta Maria had been impeached for involvement in the Irish rebellion and for bringing arms and ammunition from abroad. She would therefore be in mortal danger if she were to be captured. In such circumstances, Charles would have had to have surrendered as a matter of honour and returned to London to bargain for her life. Parliament would thus have achieved its war aims without the need for any more fighting.

Second, in mid-April the need for Maurice's army to join the king's field army had not yet become urgent. Essex's infantry was unlikely to leave winter quarters for some time, Waller showing no signs of stirring from Farnham, and the Eastern Association army had new orders to advance north into Lincolnshire to recover the territory lost as a result of Rupert's victory outside Newark. A window of opportunity had therefore opened, which should have been wide enough to give Maurice time to capture Lyme and to complete his march eastwards before the strategic situation in the Thames valley deteriorated. By mid-April, the prince's personal commitment to capturing the port in double quick time was also probably greater than it had been a month earlier, as he must have had worries about how long the Western army would last (and with it his independent command) if he did not achieve some spectacular success. Hopton's corps had been absorbed into the king's field army, and the king had appointed a successor to Lord John Stewart, lieutenant-general of cavalry in the Western army, who had been mortally wounded at Cheriton, without fully consulting Maurice. Maurice may also have heard rumours that he was to be replaced when the Prince of Wales moved to the west of England, and that the king had suggested that in recompense he should be given command of the cavalry in the field army during Rupert's absence. This Maurice cannot have regarded as anything other than a demotion. Moreover, he had reasons for thinking that Lyme would be easy to capture by assault. On 11th April, some of his Irish regiments had successfully stormed the town of Wareham in east Dorset, which, like Lyme, had no castle and was defended only by earthworks.[3]

On 20th April, Maurice's siege of Lyme at last commenced. Optimism as to its outcome prevailed for a time. On 15th May, for example, Sir Edward Nicholas informed Lord Forth that the prince hoped to be master of Lyme within the week. However, an excellent train of artillery, as well as infantry experienced in siege warfare, were not enough. Lyme, supplied by sea with men, food and ammunition, and its garrison inspired by the indefatigable Taunton shopkeeper Lieutenant-Colonel Robert Blake, was not another Wareham. Maurice's army was still before the town at the end of May, having suffered heavy infantry casualties in assaults on the mud walls and forts. Moreover, the strategic situation in the Thames valley had changed very much for the worse. Essex's and Waller's armies were approaching Oxford, whereas Rupert was in Lancashire and thus too far away to provide immediate assistance. On 28th May, the king sent Maurice a peremptory command that he should abandon the siege immediately and march to Bristol to await the arrival of the field army. The scaling down of operations against Lyme around 1st June may be a sign that the prince was preparing to disengage, but within days the situation in the Thames valley had deteriorated still further, making the king's command irrelevant. The field army's withdrawal to Bristol was now out of the question. Despite Walker's claims that the decision not to march was taken on 5th June, Sir William Waller controlled both major roads from Oxford to Bristol by the first day of the month, with Essex's army in close support.[4]

Why had the situation in the Thames valley changed so dramatically during May? One thing that can be said with great confidence is that it was not due to lack of forward planning on the part of the king and his military advisers. When the Royalist council of war met at Wallingford during the lull in fighting in late April, its decisions were predicated on the possibility that neither of the princes would be in a position to provide immediate military assistance if Essex and Waller took the field simultaneously. Responsibility for the defence of Oxford would therefore fall upon the king's army alone. Rupert's suggestion, which the council initially accepted, was imaginative and bold. The king was to put his infantry into Oxford and four of its neighbouring garrisons: Banbury, Abingdon, Wallingford and

Reading. The garrisons were to retain sufficient cavalry to bring in supplies from the surrounding countryside, but the rest of the horse were to escort the king into the West Country to join forces with Maurice. In the meantime, Rupert would attend to the problems in the north, while Maurice continued to besiege Lyme. Once they had succeeded in their objectives, they would both march back to the Thames valley and rescue the king's infantry. On 5th May, Rupert returned to Shrewsbury to prepare for the northern expedition, having gained approval for it to be on a much larger scale than originally envisaged, although still with a time constraint. However, within a day or so of his departure, the king and his military advisers reverted to an earlier strategy favoured by Lord Forth. Reading was abandoned and its defences demolished, and the field army was kept together in central Berkshire. The justification for this was that there was insufficient infantry to man all five garrisons. Another factor was that Reading's geographical position made it difficult to relieve in the event of a siege, as had been shown in April 1643.

Parliament's objectives in the third Thames valley campaign were, as in the previous year, to destroy Charles's field army and bring the king back to Westminster. If this proved impossible, the very size of Essex's and Waller's armies should enable them to capture Oxford and thus drive his field army from the Thames valley. This should be easier as Waller was now under Essex's direct command, and both were subject to the strategic instructions of the two Houses as relayed to them through the Committee of Both Kingdoms.

As Essex advanced to Reading and Waller to Basingstoke, the Royalist field army drew back towards Abingdon in an orderly manner. This was almost certainly because the council of war, now consisting of Forth, Wilmot, Astley and Lord Percy, the general of artillery, and three civilians, Digby, Sir John Culpeper and the Duke of Richmond, knowing well the degree of hostility between the two enemy generals, assumed that one enemy army would move towards Oxford along the north bank of the Thames and the other along the south, thus enabling them to throw their entire army against one or the other as opportunity offered. Even if this did not happen, Essex and Waller were likely to behave cautiously, as in 1643, possibly laying siege to Wallingford, whose garrison horse could easily attack their communications if they decided to blockade Oxford.

Essex, however, knowing that he had a very considerable numerical advantage over the king's army in both horse and foot, had a bolder strategy in mind. He marched from High Wycombe to Reading and then crossed to the south bank of the Thames in readiness to cooperate closely with Waller, who was moving into Berkshire via Basingstoke. In their way lay the garrison of Abingdon, which the Royalists swiftly abandoned. There was some talk among the king's advisers of fighting a battle to defend the town, but with no natural features in the landscape to offset their lack of infantry, this was rejected, while the speed of the enemy advance was such that there was no time for Culham camp to be refortified. Shock at the unexpected determination shown by the Parliamentary generals played a part in the decision, but there were also sound military reasons. The Thames had protected Abingdon against assault during Essex's advance along the north bank of the river in 1643, but it did not have proper walls or a castle and was vulnerable to attack from the south. However, this did not deter the Committee of Both Kingdoms from establishing a garrison at Abingdon later in the year.[5]

Almost immediately, the Royalist high command came to regret the decision to withdraw from Abingdon, as the town was too close to Oxford for comfort. If the enemy occupied it permanently, the city would be cut off from the villages of central Berkshire, which had provided pay and provisions for the royal army and for the garrison. A letter from Lord Digby to Rupert written too soon after the incident for it to have been a reply to an angry protest from the prince placed the blame firmly on the generals. Although the withdrawal had been discussed with the king, the orders had been issued by Lord Forth on the advice of Lord Wilmot without seeking Charles's final approval. Subsequently, the episode was used as one of the reasons for removing the latter from his command. However, Digby, who was beginning both to see Rupert as his principal rival among the king's military advisers and to acquire a taste for grand strategy, could not resist pointing out that there would have been no need for the town to have been abandoned had one or other of the princes been present with his army.

With Abingdon in their hands, Essex and Waller decided to put further pressure on the king by advancing around the north and west sides of Oxford until their armies met again at Witney or Woodstock, thus cutting the king's headquarters off from the rest of Royalist-controlled England and Wales. This involved a measure of danger, as the two armies would have to separate for a while, but it would also make it almost impossible for Charles to escape from Oxford without fighting a battle. He could retreat back into the city, but its magazine contained sufficient provisions to feed a large army for only a fortnight (although Essex may not have been aware of this). The lord general's army therefore crossed the Thames on the night of 28th May using a ford between Abingdon and Oxford. Meanwhile Waller's advanced westwards in the general direction of the so-called New Bridge, which carried the Abingdon to Witney road over the Thames on the other side of the city. In doing so, Sir William cut the principal road between Oxford and the west. If he could also cross New Bridge, he could threaten the other. At this point, however, the Committee of Both Kingdoms complicated the strategic situation by drawing the Earl of Essex's attention to the plight of the besieged garrison at Lyme.

At first, with Essex on one side of the river and Waller on the other, the king's advisers felt more secure. For the first time they might have a chance of attacking one of the enemy armies without the other being able to come to its assistance. However, their optimism was short-lived. Essex, who was facing the bulk of the king's infantry, had difficulty in forcing his way across the River Cherwell, which ran north out of the city, although he claimed not to have pushed his advantage in the hope of provoking the king's army into fighting a battle. However, the Royalists chose to defend New Bridge with only a party of dragoons, and as a result they quickly lost it, thus making it easy for Waller to rejoin Essex by marching around the far side of the city towards Woodstock. On 2nd June, Sir William prepared to advance to Witney, thus blocking the road from Oxford to the Cotswolds, but Essex ordered him to remain where he was until his own army had crossed the Cherwell. Waller's army therefore spent the day reinforcing the bridge so that it was strong enough to carry the heavy wagons of his artillery train, but he also sent a force of cavalry into the corridor of land between the Thames and the Cherwell to make contact with the lord general. The king's army responded by retreating down the west bank of the Cherwell to Oxford, allowing Essex to cross the river and send patrols as far west as Woodstock. This left only a thin corridor of land to the northwest of the city under tenuous Royalist control, and this was likely to be closed on the following day as the Parliamentary armies converged on Witney.

In desperation, the king (who according to Walker was the only person to keep a cool head) browbeat the council of war into trying to implement what they could of the only plan they had on the table, the one agreed with Prince Rupert a month before. A threat to attack Abingdon on 3rd June drew Waller's army back across New Bridge. That night the king and the Prince of Wales, accompanied by the bulk of the cavalry and 3,000 musketeers, made their way through the gap between the enemy armies using country roads to avoid cavalry patrols. Some days later, Digby wrote that the king's intended destination was Lancashire and Prince Rupert's army, but if this had been the case marching there via the Severn valley and the Cheshire plain would have been an exceedingly risky operation. In the central Midlands sat a new enemy army under the Earl of Denbigh drawn from the Midlands garrisons, and beyond them were the troops of Sir William Brereton's command. If the king was truly intending to join Prince Rupert, a better plan would have been to make for territory controlled by the Earl of Loughborough and then to march through the southern Pennines into Lancashire, as there were no major concentrations of Parliamentary troops barring the way. In our opinion, Charles's first objective when he left Oxford was to put the River Severn between himself and his pursuers and then to wait on events. Shrewsbury was probably his next destination, as Worcester was too weakly fortified to serve as an army base, and a defensive line based on the middle and lower Severn could not be held for long as it could easily be outflanked by enemy troops crossing the river at Gloucester. It also needs to be said that there is no evidence for a week or so after the king's 'flying army' arrived in the Severn valley that it intended to return to Oxford in the near future to rescue the pikemen and musketeers that had been left behind.[6]

After some confusion, both Essex and Waller set off after the king. However, Charles and his army were already well ahead, as on 6th June they reached Evesham, which enabled them to put the River Avon between themselves and the enemy. That day, Essex and Waller held a council of war at Chipping Norton to consider their next move in the light of their changed strategic objectives. Should they pursue the king or lay siege to Oxford, and what ought to be done about the relief of Lyme? They decided to divide their forces. This has been seen as a mistake, but to see it as such involves a heavy dose of hindsight. If Essex and Waller had kept their armies together, they could hope to achieve only one of their objectives at best. If they separated, they might achieve two, but not the third. Both generals considered that only one army was needed to pursue Charles because of the strength of Denbigh's forces, which were now in the Birmingham area and were likely to be reinforced by regiments from Derbyshire and Cheshire. The least important consideration was the Thames valley, as the king and the troops he had with him might have left the area for good, and the infantry that he had left behind could not take the field without cavalry support. Oxford could therefore be ignored. Essex then ordered Waller to follow the king, as his army was more mobile. It was stronger in cavalry, and also unimpeded by a large train of heavy artillery. In the meantime, the lord general himself was to relieve Lyme.

Initially, after a very short-lived initial gripe about the roles of the two armies being reversed, Waller gave every appearance of accepting his lord general's plan with considerable enthusiasm, probably because he saw himself as having the opportunity not only of defeating the king in battle but also of bringing him back in triumph to Westminster. However, Sir Arthur Haselrig, who accompanied Waller's army on all its campaigns until the spring of 1645 as a kind of political commissar, had second thoughts after putting his signature to their joint letter to the Committee of Both Kingdoms. When he arrived back in London, he aroused a storm of anger against Essex in both the committee and the House of Commons. The committee agreed that the armies should have separated but was adamant that Waller should have been ordered to relieve Lyme while Essex blockaded Oxford and sent assistance to any part of the Midlands threatened by the king's flying army. It therefore ordered Sir William to set out for the west and tried to recall the lord general. However, it should have realized that by the time Essex and Waller received their instructions they would have been so far apart as to make a reversal of roles totally impracticable. In its anger, the committee appears temporarily to have forgotten that trapping the king, not bringing its generals to order, was its first priority, ignoring the impassioned words contained in Waller and Haselrig's letter of 7th June:

We believe the war can never end if the king be in any part of the land and not at parliament, for break his army never so often his person will raise another: all the histories of England, and our experience at Shrewsbury [in 1642] will manifest that sufficiently.[7]

Waller's pursuit of the king's flying army was carried out with characteristic speed and thoroughness. As Charles moved to Worcester and then to Bewdley on the west bank of the Severn, Sir William followed a parallel course along the east bank, reaching Stourbridge on 14th June, where he met Denbigh's army of 4,000 or so men, and also Sir William Brereton at the head of some regiments from Cheshire. With a force now over twice the size of the king's, Waller would willingly have given battle, but he was unable to cross the Severn as the bridges at Bridgnorth, Bewdley and Worcester were defended against him. However, by taking a route that went well to the north of the river, his army would be able to travel along good-quality roads, thus enabling it to reach Shrewsbury, Charles's most likely next destination, before the king. He thus had every confidence of carrying out his strategic role. It was just a question of waiting for Charles's next move.

However, Sir William was beginning to have second thoughts about the wisdom of the strategy that he and Essex had agreed at Chipping Norton. He tried to avoid blame by maintaining that he was merely obeying his superior officer. However, when the Committee of Both Kingdoms repeated its order that he should march into the west, he made common cause with his fellow commanders at Stourbridge by drawing the committee's attention to what damage the king might be able to do in central England with no large army to oppose him. This was a bold statement to make to one's political masters, but as a lesson in basic strategy it in no way compares with the magisterial reply of the Earl of Essex to the committee's order that his army stop in its tracks, despatch a force of cavalry to relieve Lyme and then return to the Oxford area. The lord general wrote that anybody with experience of military affairs would know that attempting to use cavalry in the enclosed country around Lyme against experienced Royalist infantry was a recipe for disaster. The town could only be relieved by a complete army.[8]

Just as Waller began to build up a head of steam against Essex, the ground was swept from under his feet. In the first place, he found that Parliament had temporarily lost interest in the campaign in the Midlands. The lord general had begun to make steady progress in the west. Maurice gave up the siege of Lyme on 15th June, and Weymouth surrendered within a week, followed not long afterwards by Taunton, and in his letters to the committee Essex claimed that all he needed to raise a large number of new troops in Devon, Dorset and Somerset was the presence and support of the western gentlemen who had been refugees in London for the past year. Second, the king's council of war took two crucially important decisions when it met at Bewdley on 14th June. The first was that the scale of the troop concentration that Waller had assembled at Stourbridge made it too dangerous either to try to join Prince Rupert or to remain in north Worcestershire. On the other hand, the situation in the Thames valley had improved immeasurably, as there were now no enemy troops in the vicinity of Oxford. Provided that the flying army could steal a march on Sir William Waller, there was nothing to prevent the field army being reconstituted.

The second decision resulted in the despatch of a letter to Prince Rupert, which allegedly lost the king the north of England. [9]

In order to evade Waller, the king's advisers employed a trick similar to that which the Earl of Essex had employed to escape from the Severn valley the previous September. Loading their musketeers onto boats sailing downriver to Worcester and using the cavalry in such a way as to suggest that the army was still in the Bewdley area, they stole two days' march on the enemy and were at Broadway on the edge of the Cotswolds before Waller had left north Worcestershire. As at Devizes his intelligence had let him down badly, and after one day's march he gave up the chase, consoling himself with the thought that the king was making for Bristol, where he would easily be trapped between Essex's army and his own. Sir William then spent the next week moving down the Severn valley to Gloucester on his way to the West Country, as he had been ordered, even when it became apparent that the royal army was marching towards Oxford, not towards Bristol. [10] By 24th June, the two armies were 100 miles apart. Having picked up his artillery and the rest of his infantry at Witney on the 20th of the month, the king quartered for four days in north Buckinghamshire, thus posing a possible threat to the Eastern Association or to London. The Committee of Both Kingdoms belatedly realized that it needed a full army to operate in the counties to the north of the capital, but all it had in the field was a scratch force of city of London trained bands quartered at Barnet in Hertfordshire under Major-General Richard Browne. Their original orders had been to assist Essex in blockading Oxford while Waller relieved Lyme, but these were clearly now redundant.

Realizing that the king was on the offensive, Waller anticipated the orders he was likely to receive from the committee and hurried rapidly across country just as the royal army was withdrawing from Buckinghamshire. After a violent difference of opinion, the king's council of war had rejected both a hare-brained scheme of Wilmot's to advance on London and a more realistic plan to raid Dunstable and do as much damage as possible to traffic passing along the A5 road. On the other hand, the council appreciated that it was not safe for the king's field army to remain where it was in case Waller, reinforced by Browne's brigade, tried to cut it off from Oxford. Charles therefore fell back on Banbury, probably in the hope of luring Waller into fighting a battle before Browne could join him.

On 29th June, as the two armies were marching northwards towards Daventry on parallel tracks either side of the River Cherwell, Sir William noticed a gap opening up between the Royalist main body and the rear-guard. This he decided to exploit in characteristic manner. There followed what is known as the battle of Cropredy Bridge, but to describe it as such is a misnomer as neither army was fully committed. The fighting was extremely fierce, but only at brigade level because, unlike at Cheriton, the generals on both sides managed to keep control of their subordinate officers. Waller's attack on the rearguard was quickly defeated, and the Royalists countered by assaulting part of the Parliamentary artillery train as it crossed the Cherwell. In the encounter Waller lost several hundred men, seven cannon and James Wemyss, his general of artillery. Two Royalist cavalry colonels were killed, but a new and able brigade commander emerged in the shape of the Earl of Cleveland. The king then rode westwards towards the lower Severn valley and settled his army at Evesham while he and his advisers decided on their next move. Waller assumed that the Royalists would try to march north again with the aim of joining Prince Rupert, and that they would choose the Trent valley route to avoid Denbigh's forces in the central Midlands. He therefore proposed to shadow them by moving via Northampton to Leicester, but much to his disgust many of the London trained band soldiers in his army decided to return home when they realized that another 'dance across the Midlands' was in prospect. This was followed almost immediately by the mutiny of Browne's brigade, which brought an end to active operations around Oxford for the next four months. It was at this time that Sir William made his famous despairing comment that Gardiner and many later historians have seen wrongly as sowing the seeds for the New Model Army:

an army composed of these men will never go through with your service, and till you have an army merely your own that you may command, it is in a manner impossible to do anything of importance.

Waller was referring merely to the inadequacies of the London trained bands, who saw themselves as under the command of the city authorities, not the two Houses of Parliament. The two Houses already had an army to command, that of the Earl of Essex, but there the problem was how to control the general, not the rank and file.

The news of trouble in Waller's army did not reach the Oxford army as it rested at Evesham waiting for accurate intelligence from the north. Rumours of a great battle were circulating by 5th July. Initially these reported a great Royalist victory. Not until a week later was it learned that

Rupert had been defeated. In the meantime, the council of war decided that the Thames valley and its garrisons were safe from attack for the moment, but that it was still not safe to try to join Rupert with Waller by that time blocking the route to Newark and Denbigh's army that to Lancashire. After three days of debate, the king and his military advisers also abandoned the idea of marching into Wales and taking up a defensive position there until Rupert arrived in case he did not and they were cut off from the rest of Royalist-controlled England. A new factor was concern for the queen's safety when news arrived that the Earl of Essex was advancing beyond Lyme into Devonshire. The king therefore resolved that the royal army should march via Bristol into the southwest of England with the aim of crushing the lord general's army between Prince Maurice's and his own.[11]

Notes

1 Walker, *Historical Discourses*, 7; BL Harleian ms 986, 82; Bodleian Clarendon ms 23, 187; Clarendon, *Great Rebellion* vii, 297. See Chapter XV for a discussion of the changing nature of Rupert's expedition.

2 Gardiner, *Great Civil War* I, 343–4; BL Additional ms 19891, 126; Walker, *Historical Discourses*, 9; HMC Bray ms, 151.

3 Dugdale, *Diary*, 50; BL Additional ms 18981, 126; *Mercurius Aulicus*, 934; CSP Domestic 1644, 128; Warburton, *Memoirs* II, 406, 411–13, 416.

4 CSP Domestic 1644, 127, 154, 162, 175, 182–3, 190; Bodleian Clarendon ms 1738, 8; HMC Bray ms, 152; BL Harleian ms 6988, 107.

5 Walker, *Historical Discourses*, 11, 12, 14; HMC De La Warre ms, 296; BL Additional ms 18981, 187.

6 CSP Domestic 1644, 181–2, 195, 199–200, 214; Walker, *Historical Discourses*, 14–15. 18–19; BL Additional ms 18981, 182, 187; BL Harleian ms 166, 83–4; TT E2 22; Bodleian Firth ms C7, 117.

7 Walker *Historical Discourses*, 16–18; CSP Domestic 1644, 206, 211–15, 226, 237; HMC 4th Report, 267; Warburton, *Memoirs* II, 419.

8 CSP Domestic 1644, 220, 232–9.

9 See below Chapter XV.

10 CSP Domestic 1644, 230, 242, 244; Walker, *Historical Discourses*, 24; Warburton, *Memoirs* II, 419.

11 Gardiner, *Great Civil War* II, 5; Young and Holmes, *English Civil War*, 189; Adair, *Roundhead General*, 197–8; Walker, *Historical Discourses*, 26–39; CSP Domestic 1644, 261–2, 267, 293, 301, 303, 324; BL Additional ms 18981, 203.

The march to York

Rupert's march to York was not a rash and unconsidered response to the crisis caused by the disaster at Selby but the outcome of lengthy, and at times agonizing, engagement with the quandary at the heart of Royalist strategic thinking, namely how to apportion scarce resources in such a way as to be able to conduct a war effectively on two fronts, one to the north of the Trent and the other in the Thames valley. For the first year and a half of the war, resources had moved very largely from the north to the south. Indeed, Oxford, the headquarters for the southern theatre of war, would have been untenable had not two large convoys of arms and ammunition arrived there from York, the northern headquarters, in May and July 1643 escorted by troops from Newcastle's command. However, the invasion of England by the Scots, promised in the Solemn League and Covenant in September 1643 and delivered when the Scottish army under the Earl of Leven crossed the Tweed on 19th January 1644, changed the situation completely. Now the northern theatre of war was the more threatened. The Scottish army combined with the Parliamentary troops in Lincolnshire, Lancashire and the East Riding of Yorkshire outnumbered Newcastle's army by two to one. Moreover, the army of the Eastern Association could operate in either theatre of war depending on military priorities. Not surprisingly, the marquis looked to the south for military assistance commensurate with that which his command had provided earlier in the war for the Thames valley theatre of war.

The council of war at Oxford did what it could to assist the northern command both before and after the Scottish invasion. The new army taking shape in the Welsh borderland from November 1643 onwards was intended, among other things, to protect the left flank of Newcastle's army by conquering Lancashire and Cheshire. Two months later, 1,000 cavalry returned to York from the Oxford area under Sir Charles Lucas. In March, whilst the marquis was conducting a war of manoeuvre against the Scots between the Rivers Tyne and Tees, Rupert had used part of the Welsh borderland army supported by local troops to destroy the threat to Newcastle's rear by dispersing the forces besieging Newark. However, despite eloquent and sustained pleas by the marquis and his area commanders, Rupert quickly returned to the Welsh borders to continue his recruiting operations for the king's field army. Finally, a couple of weeks later a single regiment set out from Oxford for the north escorting Lord Goring, Newcastle's general of cavalry, who had been a prisoner of war since June 1643.

This drying-up in the resources passing from the Thames valley to the north of England is explained by the steady deterioration in the strategic situation in the south beginning with Hopton's defeats in Sussex and Hampshire and Maurice's failure to capture Plymouth.[1] In the autumn, the council of war had been keen to move troops from the centre to the regions to ease the pressure on food and fodder. Now it needed to retain all the military resources it could to counter the threat from the Earl of Essex and Sir William Waller. Not surprisingly, Newcastle was very disappointed. However, the relative importance of the northern and southern theatres of war in 1644 was made absolutely clear in a letter that the king wrote to him on 11th April, immediately after returning to Oxford from the rendezvous at Aldbourne Chase. It also threw back into Newcastle's face the argument he had used the previous year to justify his refusal to march south and either join the Oxford army or invade East Anglia:

you must consider that we, like you, cannot do always what we would; besides our task is not little that we struggle with in which, if we fail, all you can do will be to little purpose. Wherefore you may be assured of all assistance from hence that may be without laying ourselves open to imminent danger.[2]

On the same day, the northern theatre of war collapsed when the Fairfaxes destroyed Lord Bellasis's army corps at Selby, only 15 miles from York. At the time Newcastle with the rest of the Northern army was in County Durham, 70 miles away, conducting a complicated war of manoeuvre against the Scots. Fortunately for him, the caution displayed by Lords Leven and Fairfax provided him with just enough time to fall back on York, which he reached without major incident on 17th April. He and his infantry remained there, but the cavalry was sent to Newark in search of assistance, where they met General Goring travelling north. In the meantime, Lord Fairfax had moved no further than Wetherby, where he and the Earl of Leven agreed on the following day to combine their forces to lay siege to York. However, although their combined armies were about 20,000 strong, the city's capture would be no easy task. Despite the great increase in the garrison's size, it was well supplied with food and other provisions. Also, the allied troops were not numerous enough to prevent the garrison continuing to bring in such supplies from the surrounding countryside.

As soon as he heard of the disaster at Selby, Rupert bent his mind towards assisting the marquis. On about 14th April, he wrote to the king suggesting 'a northern design'. The original despatch and Charles's initial reply no longer survive, but replies penned by Charles himself on the 20th and 22nd of the month to a second despatch show very clearly that the king's council of war had misgivings about the commitment of further resources to the north. Charles gave provisional approval to Rupert's plan, but he was to send some troops to Oxford and rejoin the main field army within six weeks. Otherwise, pressure from the armies of Essex and Waller would mean that Oxford had to be abandoned. Not surprisingly, the prince was unhappy with his instructions and went to Oxford to argue his case.[3]

The exact nature of Rupert's 'northern design' as first conceived can be no more than a matter of speculation. However, although the force involved would have been more heavily outnumbered than the one that Rupert organized in June, it stood a good chance of success provided that it could be organized quickly. By bringing together at Newark the so-called Northern Horse under Goring, Byron's cavalry regiments, and the horse and mounted infantry he had used in the Newark expedition, Rupert could have assembled a force of over 8,000 men in the lower Trent valley before the end of April. This would have been quite sufficient to face Leven and Fairfax in open country, as they had only about 6,000 horse and dragoons. However, lack of infantry would have meant that he could not have fought a conventional battle. His prime intention must have therefore been to out-manoeuvre the allies, presumably by approaching the city from an unexpected direction as he did ten weeks later in much more difficult circumstances. What would have happened next is impossible to say, but we think it more likely that Rupert would have tried to extricate Newcastle and his troops from the northern theatre of war as quickly as possible rather than seek to restore the situation in the north by inflicting a defeat on the enemy (unless he

saw a chance of cutting off and destroying part of the allied army). However, breaking out would have been more difficult than breaking in. The
most obvious escape route was via the bridge over the Wharfe at Cawood,
which was guarded by a castle still occupied by Newcastle's men, and so to
Newark or the garrison at Sheffield. Cawood was only eight miles south of
York, but its advantages would have been equally obvious to the enemy.
Nevertheless, with 20,000 men to Rupert and Newcastle's 12,000 they
would not have dared divide their forces, and the prince would doubtless
have devised a way of wrongfooting them.[4]

However, Rupert's long visit to Oxford between 24th April and 5th May,
the outcome of which is discussed in Chapter XIV, caused a major delay.
Admittedly there were positive results. The council of war gave the expedition its formal approval; Rupert secured permission to retain the regiments
he was to have sent from Shrewsbury to reinforce his uncle's army; and the
deadline for returning to the south was extended. However, by the time he
had returned to his command the odds on mounting a successful raid on
York from Newark had worsened considerably. In the first place, the potential size of the enemy forces opposing him had increased. By then the Earl
of Manchester's army was besieging Lincoln, only 16 miles to the northeast of Newark. Admittedly it was on the wrong side of a river in flood
and so could have done nothing to impede Rupert's advance northwards,
but it could have crossed the Trent at Nottingham while he was at York
and intercepted him as he returned towards Newark or Sheffield. If not
quite strong enough in cavalry to engage Rupert's and Newcastle's forces
in battle, the Eastern Association army could have slowed them down, thus
giving time for Lord Fairfax and the Scots to catch up. Second, the delay
caused by the discussions with the king and his military advisers had removed
the element of surprise. Sir Samuel Luke's informants knew of the York expedition by 6th May, and Rupert's intentions were all over the London newspapers not long afterwards.

The change in the military balance in the lower Trent valley resulting
from the advance of the Eastern Association army caused Rupert to order
Goring's cavalry, which had been quartered there and in Leicestershire, to
withdraw up the Trent valley to safer billets near Lichfield and then into
the Peak District. The prince now had two options. He could advance on
York via Lancashire, whose Royalist landowners led by the Earl of Derby
promised to provide him with large numbers of additional infantrymen once
he had reconquered the county. This would make a conventional battle with

the Scots and the Fairfaxes possible if it was needed or unavoidable. More-over, an operation mounted from Lancashire had the added advantage of providing an army returning from York with an escape route, as the Pennine passes could be defended against a pursuing enemy by small bodies of infantry. Alternatively, a raid on York similar to that originally planned to set out from Newark could be mounted from Sheffield. Nevertheless, time was still limited. Although he had convinced the king's council of war that the early June deadline was now impossibly close, Rupert was still under orders to return to the south as soon as possible.

The eventual decision to march to York via Lancashire almost certainly took place later than is normally thought, largely because historians have confused aspirations to restore Royalist control over the county with the practicalities of mounting an expedition to relieve York. What the prince did in June 1644 was to attempt to kill both birds with one stone. Clear signs of a plan to reconquer Lancashire can be found in Byron's instruc-tions issued in November 1643. Lord Digby also referred to it very briefly as a possible strategic objective in a letter written to Rupert in late March after the relief of Newark. Finally, at about the same time, Byron tried to persuade Rupert against taking such a course of action, the prince's inter-est having been aroused by a letter from the Earl of Derby begging him to go to the relief of his countess besieged in Latham House, near Preston, and emphasizing the number of recruits he would obtain by visiting the county.

The first sign that Lancashire rather than somewhere else was to be the rendezvous for the army intending to relieve York is a comment made in *Mercurius Aulicus* to the effect that the prince had left Shrewsbury on 15th May and was intending to rescue the Countess of Derby. The first stage of his march was to Whitchurch, where the prince was joined by reinforce-ments led by Lord Byron. As a result, Rupert had an army of about 6,000 infantry and 2,000 cavalry, but these varied very considerably in quality. Alongside the very experienced cavalry regiments commanded by the two generals and the infantry regiments that had crossed over from Ireland were garrison troops like Thomas Leveson's regiment of horse from Dudley Castle and Byron's regiment of foot from Chester, and large numbers of impressed men.

Instead of making for a crossing of the Mersey, the army marched almost due east from Whitchurch as if heading for the garrison at Sheffield, around which the Northern Horse were by then quartered. It is therefore possible to take at face value the statement made by Byron in a letter written to the Marquis of Ormonde on 12th June that it was he who finally convinced the prince to go north, not the Earl of Derby and the Lancashire gentlemen's promise of recruits in Lancashire or the need to raise the siege of Latham House. However, the final decision for the troops from Shrewsbury and Chester to advance into Lancashire rather than towards Sheffield cannot have been taken until just before the army marched northwards from the Newcastle-under-Lyme area on 22nd May. Rupert's diary does not tell us why he changed his mind, but the deciding factor is likely to have been intelligence from further east, which made the relief of York from the southwest rather than the northwest much less attractive. This would probably have included news that Cawood Castle had surrendered on 19th May and that the Earl of Manchester's army had captured Lincoln and lain siege to Gainsborough, which was expected to surrender very quickly and thus provide the earl with a first-class crossing point over the Trent only a day or two's march from the allied armies at York. Moreover, Manchester's cavalry had joined the horse of the other two armies in the lower Trent valley to the west of Gainsborough, thus giving the allies a numerical advantage in horse and making an advance on York from Sheffield almost as dangerous as one from Newark.[5]

Once it had left the Cheshire/Staffordshire border, Rupert's army headed for the easiest crossing over the Mersey at Stockport. It brushed aside the opposition that had been hastily gathered to defend the bridge and then quickly captured Bolton and Liverpool by assault, destroying much of the Lancashire Parliamentarians' infantry in the process. On or before 4th June, Goring met Rupert's army at Bury, allegedly bringing with him well over 4,000 cavalry and 800 infantry, not merely the Northern Horse but also regiments from the Nottinghamshire and Derbyshire garrisons.[6]

Meanwhile, the siege of York was proceeding at a somewhat leisurely pace. An assault was out of the question given the size of the garrison and the strength of the fortifications, but so was a total blockade. As a result, the first six weeks of the undertaking were more like a stand-off than a siege. Lords Fairfax and Leven therefore approached the Earl of Manchester and the Committee of Both Kingdoms for assistance. Although determined to capture Gainsborough, the last major Royalist garrison in Lincolnshire, Manchester decided not to lay siege to Newark, despite the humiliation that some of his troops had received there two months earlier. Before 22nd May his horse were cooperating with the Scottish horse in the lower Trent valley, presumably to block any attempt by Rupert to move in that direction, and on 3rd June he arrived before York with six regiments of infantry amounting in total to about 5,000 men. This was not in strict accordance with the orders he had received from the committee, but he reasoned that, as Rupert was widely believed to be intent on relieving York, he was pre-empting not disobeying earlier orders to follow the prince wherever he went. However, he did promise that he would head southwards if Rupert made any move to join his uncle instead. The committee seems to have tacitly accepted the strength of the earl's argument that three armies were needed to besiege York, but it showed concern that Manchester's army might become so committed to the siege of York that it would be unwilling to play an active role in curtailing Rupert's activities. Nevertheless, as soon as it became apparent that the prince was on the march into northwest England, Leven and Fairfax sent two of their infantry regiments across the Pennines under Sir John Meldrum's command to strengthen the county's defences. They arrived too late to take part in the engagement at Stockport, but Meldrum nevertheless managed to reach the town of Manchester safely, where he was forced to play a purely defensive role until Rupert had left the county. He spent the time writing for assistance to other generals in the northern theatre of war and outside, and weaving elaborate but implausible strategies for bringing Rupert to battle in Lancashire before the prince's strength became overwhelming.

When it learned of the storming of Bolton and Liverpool, the Committee of Both Kingdoms urged Leven, Fairfax and Manchester to send more troops across the Pennines, but the request was met with a firm refusal. While acknowledging that Manchester had orders to follow Rupert, the three generals were confident of capturing York quickly. They would therefore have plenty of time to deal with Rupert, whether he decided to return to the south, stay where he was or head for Scotland. Starving York into surrender would be time-consuming, as they were still unable to cut the city off completely from the surrounding countryside, but with a combined force of almost 30,000 men they felt strong enough to storm its defences once they had exploded the mines that were being currently dug under part of the walls.[7] They would have been even firmer in their resolve had they known that Rupert was not that eager to leave Lancashire for the moment.

Reading between the lines of several letters that Rupert received in early and mid-June, it is almost certain that he had another project that he wished to complete before advancing on York, namely the capture of the remaining garrisons in Lancashire and Cheshire held by the Parliament-arians, after which he was confident of raising an army of 20,000 men there and in Wales. Whether York fell or not in the meantime did not matter, as he would have plenty of troops with which to recapture it. This did not meet with the approval of the king or the council of war.[8] They were deter-mined that he should spend as little time as possible in the north, as the strategic situation in the Thames valley was deteriorating rapidly. They were also worried that the allied armies would march into southern England after capturing York. From the last week in May until 17th June, Rupert was sent a stream of letters containing a reasonably consistent set of instructions urging him to concentrate on Yorkshire rather than Lancashire, defeat the allied armies there as speedily as possible, and then rejoin the king to face Essex and Waller. However, Rupert now knew that Manchester's army had joined the forces besieging York, which would make the task of rescuing the Marquis of Newcastle more problematic until such time as he could raise a larger army.

The crucial letter in the series has always been seen as the one written by the king to Rupert from Tickenhill House in Bewdley on 14th June in that its contents can be read as clear instructions not merely to relieve York but also to fight the armies besieging it. However, Young and Newman have expressed reservations about the firmness of the royal command, which is hardly surprising as the language used is clumsy with all the hallmarks of being written by a committee. It is also ambiguous in that it can be read in such a way as to suggest that the loss of York would be a major personal blow to the authority and prestige of the Crown, or the exact opposite. Although initially we favoured their reading of the Tickenhill letter, other letters written on the same or the following day by the Duke of Richmond and the king himself show very clearly that it was the former meaning that was intended.[9] This neatly makes the point that Rupert's instructions can only be understood by analyzing information contained in all the corres-pondence he received from the king and members of his council of war in the run-up to the battle of Marston Moor.

No letters relating directly to the relief of York survive for the period between 25th May and 6th June, when Essex and Waller were tightening the noose around Oxford, but Rupert's diary suggests very strongly that there was one that has subsequently disappeared, as he claimed to have received his first orders to go to York on about 1st June while he was at Bolton. However, eight exist for the period between 7th and 17th June. The first seven, including the Tickenhill letter, were written when the flying army was in Worcestershire and before the king's council of war realized that the Earl of Essex's army had marched too far west to affect operations in the Thames valley theatre of war. They are full of gloom and reiterate earlier orders for Rupert to return to the south as quickly as possible.[10] The eighth, written on 17th June at Broadway, is of a different character. Although it evinces some caution, the tone is upbeat. The flying army was on its march back to the Thames valley and would be able to join up with foot soldiers that had been left behind in Oxford before Waller caught up. However, the letter was penned by Lord Digby, an eternal optimist whose judgement Rupert mistrusted, and Rupert may not have received it until he was crossing the Pennines on his way to York.[11]

The really important insight provided by analysis of the series of letters is that the order to fight the armies before York was not something novel. The very first letter in the series, written by the king from Worcester on 7th June, clearly states that Rupert must fight the Scots. The only difference between it and the Tickenhill letter is that the latter mentions fighting the armies before York, not just the Scots. However, this cannot be seen as a fundamental change in the prince's orders, as he would have found it very difficult to separate the Scottish army from the rest and attack it without the others intervening. The most likely explanation for the difference in wording between the two letters is that the king did not know on the 7th that Manchester's army had arrived outside York, but did on the 14th, although it is possible that the earlier letter was written in a hurry and as a result was less exact in its use of language than it should have been. What is new about the Tickenhill letter is that it orders Rupert to set aside all other plans and to march on York immediately so that he can return to the south without any lengthy delay. This point is strongly reinforced in a more personal letter almost certainly written by the king on the following day, which probably lacks a date because it was sent in the same package. The undated letter, which has been totally ignored by historians, reads as follows:

To what I wrote yesterday I can only add that the relief of York is that which is most absolutely best for my affairs whereof again I earnestly conjure you speedily to prosecute that if you have but the least hope to do good there, but as I have told you my business can bear no delay for you must either march presently northwards or hitherward, and that without engaging yourself in any other action.

Further pressure on the prince to relieve York is apparent in other correspondence he received in the third week in June. A letter written on the same
day as the Tickenhill letter by Richmond, the only member of the king's
inner council whom Rupert trusted completely, claimed that the condition of York was more serious than he may have been led to understand
from intelligence obtained locally, and that speed was therefore essential.
Sir William Davenant, a general officer belonging to Newcastle's army, took
a different approach. In a letter written from Haleford on the Mersey on
13th June, he reminded the prince of the demoralizing effect on the besieged
garrison of uncertainty as to his intentions:

*I fear lest the rumour, which is common at Chester, of the king's necessities,
and consequently of your Highness's, marching towards him . . . would prevail
more on the people [at York] than their want of victual or the enemy's
continual assault.*[12]

What is surely significant about the Tickenhill letter, Richmond's letter
and the king's undated letter is their emphasis on speed: Rupert must drop
all other schemes and concentrate on the relief of York, after which he
must return immediately to the south. Their context was almost certainly
rumours that Rupert wanted to campaign in the northwest for a number
of weeks to complete the plan described in his diary.

On 18th June, having received the package of letters from Bewdley,
and probably against his better judgement, Rupert decided that the march
to York must take precedence over securing Lancashire or immediately
returning south. The following day, having assembled most of his army
near Liverpool, he advanced up the Ribble to Clitheroe and so across the
Pennines into the valley of the River Aire. The army's line of march was
well to the north of the most direct route from Lancashire into Yorkshire.
However, the latter ran too close to the enemy garrison at Manchester, and
Rupert was determined to have his line of retreat protected by a string of
Royalist garrisons, not threatened by an enemy stronghold garrisoned by a
thousand or so soldiers. The route taken also made it much easier to link
up both with George Goring's cavalry, which had been sent north from Bury
to pick up regiments and new recruits in Westmorland and Cumberland,
and with Sir Robert Clavering's brigade, which had been operating against
the Scottish army's lines of communications in Northumberland. The army
rendezvous was to take place at Skipton on 26th June. Goring duly arrived
the day before with 1,000 additional men, but Clavering's brigade, which

was of an equivalent size, had been delayed. Rupert decided not to wait for its arrival, a very significant mistake that it is tempting to blame on his uncle and his uncle's advisers, who were urging him not to delay, but this is unlikely to have been the only consideration. Rupert would probably have been aware that reinforcements for the allies from the Midlands and from south Lancashire were on the march towards York and might arrive there before he did if he waited for Clavering.[13]

Parliament's strategy from mid-June onwards was a compromise between the views of the army commanders in Yorkshire and elsewhere, and the Committee of Both Kingdoms. All agreed that the first priority was to capture York, but the differences as to what was to be done about Lancashire persisted. As the three generals had refused to be deflected from their siege, the committee put pressure on the Earl of Denbigh. His army had been ordered in early June to block any route by which Rupert might march south to join his uncle, but before the earl could leave he was drawn into Waller's pursuit of the king's flying army. When Waller and the king marched south, Denbigh was ordered to advance into Lancashire. To this end he moved from Wem to Nantwich and then to Knutsford. When it became apparent that Rupert was heading for York, not for the Thames valley, he was ordered by the generals of the allied armies to join Sir John Meldrum at Manchester and then to head for York. However, having visited Meldrum, Denbigh decided that it was unsafe for his army to advance further north because of a threat to his rear from Royalist forces in Shropshire. He was also unwilling to take orders from the three generals without a direct instruction from the Committee of Both Kingdoms. However, he did leave some horse with Meldrum when he returned into the Welsh Marches to counter a threat to Oswestry.[14]

When they first learned that Rupert was on the march towards York, Fairfax, Leven and Manchester agreed to engage Rupert in battle while maintaining the siege of York. However, this could only be accomplished if the troops gathering in Lancashire were able to join them. They received a letter from Meldrum on 30th June that he could reach Wakefield, 20 miles from the city, by 3rd July, but this would be far too late, as they knew by that time that Rupert had advanced from Skipton to Knaresborough, only 15 miles from his destination. They therefore abandoned the siege and took up a position on moorland, variously described as Ouse Moor and Hessay Moor, about three miles from the city covering the Knaresborough road, in the expectation that Rupert would advance along the south side of the

Nidd. Instead, he crossed the river and approached York from the north by a very circuitous route, which put two rivers between his army and those of the allies. The prince also sent a force to capture the bridge of boats that Fairfax and Leven had erected over the Ouse just to the west of York, his object being to prevent the allied armies crossing to the north bank to intercept him as he neared the city. This was easily accomplished, as the three generals had left only a small force of dragoons to guard it. As a result, Rupert was able to enter York without opposition on the night of 1st July, leaving his army to quarter in the meadows close to the bridge. Rupert has received much praise for his imaginative tactics, but he had been lucky. If the generals had stationed cavalry patrols close to Knaresborough on both banks of the Nidd, they could have observed the prince's progress and used the bridge of boats to move troops from one side of the river to the other as appropriate. Their subsequent claim that the bridge was too weak for this purpose cannot be believed, as the Royalists used it a day later to move their army to the south bank. Rupert had thus achieved his first objective; York had been relieved.[15]

Notes

1 Carte, *Ormonde*, 418–19; Slingsby, *Diary*, 102–3; Dugdale, *Diary*, 65.

2 BL Harleian ms 6988, 106; Warburton, *Memoirs* II, 482–3.

3 Bodleian Firth ms C7, 63, 72, 77; Fairfax, *Short Memorial*, 437; BL Additional ms 18981, 155.

4 Rushworth, *Historical Collections* V, 604, 618.

5 *Rupert's Marches*, 766; *Mercurius Aulicus*, 989; Luke, *Letterbook*, 649; Bodleian Firth ms C7, 103; *ibid.*, Carte ms XI, 87.

6 Bodleian Carte ms X, 664.

7 HMC Bray ms, 152; CSP Domestic 1644, 173–4, 191–2, 200, 206–8, 217, 246.

8 Warburton, *Memoirs* II, 434, 439n; Bodleian Firth ms C8, 253.

9 Bodleian Firth ms C7, 122–3; BL Additional ms 18981, 194; Newman, *Marston Moor*, 40–1; Young, *Marston Moor*, 79.

10 The letters are dated 7th, 8th and 9th June (Warburton, *Memoirs* II, 414–18); 14th June × 2 (BL Additional ms 18981, 191, 194); and 14th June and n.d. but almost certainly 15th June (Bodleian Firth ms C7, 123; *ibid.*, C8, 253).

11 Warburton, *Memoirs* II, 419–20, 434–6; Wilts CRO 413/444A 35; Bodleian Carte ms XI, 86.

12 Warburton, *Memoirs* II, 434.

13 *Rupert's Marches*, 766–7; BL Additional ms 18981, 189–99; HMC Portland ms I, 179; Wilts CRO 413/444A 35.

14 CSP Domestic, 1644 176, 230–1, 252–3, 272–3, 286–7; HMC Appendix to the 4th Report, 267–8.

15 *Rupert's Marches*, 766; CSP Domestic 1644, 337. Stockdale's account is printed in Young, *Marston Moor*, 213–16.

chapter XVI

The battle of Marston Moor

Having failed to prevent Prince Rupert reaching York, the allied generals decided to retreat to the line of the River Wharfe, assuming that
his next destination would be Newark. The armies were strung out along
the road to Cawood and Tadcaster when the lieutenant-generals of horse,
Oliver Cromwell, David Leslie and Sir Thomas Fairfax, commanding the
rearguard reported signs that the Royalist armies, instead of taking time to
rest and reprovision the city, were in full pursuit. They therefore recommended that the generals should stop the retreat and lead the armies back
to the only place of advantage on the plain between the Ouse, the Nidd
and the Wharfe, a shallow ridge between Tockwith and Long Marston.
Leven, Lord Fairfax and Manchester agreed.[1] During the afternoon and early
evening, the two army groups slowly took up positions facing one another,
with the allies on the ridge and the regiments of Newcastle and Rupert to
their north on Marston Moor between the ridge and the River Nidd. Separating the moor from cultivated ground were a number of obstacles: in the
west a marsh and a rabbit warren; in the east a hedge; and across much of
the front a ditch, which varied in depth. During the afternoon, both sides
drew up their troops in the conventional manner for a battle fought in open
country with the infantry in the centre and cavalry on the wings. The allied
armies were half as large again as the Royalists, about 28,000 as opposed
to 18,000 men, but the imbalance was mainly in infantry. Possibly to compensate for this, Rupert placed a brigade of Northern Horse under Sir William
Blakiston behind the Royalist infantry brigades to act as a reserve.[2]

The battle began at 7.30p.m., an unusually late hour in the day, but it
was not by accident. The allied generals had ordered a concerted attack

Map 5 The north of England, 1642–45

on the Royalist armies in the belief that Rupert would have permitted his officers to stand down for the night. At first the allies achieved considerable success. Rupert's commands had been to wait for the enemy to attack, but on the right wing Lord Byron moved forward prematurely with some troops of horse, possibly because most of the regiments on his wing had

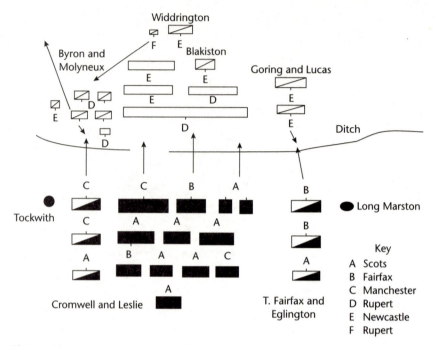

Figure 12 The battle of Marston Moor, about 7.30p.m.

been taken completely by surprise and were still mounting their horses. Byron's men were quickly overwhelmed by their adversaries, Oliver Cromwell's Eastern Association horse, as they attempted to cross the marsh and rabbit warren, but he had won enough time for the remainder of his wing to organize themselves and attack, supported by Rupert with part of the reserves.[3] Elsewhere things seemed to be going well for the allies. In the centre the English and Scottish regiments that formed the first line of the infantry formation had crossed the ditch and were making steady progress against the Royalist foot, whereas Sir Thomas Fairfax leading the first line of the allies' right wing was involved in close combat with the Northern Horse under Lord Goring in and about the ditch.[4]

The first crisis came in the centre. The Yorkshire regiments in the middle of the allies' first line broke through the ranks of the Royalist infantry facing them only to be charged by Blakiston's brigade and put to flight. They carried with them almost all the regiments directly behind them and to their right in the second, third and fourth lines of allied infantry, Scots, Yorkshiremen and Eastern Association alike, although the Eastern

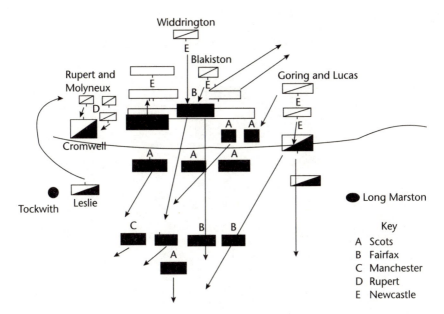

Figure 13 The battle of Marston Moor, about 8.30p.m.

Association regiment commanded by the Earl of Manchester appears to have retreated, not to have fled the field in panic. At about the same time or slightly earlier, Sir Thomas Fairfax's cavalry were broken by the Northern Horse when they failed to receive the expected support from their second and third lines. The only exception was Sir Thomas's own regiment, but, having forced its way through the enemy ranks, it rode off in pursuit of the regiment it had routed leaving Sir Thomas almost on his own.[5] To make matters worse, most of the victorious Royalist horse rallied when they reached the crest of the ridge, and some turned their attention to two Scottish regiments of the first line, the sole survivors of the centre and right of the allied infantry formation.[6]

On the left, however, Cromwell and his Scottish reserves under Leslie had routed Rupert's cavalry, probably by sheer weight of numbers, after a fierce fight lasting about half an hour. At about the same time, the Eastern Association infantry regiments to Cromwell's right under General Crawford had driven back the Royalists' foot facing them, who, like the defeated cavalry, took refuge in the woods beside the Nidd. Instead of chasing after them, the allied cavalry halted. After considerable discussion, which may

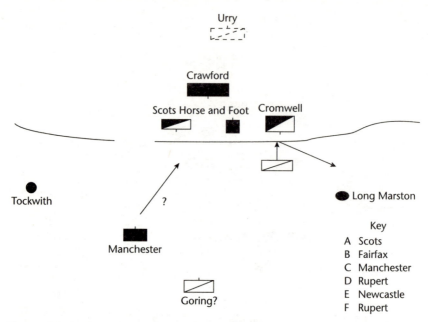

Urry

Crawford

Scots Horse and Foot   Cromwell

Tockwith

?

Long Marston

Manchester

Goring?

Key

A Scots
B Fairfax
C Manchester
D Rupert
E Newcastle
F Rupert

Figure 14 The battle of Marston Moor, about 9.30p.m.

have been informed by Sir Thomas Fairfax arriving with news of what had happened elsewhere on the battlefield, it was agreed that the cavalry and infantry should wheel to their right and attack the victorious, though disorganized, Royalist formations as they encountered them.[7] The only body of infantry to put up any resistance was Newcastle's infantry regiment, the Whitecoats, which held its ground until annihilated. As darkness fell, the Eastern Association forces had roughly reached the position where the Royalist left wing had been deployed when the battle began. Here took place the final cavalry engagement of the day, in which Cromwell easily routed some of the regiments that had defeated the allied right wing horse two hours earlier. However, most of Goring's troopers were probably on the far side of the ridge, well able to fight but not prepared to do so because by that time it was impossible to distinguish friend from foe. Only in the morning did they reluctantly obey orders and leave the battlefield.[8]

Although the victory had been a significant one, it was not decisive. Too many Royalists had escaped under the cover of darkness. It took the allies several months to evict Prince Rupert and the remnant of his army and another year to complete the conquest of the north of England.

Notes

1 Fairfax, *Short Memorial*, 437–8; Newman, *Marston Moor*, 47–55; TT E2 14; Wilts CRO 413/444A 37; SRO 445/277.

2 BL additional ms 16370, 65; Young, *Marston Moor*, plate 21 (Lumsden's plan); TT E2 14. the figures are taken from Barrett, *Battle for York*, 92–5.

3 *Ibid.*; Wilts CRO 413/444A 37; James II, *Life*, 22–3.

4 TT E2 14; TT E54 19; Fairfax, *Short Memorial*, 438; Slingsby, *Diary*, 114.

5 *Ibid.*; Terry, *Leven*, 282; Fairfax, *Short Memorial*, 438; TT E2 1; TT E54 19; SRO 445/277, 278.

6 Bodleian Clarendon ms, 1764; Slingsby, *Diary*, 114.

7 Fairfax, *Short Memorial*, 438; Baillie, *Letters and Journals* II, 214, 218; TT E2 14; TT E54 19.

8 TT E2 14; Young, *Marston Moor*, 112–3, 234; Cholmley, *Memorials*, 350.

chapter XVII

The Royalist recovery

On 12th July, the king and his council of war at last received a definitive report from Rupert himself on the outcome of the battle of Marston Moor. At the time the field army was at Coberley, near Cheltenham. Its aim was to steal a few days' march on Sir William Waller and with luck to fight the Earl of Essex before he could catch up. If this proved impracticable, they were confident of defeating Waller himself in battle with the support of reinforcements from the Bristol garrison. The document itself does not survive, but something of its contents can be inferred from letters written during July by Digby to Rupert and to Lord Goring, and by Sir Edward Nicholas to the Marquis of Ormonde.

Rupert admitted he had suffered a defeat but pointed out that he had saved most of his cavalry and some of his infantry by retreating into Lancashire and Cumbria, which were firmly in Royalist hands, and that he had left sufficient soldiers in garrison at York to enable it to withstand another siege. He may also have claimed that he had, or soon would have, a sufficiently large army in the northwest to relieve the city garrison again if that became necessary. If not stated in so many words, the implication was that the northern campaign was still in progress with the prospect of plenty of serious fighting in the weeks, if not months, to come. There were similar views in the allied camp. The drubbing that Rupert had given to the Fairfaxes' army at Marston Moor meant that Eastern Association troops were still needed in the north of England. As a result, the king's fears expressed in the Tickenhill letter of 'the effects of their northern power' being experienced in the southern theatre of war vanished for the time being. It is not therefore surprising that Rupert's letter strengthened the king's resolve to pursue Essex's army. Two days later, the decision to do so was further vindicated by news that Waller's infantry had melted away and that he was in no condition to undertake an active pursuit or to threaten Oxford. The pace of the advance then increased, with the result that within two weeks of leaving Evesham the king's army was close to the Somerset/Devon border and anticipating a rendezvous with Prince Maurice's Western army, which, after some adventures, was encamped just to the east of Exeter. The strategic objectives were now not merely to defeat Essex but also to 'prepare a reserve in case of further disaster . . . northwards, and, in case of success there, [to] be likely to finish the work', that is presumably to bring the war to a successful conclusion.[1]

The next four months was to be a period of almost unbroken success for the Royalist armies in the south of England, although, as will be shown, this owed far more to mistakes made by the enemy than to the strategic competence of the king and his advisers. However, the Royalist high command could not have achieved what it did without the prudence and cool-headedness shown by Prince Maurice in the second half of June and the first three weeks of July. Having abandoned the siege of Lyme at the approach of Essex's army, which outnumbered his forces in Dorset by more than two to one, the prince retreated to the other side of Exeter via Chard and Honiton instead of marching to Bristol as the king had instructed him to do a fortnight before. Maurice had sound reasons for remaining in the west. In the first place, he probably knew some time before leaving Lyme on 14th June that the king's army had been unable to retreat from Oxford to Bristol. He may also have known that it was in Worcestershire, apparently heading for Shrewsbury and the north, having abandoned any notion of retreating into the west of England. There was also a second consideration. Given that Chard was his first night's quarters after leaving Lyme, Maurice could almost certainly have reached Bristol before the Earl of Essex, who was in deepest Dorset, but this would have meant not only abandoning the queen, who was at Exeter about to give birth, but also the almost certain destruction of 2,000 of his troops who were blockading Plymouth.[2]

Henrietta Maria duly gave birth to a daughter on 16th June but was very ill both before and after the event and terrified of being shut up in Exeter, which the western Royalists and the king's council of war thought would be Essex's next target. When the lord general at last advanced into Devonshire after a week's rest at Chard, the queen fled the city heading for Falmouth, the safest port from which to set sail to France, as it was at the boundary of the operational areas of Parliament's Channel and Irish Sea fleets. Maurice escorted her as far as the Cornish border with the troops that had besieged Lyme using a route that went well to the north of Dartmoor, a sensible precaution against the enemy garrison at Plymouth mounting a successful kidnapping operation. He then took up a strong defensive position at Okehampton guarding the approaches to Cornwall reinforced by the corps of his army that had been blockading Plymouth. He also withdrew troops from Barnstaple, whereupon the town reverted to its original allegiance and declared for Parliament. Essex made no attempt to follow him. Instead his army rested for a fortnight at Tiverton close to the eastern border of Devon. Maurice remained at Okehampton until he received news that the queen had left for France. One mission successfully accomplished, his next priority was to save the Western army from being destroyed or forced to surrender, which was one of Essex's declared objectives after he had relieved Lyme.

The lord general's plan was to trap Maurice's army between troops from the Plymouth garrison, which would presumably have guarded the bridges across the Tamar, and his own army as it moved westwards, but he was slow to leave Tiverton. His reasons were that he was waiting for his troops' pay to arrive, and that he had sent some of his regiments to assist in the fortification of Weymouth and Barnstaple, but one suspects that Essex did not want to place himself in the embarrassing position of capturing the queen and then having to hand her over to Parliament.

In the light of Essex's inactivity, Maurice decided to risk returning towards Exeter with his entire army while leaving the trained bands of west Devon and Cornwall under Sir Richard Grenville, Waller's former lieutenant-general of horse, to resume the blockade of Plymouth. Maurice was almost certainly not intending to engage Essex in battle given the disparity in size between the two armies and the fact that his cavalry had little or no battle experience. A more likely explanation for his marching eastwards directly towards the enemy army is that, as Exeter's fortifications had been thoroughly refurbished and its magazines reprovisioned, it was the safest place for him to quarter his infantry until such time as the king's army could march to his rescue or cause such alarm in the Thames valley that the Committee of Both Kingdoms ordered Essex to return east. However, when Maurice decided to leave Okehampton, he knew nothing about the whereabouts of the king's army other than that it had been in the south Midlands a month earlier. Charles had sent a letter from Evesham on 11th July informing him of his determination to follow Essex into the southwest of England provided that Waller remained inactive, but it does not appear to have reached him in time.[3]

When the Barnstaple brigade, comprising three regiments of infantry and two of cavalry, returned to Tiverton on about 17th July, Essex and his council of war discussed the various strategic options available to them. Although they were aware that the king's army had reached Bath, they did not see it as being strong enough or close enough to influence their decisions. Essex believed that the forces Waller and Browne had assembled near Oxford would deter the king from marching further west by threatening his headquarters or by dogging his steps as he advanced. Moreover, if Essex's army moved back towards Bath, the local Parliamentarians would probably lose control of Taunton and Weymouth. Instead, the council of war decided that the army should relieve Plymouth, whose garrison was severely demoralized by lack of pay and fodder, but this was almost certainly not the major reason for marching further west. Despite some energetic campaigning over the past three months by local Royalists, the town was in no danger of surrendering. Moreover, the fleet could supply its needs more easily than a land army, as it had done very effectively for over a year and a half. Essex's real intention was to conquer the whole of the west of England and thus silence his critics at Westminster and in the city of London. Surprisingly, his letter to the Committee of Both Kingdoms explaining his intentions mentions the fate of the Royalist army of the west in only vague terms, but presumably he thought that it would either fight him at Okehampton and be defeated or retire into Cornwall, where he could deal with it at a later date. It is also odd that Essex did not consider remaining at Tiverton, a position from which his army could attack one or other of the enemy armies as occasion offered, but presumably it had consumed all the available food supplies in east Devonshire. This may also explain why Essex did not lay siege to Exeter.[4]

On the very day that Essex set out from Tiverton heading for Crediton with an army of about 10,000 men, Maurice's army was approaching the town from the opposite direction with just over half that number. A collision seemed inevitable, but Essex missed his opportunity to fight a battle on 20th July, largely because he failed to send out scouts and was therefore unaware of the approach of the Royalists. Walker claimed that the prince would have risked a battle at Crediton had he not received a message that day that the king's army was at Ilchester, only 60 miles away.

He therefore redirected his march to Exeter 'to make the game surer'. Walker is not often wrong in a factual sense, but in this case he must be, as the king did not reach Ilchester until the evening of the 20th. For this reason, we accept Joseph Bamfield's account of what happened. Maurice, learning while on the march that the Parliamentarians had left Tiverton, took steps to avoid the earl's army. Hurrying past Crediton, he apparently crossed to the east bank of the Exe at North Exe, thus putting the river between himself and the enemy. Then, leaving 1,000 infantry and some horse to defend the bridge, he and the rest of the army took up quarters at Heavitree on the far side of Exeter just before nightfall. It was only then that he heard that his uncle's army was less than four days' march away.

All Essex managed to do on 20th July was to capture a few stragglers, but instead of pursuing Maurice towards Exeter, his army continued its march westwards to Okehampton and then to Tavistock, where it made contact with the Plymouth garrison. This looks like yet another case of Essex reacting lamely to an unanticipated turn of events, as for example when the king's army left Shrewsbury in October 1642, but in the circumstances it was probably the best course of action. The distance from Crediton to Heavitree via Tiverton, the nearest bridge over the Exe under Parliamentary control, was about 30 miles, a two-day slog given the disruption that would result from reversing the army's line of march. Moreover, Maurice was likely to have drawn up his army in such a position that it could retreat behind the walls of Exeter if real danger threatened. These were the kind of factors that would have convinced Essex that he had only a slim chance of inflicting a decisive defeat on the western Royalists before the king's army arrived.[5]

Until his arrival at Tavistock, it is possible to construct some form of logical defence of the Earl of Essex's strategic decisions, but his next move across the River Tamar into Cornwall is difficult to explain. At the time, Royalists and Parliamentarians alike thought that he was about to do some sort of deal with the king. However, despite renewed attempts by Charles to win him over, Essex had no intention of changing sides. Bamfield hints at a deeper motive, possibly some hare-brained plot devised by Lord Wilmot to seize the king, after which all the armies would march east and force the politicians on both sides to negotiate, but unfortunately he provides no details. Nevertheless, Wilmot was removed from command of the cavalry and replaced by Lord Goring, who had distinguished himself at Marston Moor. Possibly Essex's strategic judgement was warped by the fact that he felt he could trust nobody outside the small circle of colonels and above who had campaigned with him since before Edgehill. Prominent among these was Lord Robartes, an infantry officer and a major Cornish landowner, who allegedly managed to convince the earl against the advice of many on his council of war that there was much support for the Parliamentary cause west of the Tamar. A strong hypothetical argument could have been made to that effect. During the first three months of the war, the Royalists had faced considerable opposition in Cornwall, and the heavy-handedness displayed by the Western army from the winter assaults on Plymouth onwards must have turned more people against the king's cause. However, Robartes was wrong, and it is therefore fitting that he was the first to admit that he had been mistaken in a letter to the Parliamentarians of Barnstaple written on 31st July following the poor response to Essex's requests for provisions made at Bodmin, the county town, on the previous market day.[6]

Two other arguments can be made in defence of Essex's invasion of Cornwall, but they are pretty feeble ones. The first is that he and his advisers still believed that Waller was following the king, which gave them a fair chance of crushing both Royalist armies between them. However, it is highly likely that before crossing the Tamar the lord general had received a letter from the Committee of Both Kingdoms to the effect that Waller's army had shrunk to about 4,000 men and was in no condition to come to his support. In a letter he sent from Tavistock on 26th July, he showed very clearly that he had read correspondence from the committee concerning the Channel Isles, which had been written to him on the same day as the letter concerning Waller.

The only other reason we can suggest for Essex's invasion of Cornwall was that he thought that his army could remain there until Waller had been reinforced and could take the offensive, or the king and Maurice be forced into a disastrous retreat due to lack of victuals, a crisis in the Thames valley, or both. If this was the case, he must have thought that his army could be supplied, and even reinforced, by the Earl of Warwick's fleet operating out of Plymouth. This would explain why, having been disappointed of support at Bodmin, he ordered his army to take up quarters in and around the town of Lostwithiel in the south-central part of the county, which theoretically had easy contact with Plymouth via the port of Fowey.[7] Unfortunately, Essex neglected to secure the east bank of the River Fowey and most particularly the fort on the headland at Polruan, which dominated the entrance to the Fowey estuary. However, even if he had had good communications with

Plymouth, the prevailing direction of the winds in the Channel during August would have made it most unlikely that supplies sufficient to feed an army of 9,000 or so men could have reached Plymouth from the nearest ports under firm Parliamentary control in southern Hampshire and the Isle of Wight.

The Committee of Both Kingdoms did little to assist Waller, but it had more luck in restricting the king's supplies. Sir William's horse and dragoons, 2,000 strong, under Lieutenant-General Middleton disrupted provisioning operations in Somerset and Dorset, causing considerable alarm to the king's advisers. This probably explains the wording of a letter written by the king to Prince Rupert in early September, when the crisis had passed: 'had our success been either deferred or of any other kind, only a direct miracle could have saved us, and certainly nothing could be so unlooked for as that Essex in Cornwall should imitate [and outdo] Meldrum at Newark', that is, surrender. However, Middleton was not strong enough to penetrate far into the enclosed countryside of east Devonshire without strong infantry support. Moreover, his communications were under constant threat from a brigade of Royalist cavalry operating in west Somerset under Sir Francis Dorrington, which had already frustrated his attempt to capture one major Royalist convoy carrying food supplies westwards.[8]

The so-called battle of Lostwithiel was nothing of the sort. Indeed, the convoluted nature of the landscape in that part of south-central Cornwall made it difficult for armies to draw up in conventional battle formation. Instead, it was a series of engagements spread over the last three weeks in August in which Essex's army was surrounded on the landward side by Royalist forces and then slowly driven back towards the port of Fowey. His infantry in particular put up a good fight until almost the end, but their fortitude was worn down by the shortage of military supplies and food, by the bad weather, and by the strong Royalist presence on the east bank of the estuary, reinforced from mid-August onwards by the king's train of artillery, which was thus able to fire into the heart of the Parliamentary position. By the last week of the month a breakout was the only answer. The cavalry managed to escape overland because the king's generals failed to take adequate precautions, but this was impossible for the infantry and the artillery train. There was some hope that Warwick might be able to evacuate them by ship, but it was probably just as well that he did not try given the strength of the Royalist barrage that could have descended on Fowey harbour. The final blow came on 31st August when some of Essex's infantry regiments abandoned a strong defensive position at Castle Dore, thus enabling the Royalists to cut them off from the sea and the faint possibility of rescue via Fowey and the tiny creeks at Menabilly and Polkerris. Essex himself escaped from the trap in a small fishing boat, but his foot regiments surrendered on 2nd September on what were generous terms, namely permission to march to Southampton provided that they left their artillery, arms and ammunition behind them.

Thus the Cornish campaign had ended in a Royalist victory, which was very good for their confidence, but of limited strategic value because of the time it had taken to achieve results and the fact that Essex's troops were neither made prisoner nor forced to promise never to take up arms again against the king. This leniency was possibly driven by propaganda considerations, as Charles hoped to persuade many of the rank and file to change sides through a combination of clemency and a clear commitment to a negotiated peace. If this was the case, he had little success. Despite the hardship of the journey, most of Essex's infantry made their way to Southampton. Another factor was that by the end of August Charles did need to bring matters to a swift conclusion. Time was of the essence if the king's armies were to take full advantage of the disasters that had happened to the armies of Waller and Essex in the south. Walker implies that the fate of three besieged garrisons on the fringes of the Thames valley theatre of war – Banbury, Basing House and Donnington Castle – also necessitated speedy action, but it only seems to have become an important consideration in strategic discussions at Chard a month later. They are not mentioned at all in an important letter concerning future strategy that Charles sent to Rupert on 3rd September. Nevertheless, the failure of the king and his generals to bring the Cornish campaign to a quick conclusion was to deprive them of their best opportunity to gain a major strategic advantage over the enemy before the end of the 1644 campaigning season, namely invading their quarters before they could assemble a large enough army to keep them out.[9]

With the defeat of both Essex and Waller, the king's military advisers conceived a new and most ambitious strategic plan. The two Royalist armies would march towards Bristol and then, having joined with the forces that Rupert commanded, they would take up winter quarters in Norfolk of all places. Sir Edward Walker makes no mention of the plan, but three different sources refer specifically to the Norfolk project: letters from Arthur Trevor to the Marquis of Ormonde; between Prince Rupert and Lord

Digby; and from Sir Edward Nicholas to the king, all written between 6th September and 27th October.[10] The scheme has all the ill-founded optimism and bravura of Lord Digby's strategic thinking about it, as the Royalist army could easily have been cut off from Oxford by a combination of allied armies marching from the north and the south, which could then trap it as effectively in East Anglia as Essex had been trapped in Cornwall. However, invading the Eastern Association was not totally out of the question if the two armies moved fast enough to prevent a rendezvous of Parliament's remaining forces in the south of England and the Midlands. This may explain Rupert's enthusiasm for the plan, coupled with the fact that invading the Association had been one of his pet projects in the summer and autumn of the previous year. However, the two Royalist armies moved far too slowly. It took them well over a month to march from Lostwithiel to the Dorset/ Wiltshire border, whereas the king's army had taken only twenty-two days to march from Evesham to the eastern parts of Cornwall. The slowness was partly explained by their much larger train of artillery, but precious time was also devoted to attempting, unsuccessfully, to browbeat Plymouth into surrender, and then to protecting Royalist-held east Devon, Somerset and west Dorset during the winter months by making arrangements for the blockade of the enemy garrisons of Lyme, Taunton and Weymouth, Barnstaple having surrendered on extremely generous terms before the royal armies left Devonshire. This reflects the tension between the Norfolk plan and another element in the grand strategy for winning the war that was gathering momentum once more. The king thought that he had seen good evidence of support for his cause in the southwest of England during the Lostwithiel campaign that could be exploited by the revival of the Western Association with the Prince of Wales at its head.[11]

Initially, the route taken by the Royalist armies was similar to the one taken by the king's army on its way to Lostwithiel, but when they reached the eastern parts of Somerset, two factors, one negative and the other positive, caused a deviation. First, at South Perrott in Somerset on 30th September the king and his advisers met Prince Rupert, who had left Chester with his troops about a month earlier. The news was not good. They were less numerous than had been hoped and were still at some distance from the southern theatre of war. The Anglo-Irish infantry regiments had suffered very heavy casualties in a battle at Montgomery ten days earlier and had retired to Shrewsbury, while the cavalry, quartered further south in Herefordshire and its environs, were afraid to march through the enclosed country that lay between them and crossings over the Severn because of lack of infantry support. Moreover, troops from South Wales under General Charles Gerard's command, with whom the king had ordered Rupert to rendezvous in a letter written from Tavistock on 6th September, and which could have provided that support, were not ready to march. It would therefore take time for Rupert to bring reinforcements into the south of England.

It was nevertheless agreed before Rupert and his uncle parted at Sherborne on 5th October that the royal army accompanied by Prince Maurice's was to turn northwards towards Marlborough, which would bring it closer not only to Rupert's corps but also to the Eastern Association. It was also agreed that Rupert would not be expected to join his uncle and brother before the beginning of November and, according to Rupert's diary, that the king would not fight the enemy until he and Gerard's forces had arrived. For a week or so after Rupert left, the two armies remained in Dorset while Portland Castle near Weymouth was being relieved, but then an opportunity occurred to disrupt enemy efforts to bring together into a single body all their troops in southern England, which by that time included the army of the Eastern Association. Therefore, instead of heading north as had been agreed, the Royalist armies made for Winchester at full speed. At about the same time, a message arrived from Oxford concerning the parlous state of the besieged garrisons of Banbury, Donnington Castle and Basing House. However, the fact that nothing was done to relieve Banbury, the most important of the three and the one most in need of assistance, until after the opportunity for disrupting enemy preparations had passed, means that the council's first consideration almost certainly took priority when it decided to change the direction of the armies' march from north to east. Moreover, both Banbury and Donnington could have been relieved much more easily from Marlborough than from Winchester.[12]

The minutes of the Committee of Both Kingdoms and the correspondence it received show little sense of urgency until mid-September, when for the first time the Royalists' slow but deliberate advance eastwards was seen as possibly culminating in an attack on London. Hurried steps were therefore taken to slow their progress and at the same time to assemble an army group large enough not only to fight them before they reached the southern approaches to the capital but also, if possible, to prevent the king from reaching Oxford or uniting with Rupert's and Gerard's forces. However, getting together such a force would take time. The troops available for the new field army were the Earl of Manchester's horse and foot, about

7,000 strong, which had been recalled from the north as soon as Rupert left Chester and was now approaching the London area. There was also the promise of a brigade of the London trained bands, and what was left of the armies of Essex and Waller. How these would compare in quality with the Royalist armies was uncertain, but it was likely that they would more than match them in numbers if only they could be brought together in time.

Delaying the Royalist advance was entrusted to Sir William Waller, who resumed command over the horse and dragoons that John Middleton had led during August. Essex's cavalry were soon cooperating with them, although under an independent command, but despite frequent claims by Waller and Haselrig that their cavalry was slowing the king's progress, all they could do was fall back as the Royalists advanced and try to keep out of trouble. These passive tactics Waller attributed to his lack of infantry: 'Horse alone will not do your work against a strong body of horse and foot with artillery'. He himself could do nothing to supply this deficiency, having previously sent the foot soldiers that he could not mount as dragoons to strengthen the garrisons of Plymouth, Weymouth, Lyme and Poole. However, as the Royalist armies moved from Devonshire into Somerset and the eastern parts of Dorset, they were left in the rear unable to rejoin their colleagues. Essex's foot soldiers could also do nothing to help for the moment, as those who had stayed with their colours during the long march from Cornwall to Southampton were being rested and rearmed at Portsmouth. The city of London trained bands were similarly not ready to march.

The crucial element therefore was the army of the Eastern Association, whose general, the Earl of Manchester, had fixed his quarters at Reading by the end of September. Some of his cavalry regiments had already been sent to assist in the siege of Banbury, and a fortnight later others joined Waller's and Essex's horse in the west, but the only infantry that Parliament had in the field in the south of England in early October was about 4,000 of Manchester's quartered between Reading and Newbury or in garrison at Abingdon. These the earl refused point blank to send any further west, arguing that their job was to protect the Thames valley garrisons and the Eastern Association against Prince Rupert, who was thought to be quite capable of assembling an army of 7,000 by combining regiments from Bristol and South Wales with the Northern Horse.[13] Manchester's critics, led by Oliver Cromwell, alleged that this was no more than an excuse to conceal the fact that he did not want Parliament to win an overwhelming victory over the king, and that subsequently he condemned himself out of his own mouth in words that have been quoted time and time again, but usually without including the sentence that preceded them:

Gentlemen, I beseech you let's consider what to do . . . it concerns us to be wary for in fighting we venture all to nothing. If we fight [the king] a hundred times and beat him ninety-nine times, he will be king still. But if he beat us but once, we shall be hanged, we shall lose our estates, and our posterities be undone.

However, the second sentence is not the main point of the paragraph but merely an explanation of the inevitable effect of rashness. The first sentence, on the other hand, probably encapsulates the reasoning that lay behind Manchester's caution towards engaging the Royalists in battle throughout the autumn other than in the week before the second battle of Newbury, the only time when he knew that the Parliamentary armies enjoyed a considerable numerical advantage over the enemy and was eager to fight. If his real fears were of this nature, then to have sent the Eastern Association infantry westwards without waiting for either the city trained bands or Essex's regiments to join them was unbelievably foolhardy, especially as his foot regiments on their own were outnumbered by the infantry of the Royalist armies combined. This could prove disastrous in a set-piece battle in open or enclosed country, and there was no reason why he should trust Waller and Haselrig not to get themselves involved in a premature engagement as they retreated across the downland of southern England before the advancing Royalists in some grim repeat of Roundway Down. Indeed, their horse and dragoons nearly fell into such a trap at Andover on 19th October. Finally, Manchester was particularly agitated that the Committee of Both Kingdoms appeared to have no clear idea as to where and how his regiments were to be used if they did advance westwards. With no clear instructions, Waller and Haselrig could be expected to do their worst. The result was an uncharacteristic outburst faithfully reported by his enemies: 'still they would have me march westward, westward ho! But they specify no place, for ought I know it may be to the West Indies or to St Michael's Mount'. However, he did obey orders to send cavalry westwards on 12th October, and he was the first to arrive at the agreed place of rendezvous, Basingstoke, with most of his infantry and the remaining cavalry. There he was joined on the 19th by the rest of his own cavalry, Waller's horse and most of Essex's. By the 21st, Essex's foot and the rest of Essex's horse had arrived from Portsmouth and four regiments of London trained bands from

Reading. The following day, this hurried amalgam of three armies marched towards the enemy.[14]

Surprisingly, the problem of command of the army group was not an issue given the differences between Manchester and some of his officers and between Essex and Waller, reinforced by the 1644 campaign, and the fact that Essex and Manchester as army generals were on the same level. However, the former was taken ill and played no part in the operations in and around Newbury during October and November, leaving Manchester to preside over a council consisting of Waller, Essex's deputy Lord Robartes, their three subordinate generals, and two members of the Committee of Both Kingdoms. Given the range of opinions, this looked like a recipe for inertia, but the strategy they initially agreed has been praised by Brigadier Young for being both bold and remarkable. Moreover, they had every reason to be confident. In early October Sir John Urry, a senior Royalist cavalry commander who had changed sides for the second time in the war, informed the Committee of Both Kingdoms that the Royalist force was much smaller than had previously been believed in London, only about 10,000 men divided pretty evenly between infantry and cavalry.[15] The Parliamentarians, on the other hand, had about 6,500 horse and nearer 8,000 than 9,000 foot.[16]

By the time Parliament's scattered infantry and cavalry had come together at Basingstoke, the Royalist armies were between Whitchurch and Kingsclere, less than 10 miles away. If they had reached north Hampshire even three days earlier, they could have prevented Essex's infantry and its cavalry escort reaching the rendezvous, but now even the relief of Basing House was out of the question. To get there would mean crossing 10 miles of open downland, where all the advantage would lie with the force that enjoyed the numerical superiority. Having thus failed to disrupt the enemy rendezvous by a whisker, the king's armies headed northwards for the safety of the enclosed country around Newbury, where they took up a strong defensive position on 22nd October and waited for Rupert to arrive with reinforcements. Such was the conviction of the king and his advisers that the armies were safe from attack by an enemy they believed to be demoralized and riven with faction that they sent a brigade of veteran cavalry 800 strong under the Earl of Northampton to relieve the garrison at Banbury. This he successfully achieved three days later, but before he could return a second battle of Newbury had been fought.[17]

Notes

1 Warburton, *Memoirs* II, 473–6; Bodleian Carte ms XI, 364; Symonds, *Diary*, 30; Walker, *Historical Discourses*, 37–8.

2 Ellis, *Letters*, 2nd 3, 316–17.

3 LJ VI 603; CSP Domestic 1644, 318, 335; Walker, *Historical Discourses*, 37; Symonds, *Diary*, 98.

4 CSP Domestic 1644, 335, 351, 358–9.

5 Walker, *Historical Discourses*, 42; Bamfield, *Apologie*, 44.

6 CSP Domestic 1644, 398–9; Bamfield, *Apologie*, 44; Cotton, *Barnstaple*, 294.

7 CSP Domestic 1644, 354, 358, 379, 380, 399, 433–4.

8 Symonds, *Diary*, 55; Walker, *Historical Discourses*, 63; CSP Domestic 1644, 436–40; Rushworth, *Historical Collections* V, 702–4; Fortescue Papers, 218–19.

9 Symonds, *Diary*, 50–67: CSP Domestic 1644, 433; HMC Appendix to the 9th Report II, 436; Bodleian Firth ms C7, 155; BL Additional ms 18981, 241; Walker, *Historical Discourses*, 38–9, 63–4; Fortescue Papers, 218–19.

10 Bodleian Carte ms XII, 469; *ibid.* Fairfax ms 32, 96; *ibid.* Firth C7, 164; BL Additional ms 18981, 376.

11 Walker, *Historical Discourses*, 85–99; Warburton, *Memoirs* III, 3–5.

12 Walker, *Historical Discourses*, 103–8; Carte, *Letters*, 64–5; Wilts CRO 413/444A 37; Warburton, *Memoirs* III, 27; BL Additional ms 18981, 262; *ibid.*, Additional ms 18983, 10.

13 CSP Domestic 1644, 404, 423, 534, 542; *ibid.* 1644–5, 2, 12–3, 28–9, 35.

14 *Ibid.* 1644, 526; *ibid.* 1644–5, 56–7, 62, 65, 67, 150–1, 156; Symonds, *Diary*, 141.

15 Young and Holmes, *English Civil War*, 217–19; Holmes, *Eastern Association*, 183–6; CSP Domestic 1644–45, 39–40.

16 Reid prefers the higher figure, but he includes a figure of 800 for Waller's infantry regiments, none of which was at Newbury (*All the King's Armies*, 185).

17 Dugdale, *Diary*, 73–4; BL Additional ms 18981, 303, 312; Walker, *Historical Discourses*, 108.

chapter XVIII

The second and third battles of Newbury

The defensive position chosen by the king's military advisers was on the north side of the town rather than in the enclosures and chalk downs to the south, where the first battle had been fought. The two Royalist armies occupied a narrow triangle of land between the River Kennet and its tributary the Lambourn, which joined the main river a mile to the east. The only bridge over the Kennet within the triangle led to Newbury itself. Instead of being destroyed, it was defended by an infantry detachment in case it was needed as an escape route. There were also two small bridges carrying roads over the Lambourn, one leading to the village of Donnington and the other to the village of Shaw. Both bridges were protected by fortified positions on the north bank of the river – Donnington Castle, which had held a small Royalist garrison since the first battle, and Shaw House, which was put into a state of defence when the two armies arrived. The third side of the triangle was a north–south line between the two rivers. It passed through the village of Speen, which was surrounded by enclosures, but there was open land beyond on all four sides of the settlement. To the south was a long narrow field between the enclosures and the water meadows lining the Kennet, to the north a piece of parkland between the enclosures and the Lambourn. The approach to Speen from the west was across a narrow piece of open common flanked by woods. Here the enclosures in front of the village were defended by Maurice's infantry, supported by artillery and winged by two brigades of horse. Beyond the enclosures to the east lay the large open field of Speenhamland. Here the Royalist reserves were deployed:

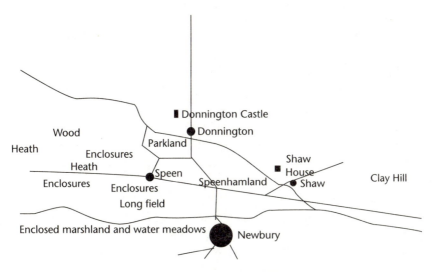

Figure 15 The second battle of Newbury: the landscape

at least four brigades of cavalry and two of the king's infantry brigades, the third being the defenders of Shaw House.[1]

On 26th October, the Parliamentary generals tried to force their way across the Lambourn, but finding its west bank heavily defended they decided to assault the position from two directions the following day. While Manchester remained on Clay Hill facing Shaw village with the Eastern Association infantry and some cavalry regiments, the remainder led by Waller marched around the north of the Royalist position to attack Speen from the west. This move, although unopposed, was very time-consuming. Even so it was followed by an artillery barrage. As a result, when the assault on Speen village began there was scarcely two hours of daylight left. Maurice's infantry put up a good fight but were eventually driven back by force of numbers to the hedge bordering Speenhamland, where the enemy advance was stopped by the king's infantry reserves. On the Parliamentary left, the Earl of Cleveland's brigade commanded by General Goring drove back the Eastern Association horse led by Cromwell when they tried to deploy beyond the ditch that separated the enclosures from Donnington Park. On the other wing, Essex's horse under Balfour working with a body of musketeers made much better progress, at one time threatening to outflank Speenhamland to the south and capture the bridge over the Kennet, but a timely charge by the king's reserve cavalry caused them to retreat in some disorder. At this point, as dusk was falling, serious fighting broke out at Shaw, delayed, it appears, by some ambiguity in the orders given to Manchester's officers, but the various attempts to cross the Lambourn were frustrated by the defenders of Shaw House.[2]

During the night, in accordance with a prearranged plan, the Royalist armies led by Prince Maurice retreated across the Lambourn via Donnington bridge and so over the downs to Wallingford, which they reached the following morning. Their remarkable speed owed much to the fact that they had left their train of artillery and their wounded behind in Donnington Castle. The king, in the meantime, had ridden with his lifeguard to join Prince Rupert, whom he met at Bath the following afternoon. No attempt was made to stop or pursue either body. The reason for this was that, although the commanders in Speen village knew a withdrawal was taking place, they assumed that the Royalists were merely taking up a new defensive position directly under Donnington Castle, which they probably saw as a trap given their own superiority in both horse and foot. Beyond Donnington was a narrow valley, where the Royalists might be hemmed in and forced to surrender. If, on the other hand, they did manage to reach the open downs beyond, they were not likely to be able to hold out for long against determined attack, as there was no cover and no prospect of their being rescued by Prince Rupert.[3]

Once the generals realized that the Royalists had escaped under the cover of darkness, they sent most of the horse off in pursuit, but by then it was far too late. What to do next caused considerable debate lasting several days. Waller and Haselrig proposed that the armies be divided, with the more mobile troops following the king, but more cautious views prevailed. On 2nd November, the armies advanced towards Oxford, but they stopped at the north slope of the Berkshire downs above Didcot because of a shortage of provisions in the Thames valley and the difficulty of transporting their artillery train across the heavy clay land between there and Abingdon. They then returned to Newbury, where Manchester's infantry resumed the siege of Donnington Castle, ignoring orders from the Committee of Both Kingdoms to attempt to prevent the scattered Royalist brigades coming together.[4]

In early November the king's armies, reinforced by Prince Rupert's and Charles Gerard's forces, two regiments from the Oxford garrison, the Northern Horse, and the Earl of Northampton's cavalry brigade, returned to Donnington without incident. They drew up on Speenhamland and offered

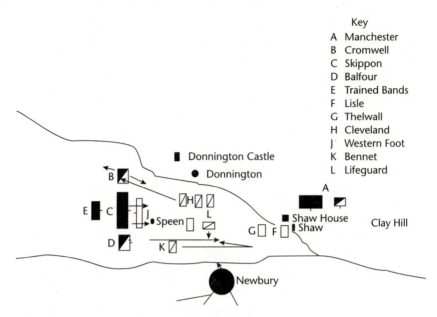

Figure 16 The second battle of Newbury, 4.30p.m.

battle, but the enemy generals declined. Despite having good intelligence of the king's approach, the committee had decided on a static defence pivoting around the bridge over the Kennet at Newbury. Admittedly, several infantry brigades supported by some cavalry and artillery pieces were stationed behind a hedge line on the north bank of the Kennet close to the bridge, but the bulk of the infantry remained in the town itself, while the rendezvous for most of the cavalry was Wash Common, two miles to the south. Some skirmishing took place between some of the king's troops and the brigades to the north of the river, but the Royalists were able to withdraw their cannon and wounded soldiers from Donnington Castle without opposition. They then gave the Parliamentary troops a second, and better, chance to fight a conventional battle, as the three armies had by that time extricated themselves from Newbury and were drawn up across the triangle of land where the second battle had been fought. It was in these circumstances that the Earl of Manchester made his famous remarks about the war reproduced in Chapter XVII, but it is worth briefly re-examining them in their correct place in the narrative. The words Manchester used were a follow-up to his dismissal of the idea that an instant victory was needed to deter a French invasion on Charles's behalf, which he rightly saw as a scare story with no grounding in fact. Indeed, it is possible that he was merely summing up the debate, as there is some evidence that other members of the committee had used virtually the same words earlier in the discussion. Oliver Cromwell protested, but in language that suggests he had misunderstood what had just been said: 'My Lord, if this be so, why did we take up arms [in the first place]. This is against fighting ever hereafter'. To us, Manchester's remarks were not an argument against ever taking up arms against the king but an abrupt and dramatic way of emphasizing the point that if the armies of the south, now drawn up in battle array facing the king's forces, were decisively defeated in the ensuing engagement, Parliament could very easily lose the war. It is also important to appreciate that Manchester's words were reported by Henry Ireton, whose testament in all other respects supported Cromwell's criticisms of his general. However, there is another interpretation of Cromwell's reply, namely that Manchester's caution was an affront to his spirituality and a rejection of God's grace. Oliver's use of language after engagements such as Naseby suggests that he saw fighting a battle at a disadvantage as affording the Lord the opportunity of showing his power by giving the victory to the godly party against all military logic.[5]

On this discordant note, the Parliamentary armies retreated from Newbury to Reading. They also abandoned the siege of Basing House, which was reprovisioned on 19th November when the king's armies returned briefly once more to the Kennet valley. The row that followed between Cromwell and the Earl of Manchester concerning the latter's military conduct from mid-July 1644 onwards led, after much political wrangling, to the remodelling of the officer corps and the establishment of a New Model Army out of the best troops that were left of the armies of Essex, Manchester and Waller, although a single army had in effect been in existence since the third week in October.

Thus the king had achieved one of his strategic objectives for the autumn, the relief of the three besieged garrisons, but it was too late in the year to pursue the other. However, three small regiments of Royalist horse, two of which had some connection with the Ouse valley counties, were chased from the Buckingham area on about the 10th of November. They need not have been a scouting party, but it is difficult otherwise to explain their presence there.[6]

At the beginning of December, the Committee of Both Kingdoms decided to put its armies into winter quarters. It stationed the infantry that had fought at Newbury in such a way as to defend a north–south line running from Portsmouth via Petersfield and Farnham to Reading and so to Aylesbury and Newport Pagnell. Abingdon, well in advance of the line, was reinforced, and a new garrison established at Henley. Waller's troops were responsible for the southern part of the line, Essex's and Manchester's and the London trained bands for the northern part. However, one final operation had to be undertaken, the relief of the town of Taunton, 100 miles to the west, blockaded since September by local forces under the governor of Bridgwater, Colonel Edmund Wyndham. Just before the 'third battle of Newbury', Waller had received orders to prepare a relief expedition to be led by his major-general, James Holbourne, comprising 1,000 horse and dragoons supplemented by his foot regiments that had been marooned in the ports of the southwest by the king's eastward march. On about 12th December, Holbourne's corps successfully accomplished its mission without a fight, the besiegers having withdrawn into nearby garrisons in the face of superior numbers.[7] However, he and his men were to be stranded in west Somerset for the next three months, their retreat blocked by Royalist cavalry in winter quarters in south Wiltshire. Thus Taunton's magnetic influence on the movement of armies in the 1645 campaigning season was beginning to take effect. However, it would be wrong to follow Reid in regarding that effect as in any way mysterious.[8] Whoever controlled Taunton would have a powerful influence on the effectiveness of the Royalist Western Association, which both sides saw as having war-winning potential.

Notes

1 BL Additional ms 16370, 61; Ludlow, *Memoirs*, 102; Rocque, Map of Berkshire.

2 Walker, *Historical Discourses*, 110–12; Symonds, *Dairy*, 145; Rushworth, *Historical Collections* V, 722–3; BL Harleian ms 166, 140; *Mercurius Aulicus*, 1232–5; *Manchester's Quarrel*, 63–4; Gwynne, *Military Memoirs*, 59–61; Luke, *Letterbook*, 366, 368.

3 Walker, *Historical Discourses*, 113–16; BL Harleian ms 166, 140.

4 CSP Domestic 1644–45, 80, 83–6, 96, 104–7; BL additional ms 34253, 36.

5 Gardiner, *Great Civil War* II, 59; *Manchester's Quarrel*, 68; Rushworth, *Historical Collections* V, 735; CSP Domestic 1644–5, 159; BL Additional ms 16370, 61; Walker, *Historical Discourses*, 118.

6 BL Additional ms 18981, 312; TT E21 15, 24; Walker, *Historical Discourses*, 120; Luke, *Letterbook*, 60. There is additional evidence that the scheme was still

alive in mid-November, when it was bracketed with the recapture of Abingdon as the next objectives for the Royalist armies in the south (Trelawney papers).

7   Bodleian Tanner ms 61, 192; CSP Domestic 1644–5, 113, 124, 135, 145, 161; Wyndham's letter, 308.

8   Reid, *All the King's Armies*, 194.

Summary of Part V

At the beginning of the 1644 campaigning season, the effective balance between the field armies of king and Parliament tipped significantly in favour of Parliament. The collapse of the Northern command in response to the Scottish invasion and the destruction of Lord Bellasis's corps at Selby ensured that the new army Prince Rupert was assembling in the Welsh Marches would be unable to take part in the war in the south, while Prince Maurice's was still in the far southwest of England. This left the king potentially facing two armies, those of Essex and Waller, and possibly part of a third, the revived army of the Eastern Association under the Earl of Manchester. Moreover, for the first time in the war the enemy forces operating in the southern theatre of war enjoyed a numerical advantage in cavalry as well as infantry. However, an encounter between the army groups was not to take place until almost the end of the campaigning season, and in much less favourable circumstances. This was primarily the fault of operational decisions taken by Parliament's new war cabinet, the Committee of Both Kingdoms.

The committee's first mistake was to treat the Earl of Manchester's army as the counterweight to Prince Rupert's. This obliged the earl to move into Lincolnshire in May, even though the Eastern Association army could have been used to much greater effect further south. If Manchester had remained in the Ouse valley, the three Parliamentary armies could have challenged the king to a battle in the environs of Oxford and almost certainly distracted Rupert from advancing north, leaving the Scots and the Fairfaxes to deal with what was left of the Marquis of Newcastle's command. Moreover, even if Rupert had managed to reach his uncle with the troops he had at

Shrewsbury, the disparity in numbers between the two sides on the battlefield would have been as large as it was to be at Marston Moor.

The committee's second mistake was its obsession with the siege of Lyme. Even without Manchester's help, Essex and Waller had the king's forces in the Thames valley in a panic in early June 1644. By placing such a premium on the relief of the town, they initiated the train of thought that led to the break-up of the very positive cooperation between the two commanders, thus saving the king's bacon. If, after Charles's escape from Oxford, the two armies had remained in the Thames valley area, the city could not have held out for long, resulting in the loss of another 3,000 or so veteran Royalist infantry. In such circumstances, Rupert would probably have aborted the expedition to York and marched south, but Manchester would have been on his tail, whereas the Earl of Denbigh's regiments in the Midlands, if incapable of fighting Rupert in a conventional battle, could have diverted his march or that of the king's flying army towards him. In such circumstances, it is difficult to see how Charles and his nephew could have joined forces.

The operational decisions taken by the king's council of war in the spring of 1644 were little better than those taken by the Committee of Both Kingdoms. Allowing Maurice to lay siege to Lyme was a risk, but trying to withdraw him from there any later than the middle of May could easily have ended in disaster. It is difficult to see how his army could have safely joined his uncle's before being intercepted by Sir William Waller, whose area of operations was to the south and west of Oxford. Fortunately, he disregarded his orders and saved his army.

Rupert's plans for the defence of Oxford and its environs against superior numbers while he was away in the north of England were too ambitious and were grounded on the false premises that Essex and Waller would move slowly and find difficulty in cooperating with one another. However, the orders he himself received to defeat the allied armies before York, and then to return south as quickly as possible, were understandable in the circumstances. Even if he had been commanded merely to rescue the marquis's infantry and relieve the city, the best he could have hoped for in the aftermath was a successful retreat into Lancashire, where the Committee of Both Kingdoms could have taken steps to prevent his being able to move south until Essex and Waller had dealt with the Oxford army.

Once the king had left Oxford, he was at the mercy of his enemies, and his subsequent successes were the result of their mistakes rather than any strategic brilliance on his own part or that of his council of war, which was bitterly divided from the end of May until the arrest of Lords Wilmot and Percy in August. All that can be said is that when firm decisions were taken, the army marched with speed and determination. Fortunately, the defeat at Marston Moor was much less disastrous than it might have been. The victorious allies were in a state of shock and unable to exploit their success in the immediate aftermath of the battle. Given the hammering they had received, it is scarcely surprising that their next thoughts were very largely for the security of the north, and the Committee of Both Kingdoms did nothing to countermand them.

In July 1644, the committee made two further mistakes. It failed to reinforce Waller's army when it fell apart after the battle of Cropredy Bridge. It also reasserted its orders for the Eastern Association army to remain in the north Midlands keeping a watch on the movements of Prince Rupert's forces in Lancashire and Cheshire. If either Waller or Manchester had been in a position to move into the Oxford area in strength in mid- to late July, the king's field army would have been forced to return to defend its headquarters, thus allowing the Earl of Essex to reconquer the southwest of England unmolested.

Finally, the strategic decisions that the committee made after Lostwithiel in order to delay the eastward progress of the king's and Maurice's armies were highly risky. Waller and his cavalry regiments were lucky not to be overwhelmed, while feeding Essex's cavalry and troops from Manchester's army into the fray as they arrived gave the king the chance of defeating the Parliamentary forces in detail if he had been sufficiently fleet of foot. Fortunately for the two Houses, the Earl of Manchester's caution, and the slowness with which the Royalist armies marched through Devon and Dorset, saved their scattered forces from destruction, but from late October onwards it was the generals who failed to keep their eye on the ball. Failure to respond positively to sounds that the king's armies were retreating from the battlefield on the night after the second battle of Newbury defies explanation, although the ultra-cautious stationing of troops around Newbury prior to the abortive third battle is more understandable.

By the end of the 1644 campaigning season, the allies had largely reconquered the north of England and gained some ground in the south, but both sides were finding it difficult to maintain large armies in the field. In November, the opposing army groups in the Thames valley theatre of war were only about two-thirds the size of the armies that the king and Essex had commanded at the start of the Edgehill campaign. More-over, although both sides appear to have been well equipped with arms and ammunition, keeping their armies supplied with pay, provisions and recruits was becoming increasingly difficult. Before the campaigning season was over, the Eastern Association declared that it no longer had the financial resources to maintain its army, while the supplies provided by the West-ern Association for the Royalist armies on their way back from Cornwall had been limited.[1] Both sides therefore faced a crisis.

Note

1 Walker, *Historical Discourses*, 63–80; CJ III, 703; Wanklyn, *The King's Armies*, 91–3, 177.

PART VI

The crisis of the war

chapter XIX

Winter quarters

Field army activity in England and Wales during the winter and early spring of 1645 followed a similar overall pattern to that of previous years; the infantry were largely rested and recruited, while the cavalry played a more active role, sometimes being employed on military operations at a considerable distance from army headquarters. The Royalist high command was, on the whole, more vigorous in its use of resources from the centre to support initiatives elsewhere, but for a number of reasons both sides were more restrained than in previous years. In the first place, for most of the troops the 1644 campaigning season had been far more exhausting than in previous years. Essex's army was almost continually on the move from mid-May to mid-November, as were Waller's cavalry and dragoons. Manchester's troops had had a quiet patch between mid-July and the beginning of September, but they had fought in two major battles and taken part in several sieges. There is therefore little doubt that the cries of distress from Skippon, Cromwell and other generals during November were real ones. Their troops had suffered as never before from shortage of food, rest and pay; they could not be relied upon to perform at their best, or indeed to perform at all, until at least some of their needs had been satisfied. Similarly, the king's and Prince Maurice's armies had been in the field since mid-May. They had marched even longer distances and taken part in some very heavy fighting. Even allowing for a measure of special pleading, Lord Goring's account of the lack of enthusiasm in what was left of Maurice's infantry when it took the field again after no more than a month's rest rings true:

I esteem myself very unhappy to be diverted from the pursuit of a distracted enemy by that which of itself is a greater misfortune . . . a universal deadness and backwardness in the officers of foot to undertake any action without refreshment.[1]

Second, political factors help to explain the inactivity of the field armies during the winter months. Knowledge that peace negotiations were to take place over twenty working days at Uxbridge in February 1645 may have reduced the tempo of warfare at the centre, although, as in 1643, they had no effect on fighting in the regions and were similarly unproductive. More important was the remodelling of the field armies, which had a much more direct impact on Parliament's military operations than on those of the king. Almost all the general officers were removed by the Self-Denying Ordin-ance, by which peers and MPs were no longer to hold permanent commissions in the army, while the best elements of the armies of Essex, Waller and Manchester were to form the nucleus of the New Model, a field army 22,000 strong comprising twelve infantry regiments, eleven cavalry regiments and one regiment of dragoons. Such drastic changes would have been disruptive whatever the circumstances. However, although it was quickly agreed that Sir Thomas Fairfax should command the new army and Phillip Skippon serve as major-general of infantry, political wrangling at Westminster between the Lords and the Commons meant that some of the essential pieces of legislation did not gain final approval until early April, thus prolonging the uncertainty until almost the start of the new campaigning season. Even so, the post of lieutenant-general of cavalry remained vacant. The reason for this was probably to give Commissary-General Vermuyden the chance to prove that he was good enough for the job, rather than to allow Oliver Cromwell, who, as an MP, had resigned his commission, to be re-engaged on a short-term contract a few weeks later when the dust had died down.

The effect on the outcome of the war of combining three armies into one and of removing the top generals has been discussed earlier in this book, but it needs to be emphasized that in the transitional period between December and the end of April command structures built up over two years or more broke down and with them commitment and discipline. Some cavalry units refused to leave their quarters either because of lack of pay or because they would not obey the officers under whose command they had been placed. Essex's army was particularly affected by insubordination, although there was also some unrest among Cromwell's cavalry regiments.

This, combined with a shortage of infantry, meant that, when it came to mounting military expeditions, the Committee of Both Kingdoms was reduced to scraping together *ad hoc* assemblages of units. It no longer had at its disposal fully integrated brigade groups. However, the committee became seriously alarmed on only one occasion, when it interpreted a concentration of Royalist troops in the northwest Midlands in late February and March under Prince Rupert's command as preparations for an attack on the Eastern Association. The only field army troops immediately available were a brigade of Manchester's army under Major-General Crawford quartered around Aylesbury, but even they were slow off the mark, managing only to get as far as Northampton before the threat subsided. More responsive was the Scottish army. A brigade under David Leslie moved into Cheshire from Yorkshire to support regional forces under Sir William Brereton's command in a diversionary attack against Rupert, but the Scottish generals probably agreed to this because they thought the prince could as easily move northwards towards the Borders as advance in any other direction. By the early spring, a force of Irish Catholic foot soldiers led by the Marquis of Montrose, with limited support from the Highland Scots, was causing fears that a new front was about to open up north of the border. However, Montrose's impact on the war in England at this stage in the 1645 campaigning season was marginal. Nevertheless, the Earl of Leven needed to be able to react to events in Scotland as they developed, which probably explains why Leslie was ordered to return to Yorkshire as soon as there were clear signs that Rupert was marching towards the lower Severn valley.[2]

On the king's side, there was considerable evidence of the revival of the practice of quartering units of the field army at a distance from Oxford, thus reducing the pressure on the Thames valley area to provide pay, food and fodder. The need to restrict the number of troops billeted there was more acute than in previous years because of the impact of the new enemy garrisons on Royalist control over central Berkshire. Brave talk about stationing cavalry in villages in the Newbury area came to nothing, probably because of the strong Parliamentary presence in and around Reading from December onwards, whereas Abingdon endangered communications between Oxford and the country immediately to the south of the river Thames. As a result, cavalry was largely billeted in Gloucestershire, Wiltshire, and Oxfordshire west of the Cherwell, infantry in the towns of the Cotswolds, and Gerard's Welshmen in Monmouthshire. Thus Colonel Massey's quarters around Gloucester were straitened for the third winter in succession. Nevertheless, one infantry brigade was kept close to Oxford, at Faringdon to the southwest of the city guarding the road to Bristol.[3]

Unlike in previous years, however, the use to which units of the field army were put during the winter months does not suggest that the Royalist high command had a clear grand strategy in mind other than the obvious, namely to recruit the Oxford army and the Western army in preparation for the 1645 campaign. This may have had something to do with the bedding down of new commanders as Rupert replaced the Earl of Forth as lord general, Maurice took over from Rupert in Wales and the Borders, and Goring succeeded Maurice, although with more limited powers. But this was as far as the remodelling of the Royalist field army went. Factional infighting, exacerbated by the new appointments, and the growing conflict between Rupert and Digby for the king's ear may also have played their part in promoting inertia. Moreover, a council of war will not function at its best if there are too many members with entrenched attitudes. This may help to explain why strategic initiatives undertaken during the winter do not appear to have been well thought through, with the result that coopera-tion between regional and national forces was not managed effectively. Important projects failed or were less successful than they might have been because of lack of support from the centre, while forces from the centre were used on their own in areas where there was little or no possibility of securing local support. As a result, they did not achieve lasting results. The removal of the highly experienced but bodily infirm Lord Forth from the council of war was not a factor in this. There is no evidence that he was a major influence on the king's decision making at any time, and his close association with the siege of Gloucester, the defeat at Cheriton and the abandonment of Abingdon makes it unlikely that he would have master-minded the 1644 campaign. Indeed the king had nearly sacked him after the Abingdon incident.[4]

In January 1645, a most determined effort was made to overrun Major-General Browne's garrison at Abingdon, which had been heavily reinforced by Parliament in the late autumn but was supposed to be mutinous through lack of pay. Using only the resources of the Oxford and Wallingford gar-risons and his own or his brother's regiment of foot, Prince Rupert's assault across the bridge over the Thames began by making very good progress against the defenders, but in the end superior numbers had their effect. The Royalists were driven back and many were killed, including the governor of Oxford, Sir Henry Gage. Had Rupert also attacked Abingdon from the west using the veteran regiments of foot quartered at Faringdon, the result could have been very different. Instead, only a party of horse appeared from that direction, much to the surprise of Browne, who at once transferred infantry to the other side of the town. It was this which almost certainly tipped the balance against Rupert's men, not advance intelligence from Oxford as was suspected at the time, as Browne does seem to have been taken by surprise.[5]

The following month, an attack on the twin towns of Weymouth/Melcombe Regis by the Dorset Royalists under Sir Lewis Dyve followed a similar pattern. Dyve managed to capture Weymouth, which lay to the west of the river separating the two, but he failed to build on his success by impressing on his superiors the need to provide him with resources to capture Melcombe Regis and defend Weymouth against a counterattack. Two weeks later, the Parliamentarians were able to recapture Weymouth from Melcombe because of reinforcements brought in by sea and poor security on the part of the Dorset Royalists, who had left the bridge between the two parts of the town intact and possibly unguarded. Another factor was the slow progress towards Weymouth of a detachment of the field army under Goring's command, which had been ordered to go to the support of Dyve's regiments three days before the Parliamentary counterattack took place. When it did arrive the following day, there was an attempt to recapture Weymouth, but it was driven back after sustaining heavy casualties from artillery pieces placed so as to be able to fire grapeshot along the streets of the town.[6]

The examples described so far were offensive operations that began hopefully but ultimately failed not because of an overall lack of resources but because resources that were readily available were not committed in an appropriate manner. Nevertheless, no territory had been lost. However, the third example was much more serious in strategic terms. Just after Christmas 1644, troops from Lancashire and Cheshire under Sir William Brereton's command lay siege to Chester. Although not itself accessible to seaborne vessels, the city was essential for the defence of the ports along the Flintshire coast through which the troops, ammunition and other military supplies arrived from Ireland. In January, a major sally led by the acting governor, Lord Byron, against the fort that Brereton had built at Christleton to guard the southeastern approaches to the city was repulsed with heavy casualties, and after that the siege became much more intense.[7]

Prince Maurice, who had just arrived in his new command with a small regiment of foot and half a regiment of horse, was immediately ordered by the king's council of war to assemble a force to relieve Chester, but no further support was to be provided by the field army. Drawing together such a force therefore entailed scouring the garrisons of the Midlands and the Welsh borderland. The biggest contingent was the so-called 'Shrewsbury foot', what was left of the troops that had come over from Ireland between November 1643 and February 1644. Since their defeat at Montgomery five months earlier, they had been quartered in the town, where they had been rested, fed and presumably recruited. However, their plundering had further alienated an urban population that had never been truly Royalist in sympathy. All that was left behind to defend Shrewsbury after Maurice's departure were a couple of hundred Anglo-Irish regiment soldiers whose colonel was the governor, and the town regiment, whose company commanders appear, significantly, to have been country gentlemen or professional soldiers.

As Maurice's army moved towards Chester, the Committee of Both Kingdoms sent out urgent pleas to its regional commanders and to the Scots to march to Brereton's support, but the forces at Sir William's disposal were too small to do anything much beyond defending the east bank of the Dee against Maurice, who was approaching Chester from the Welsh side of the river. Maurice entered Chester on 20th February, and Brereton abandoned his siege works. However, two days later the Shropshire Parliamentarians supported by some companies of foot from Nantwich and Stafford provided by Sir William captured Shrewsbury by a well-executed night attack informed by first-rate intelligence, which not only pinpointed a weak spot in the fortifications but also revealed that the town was guarded by only a handful of experienced soldiers. As a result, the Royalists lost an army base containing a huge quantity of military supplies and foodstuffs that had been patiently built up by Rupert, Maurice and their commissioners.[8] In strategic terms, Shrewsbury's capture caused a major blockage in the route between Oxford and North Wales, a major recruiting ground for the royal armies. It also made Chester even more isolated. On the other hand, Maurice had lost only about 200 foot soldiers who could have taken part in the field army's spring campaign. Moreover, in the short term, recruiting operations in North Wales were not adversely affected because of the reaction of the king's council of war.

The loss of Shrewsbury was followed by what should have happened in the first place, the commitment of substantial elements from the field army to winter operations in the Welsh Marches. Several thousand infantry and cavalry marched speedily from Gloucestershire to Ludlow under the command of Sir Jacob Astley, now Lord Astley, as did Charles Gerard's troops from Monmouthshire. Rupert himself and Langdale's Northern Horse soon followed, with the result that by mid-March the two princes had a force of about 8,000 men in Denbighshire and Flintshire. As has already been mentioned, this was a matter of great concern to the Committee of Both Kingdoms, who thought that Rupert and Maurice would overrun the parts of Cheshire and Shropshire controlled by Parliament's supporters and impress large numbers of men, as Rupert had done in Lancashire in 1644, and then march into the Eastern Association at a time when most of the cavalry brigades of the field armies that could be used for active operations were in the West Country.[9] A force was nevertheless got together to bar the two princes' march eastwards, but after they had reprovisioned Chester, relieved its out-garrison at Beeston Castle and drawn new recruits from North Wales, they set off southwards towards the lower Severn valley, having achieved objectives that were less ambitious than the committee had supposed. Rupert and Maurice spent April dealing with neutralist insurgents, the Clubmen, who had risen in rebellion against the exactions of the Royalist soldiers in Herefordshire and Worcestershire. This was followed by further recruiting operations in the southern part of the borderland and the defeat at Ledbury of a large party of Edward Massey's troops from Gloucester, which had been trying to exploit the Clubmen uprising. In mid-March, however, Gerard's infantry and cavalry had been allowed to march back into Pembrokeshire to counter a major threat from the local Parliamentarians, who looked likely to overrun the whole of southwest Wales. This was very late in the day for troops from the field army to be allowed to return to their region, but Rupert and the king probably felt that Gerard would be able to restore the situation very quickly and rejoin the army in time for the summer campaign, given the delay in Parliament's preparations likely to be caused by problems associated with the birth of the New Model Army.[10]

Campaigns during the winter months involving elements of the field army that were defensive in character or mere tidying-up operations had been at best unimpressive and at worst misdirected, although not massively wasteful in manpower. They had also been the cause of new enmities, as between the Dorset Royalists and Lord Goring. Pushes into enemy territory, on the other hand, were sometimes spectacular and often of considerable importance for their propaganda value, but in the end they were of little real military significance. In mid-December, Lord Goring was allowed to use what remained of the Western army's infantry regiments and several brigades of horse for an expedition into Hampshire. The purpose of the expedition is not wholly clear, but he almost certainly had hopes of capturing one of the string of ports around the Solent that Parliament had held since the start of the war, most probably Portsmouth, where he had been governor in 1642. Having apparently failed to bribe a guard to deliver up Portsea bridge, he attacked the small enemy garrison at Christchurch but hurriedly withdrew at the approach of a relieving force.

After this failure, the expeditionary force moved northwards to carry out an attack on Parliament's winter defence line where it ran close to the Hampshire/Surrey border, a section that Waller's army was supposed to defend. Knowing that many of Waller's troops had gone with Holbourne to Taunton, Goring probably thought that the line would be only lightly defended, but the enemy was sufficiently prepared to prevent his achieving a major success such as the capture of Farnham Castle. Gardiner implies that he had succeeded in doing precisely this in early January through misreading the last line of a letter from Goring to Rupert, which was clearly written from Fareham, between Southampton and Portsmouth, not from Farnham. Probing attacks against villages in northeast Hampshire caused a stir in the London newspapers and livened up the minutes of the Committee of Both Kingdoms, but they did little more than capture a few soldiers who were too slow to move out of the way and deprive some farmers of their produce and stock. Moreover, there was no Royalist uprising, which is scarcely surprising as the Surrey/Hampshire borderland, unlike some parts of Kent and Sussex, had shown no sympathy for the king's cause when given the chance to do so in November 1642 and again in November 1643. There was also no incentive for an army to remain there for long, as much of the countryside around Farnham was infertile sandy heath, woodland and chalk down, and as such quite incapable of keeping a force of 3,000 men supplied with food and fodder, as Hopton had discovered in 1643. By 23rd January, therefore, Goring and his troops were quartered once more around Salisbury, where they remained for the next six weeks.[11]

The second push was much more spectacular but almost as bereft of long-term benefits to the king's cause. Two brigades of horse that had fought under Langdale in the Marquis of Newcastle's army, quartered in Wiltshire for the winter, begged the king for permission to return to the north in order to relieve the remaining Yorkshire garrisons still in Royalist hands. By the time they set out on 20th February, only a handful were still holding out, the most important of which were Scarborough, Skipton Castle and Pontefract

Castle. Riding via Banbury and the East Midlands garrisons, Langdale's men defeated a strong force of Eastern Association cavalry at Melton Mowbray and completely routed the besieging force outside Pontefract under Colonel John Lambert, an amazing feat as they had little infantry support. Having given the garrison a brief respite in which to collect provisions, the Northern Horse returned to Royalist-held territory in Staffordshire by 9th March, before the Committee of Both Kingdoms was able to assemble a force to cut them off. *Mercurius Aulicus* exploited 'Langdale's ride' for all it was worth, but its only achievements were to enable Pontefract to hold out for another four months and to whet the appetite of the Northern Horse for another expedition northwards, but this time taking the main field army with them.[12] However, it would be wrong to argue that Langdale's men would have been better employed helping Prince Maurice to relieve Chester. Horsemen could not have defended Shrewsbury, while the infantry regiments in its garrison took part in the relief expedition. Neither could they have gone in their stead, as the countryside between Shrewsbury and Chester was unsuitable for cavalry operations, being very extensively enclosed on both the Welsh and the English sides of the Dee.

Insofar as Parliament's field armies were concerned, the only offensive operation undertaken between December and the emergence of the New Model Army from Essex's old army base at Windsor on 29th April was the rescue of Holbourne's men from Taunton, a task committed to Waller and Cromwell, whose force consisted largely of cavalry and dragoons. The campaign began in vintage Waller style with Colonel James Long's large regiment of Wiltshire horse being surrounded in their quarters and comprehensively destroyed in a running fight on 12th March. The two generals then divided their forces, with Waller advancing towards Bristol in the mistaken belief that the city would be betrayed to him, while Cromwell moved into west Dorset to be as close to Holbourne as possible. General Goring, still commanding the bulk of Maurice's army but strengthened by more cavalry from the king's army, moved against Waller, considering the threat to Bristol to be the more serious. He seems to have assumed that his infantry, supported by the western Royalists besieging Taunton and two large brigades of infantry from Devon and Cornwall that were between Exeter and the Somerset border heading for Taunton, would be sufficient to deal with Cromwell. However, the commanders of the Devon and Cornwall contingents, Sir John Berkeley and Sir Richard Grenville, decided that discretion was the better part of valour and remained in the enclosed country on the Devonshire side of the border, while the foot already around Taunton retired into the nearest Royalist garrisons as they had done in similar circumstances in December. These were sensible precautions, as the various Royalist formations were in danger of being destroyed in detail, Cromwell having got his cavalry into a position in the Blackdown Hills from which he could attack each in turn. As the Royalists fell back, so Holbourne marched out of Taunton, rendezvousing with Cromwell at Axminster near Lyme without any opposition on 26th March. The Dorset Royalists claimed that he brought out nearly 2,000 horse and foot, but the force is likely to have consisted almost entirely of horse and dragoons given the size of the garrison after he left.

Cromwell, Holbourne and Waller joined forces near Shaftesbury at the end of March, and Goring advanced towards them. A battle seemed imminent, but both sides were cautious because of their shortage of infantry. Nevertheless, Goring raided the quarters of Waller's and Cromwell's cavalry regiments on three occasions between 30th March and 4th April, causing a considerable number of casualties. When the enemy troops began to withdraw eastwards in mid-April in preparation for the birth of the New Model Army, he received orders to set off in pursuit, taking with him several thousand infantry from the forces surrounding Taunton, which now included the brigades from Devon and Cornwall. However, before he could set out, his orders were rescinded. Grenville had discovered that the governor of Taunton, the redoubtable former defender of Lyme Robert Blake, had 1,200 men in his garrison, and he refused point-blank to allow his Cornishmen to march eastwards leaving forces in their rear strong enough to disrupt, or even destroy, efforts to raise new regiments in Somerset and Dorset for the Western Association. Moreover, Sir Richard was confident of storming Taunton within a fortnight, provided that he was reinforced by some of Goring's infantry. Goring was therefore ordered to stop, to send most of his foot soldiers back to Taunton, and to use his cavalry as a screen to protect the siege operations against any attempt by Cromwell and Waller to intervene. In the event, Grenville never had the chance to prove his hypothesis. He was seriously wounded in an attack on Wellington House, one of Taunton's out-garrisons, on about 11th April, and command passed to the leader of the Devonshire division, Sir John Berkeley, who contented himself with blockading the town.[13]

If the achievements of both sides in strategic terms had been unspectacular during the winter months, what assessment can be made about their other priority, recruitment? The number of rank-and-file infantry soldiers that Essex's and Manchester's armies were able to contribute towards the New Model Army in March 1645, 3,048 and 3,578 respectively, suggests that they had lost little by way of attrition during the winter, although the figure for Manchester's brigade may include a regiment of foot at Abingdon raised in Essex in the summer of the previous year, which did not fight in the Newbury campaign. Waller's army contributed only 600 foot, the rest being in garrison at Taunton and elsewhere in the West Country. Thus a further 7,000 infantry had to be impressed in order to fill up the ranks of the twelve New Model Army regiments, all of which were supposed to be 1,200 strong. However, new musketeers and pikemen came in only gradually during the spring, some well after the New Model Army had taken the field. Insofar as cavalry was concerned, there were more than enough troopers to meet the figure of 6,600 from the armies of Essex, Manchester and Waller. Another 2,000 not selected for the New Model were kept in pay during 1645 to support the regional armies.[14]

The king's armies were also recruited during the winter with considerable success. Sir Richard Grenville raised four new infantry regiments in Cornwall, which fought in the Western army from April onwards, but attempts to raise regiments for the Prince of Wales elsewhere in the Western Association were less successful. Despite the hopeful noises made from time to time in letters written by the prince's council, only his lifeguards of foot and horse enjoyed more than an ephemeral existence, and the latter were only brought up to something like full strength by absorbing three existing regiments.[15] Rupert and Maurice, on the other hand, managed to recruit well over a thousand infantry via impressment in Wales and the borders, but this was counterbalanced by the loss of several hundred veteran infantry from the Faringdon garrison, which were intercepted by Oliver Cromwell while marching to Woodstock in late April. Nevertheless, when the king's army came together at Stow on the Wold ten days later, its infantry strength was 2,000 or so larger than it had been at the second battle of Newbury.[16]

Notes

1 CSP Domestic, 1644–5, 110, 125, 139; BL Harleian ms 166, 141; BL Additional ms 18982, 11.

2 Brereton, *Letterbook* I, 119, 136, 140–1, 156–7; CSP Domestic 1644–5, 264, 307, 341, 351, 370; Gentles, *New Model Army*, 10–24.

3 Corbet, *Military Government*, 130–2; Bodleian Firth ms C7, 325–64; Hutton, *Royalist War Effort*, 167–9.

4 The highly positive view of Forth's generalship begins with Gardiner, but for him it was no more than a rhetorical trick to discount the idea that the king himself could have been responsible for the successful Royalist strategy in the south in 1644. Despite the fact that contemporary evidence for Forth's competence is slight and thinly spread, Barratt has recently revived the notion (*Great Rebellion* ii, 63–5; *Cavaliers*, 16, 23, 80).

5 CSP Domestic 1644–5, 245–7; Walsingham, *Alter Britannicae Heros*, 20–1.

6 LJ VII 263; TT E269 7, 15; William Salt Library Salt ms 2007, 7th April 1645.

7 Malbon, *Memoirs*, 155–6; BL Harleian ms 2155, 24.

8 Dugdale, *Diary*, 77; BL Additional ms 18982, 23; CSP Domestic 1644–5, 311–12; Malbon, *Memoirs*, 161–7; Kitson, *Rupert*, 224–5; Maurice, *Account*, 38–9; TT E270 33; Luke, *Letterbooks*, 164–5; Bell, *Memoirs*, 171–2. Rupert is said to have regarded the loss of Shrewsbury as more important than his defeat at Marston Moor, probably because he valued his personal achievement in creating an army base in the face of local indifference or hostility without interference from Oxford.

9 Malbon, *Memoirs*, 166–8; Brereton, *Letterbook* I, 142.

10 Brereton *Letterbook* I, 66, 130, 141–2; Corbet, *Military Government*, 142–5; *Mercurius Aulicus*, 1563–4.

11 TT E24 10; TT E25 7; Whitelock, *Memoirs*, 126; Walsingham, *Hector Britannicus*, 107–8; BL Additional ms 18982, 11; Gardiner, *Great Civil War* II, 113; Dugdale, *Diary*, 76.

12 Barratt, *Cavaliers*, 151–60; Warburton, *Memoirs* III, 68–9, *Mercurius Aulicus*, 1401–9.

13 Wanklyn, *King's Armies*, 135–49; Sanford, *Great Rebellion*, 620.

14 Gentles, *New Model Army*, 32–9; CSP Domestic 1644–5, 415, 429.

15 Wanklyn, *King's Armies*, 179–92; Carte, *Letters*, 97; Stoyle, 'Grenville's creatures', 28–9; Bodleian Wood Pamphlets 378 9, 10.

16 Symonds, *Diary*, 160–6; Hutton, *Royalist War Effort*, 173–5; Tucker, *Royalist Major General*, 43; Rushworth, *Historical Collections* VI, 160, 163–4.

chapter XX

The Naseby campaign

The opening of the 1645 campaigning season was a period of great uncertainty for both king and Parliament. Although the king's prospects
in the south of England had revived very significantly in the second half of
1644, it had not been possible to keep up the momentum over the winter.
Elsewhere it was a similar story, if not worse. Langdale's ride had done
nothing to recover lost ground in Yorkshire and the northeast; there were
no troops in the field and the few garrisons that remained were closely
besieged. In the northwest of England and the northern part of the Welsh
borderland, the situation had deteriorated. With the surrender of Liverpool
in November, the Royalist position in Lancashire had reverted to what it
had been before Prince Rupert's arrival in May 1644. Further south, the king's
supporters had lost territory that had been theirs since the start of the
war. Shrewsbury had been captured, Chester was under siege, and the enemy
controlled a belt of country stretching across north Shropshire almost
as far as Cardigan Bay, separating Royalist North Wales from the Severn
valley and Oxford. Only in the southern borderland had the tide of conquests been pushed back with the reconquest of parts of Gwent, but the
gains were not strategically significant. Not surprisingly, there was an air
of despondency among the king's advisers, which even Prince Rupert felt
at times, despite his promotion.[1] However, there were several important rays
of hope. Digby and his supporters at court firmly believed that the balance
of military resources would tip in the king's favour during 1645 as developments in Charles's other kingdoms impacted on the war in England. The
Marquis of Montrose's string of victories should weaken the resolve of the
Scottish army if not cause it to go home, while a peace treaty with the Irish

rebels would allow the king for the first time to recruit troops systematic-
ally in the parts of that country they controlled. Moderates among the king's
advisers, on the other hand, had great faith in reviving popular royalism via
new associations of counties raising forces under civilian control pledged
to fight for a negotiated peace. To this end the Prince of Wales, supported
by a sub-committee of the Privy Council consisting of moderates, had moved
in March from Oxford to Bristol to breathe new life into the Western Association. However, success in this endeavour was dependent on bringing the
siege of Taunton to a successful conclusion. Finally, there were great hopes
that cracks in the enemy coalition apparent in the autumn of 1644 in the
quarrels between the supporters of Manchester and Cromwell would open
up once more, which, if they did not cause the coalition to disintegrate,
could well limit its military effectiveness. Parallel with this ran the conviction that the 'New Noddle' would be fatally flawed as a fighting machine
due to tensions associated with the traumas of its birth. Such sentiments
caused the king to enter into the new campaigning season in an optimistic
frame of mind, which it is easy to dismiss as self-delusion or whistling in
the wind.[2] However, it is important that hindsight and determinist views
of the war do not obscure the real possibility that, if things had gone dif-
ferently, the field army might have benefited, as in 1644, from enemy mistakes and this time achieved a favourable peace, or even outright victory.

Many on the opposite side shared Royalist doubts about the New Model
Army. During the winter, even the best of the troops had been restive, on
occasions refusing to obey the officers sent down to command them,
whereas newly impressed men had rioted, spreading lawlessness in the counties where they were quartered. Even when it became apparent that combining the three English armies into one had worked, and that the soldiers
were 'lusty, well armed and well paid', the Scottish leadership remained concerned about the wholesale removal of Parliament's senior generals and the
inexperience of the new officers, most particularly Sir Thomas Fairfax. In such
circumstances, they not surprisingly put their own military interests first,
most particularly the defence of the Scottish Lowlands against Montrose and
the prevention of reinforcements reaching him from England. This explains
their cautious behaviour during March, April and May 1645, which gave
the king's field army much more freedom of movement than it would otherwise have had.

The Committee of Both Kingdoms' initial plan for the 1645 campaigning season had been for the Scottish army to advance southwards so that

there could be an early encounter with the king's field army, a second Marston Moor. The sorts of ideas that were flying around in correspondence between soldiers and politicians in the winter and early spring were that the king could be trapped between the allied armies if he advanced from Oxford into the northwest or the northeast of England or into the Eastern Association. On the other hand, if he went on the offensive to the south of the Thames, a Scottish siege of Chester in association with Sir William Brereton's troops would force him to divide his forces, thus hopefully enabling the allies to achieve final victory by defeating each in turn. However, if the king decided to remain on the defensive, the Scottish and the New Model armies combined would be strong enough to lay siege to Oxford and to deter any relief expeditions. In the event, both sides did take the offensive, but the result was not an early encounter between them. The New Model Army and the king's army marched off in different directions, while the Scottish army moved northwards into the Eden valley.[3]

Since the time of Gardiner and Firth, it has been customary to portray the strategy pursued by the Committee of Both Kingdoms during April and May 1645 as blundering and amateurish, the work of civilians rather than soldiers. Instead of giving independence to its new general, Sir Thomas Fairfax, it irritated him with a plethora of conflicting commands. As a result, the New Model Army lost the strategic initiative, reacting to events as they happened rather than pursuing an aggressive line of its own such as pursuing the king and seeking an encounter at the earliest opportunity. What was needed was a new model strategy, which duly came into being after the unexpected storming of Leicester by the Royalist army. From 10th June onwards, decisions about where the New Model was to march were taken by its council of officers, not the committee. As a result, the army won two decisive victories in six weeks, which brought to an end any real prospect of the king winning the first Civil War. We wholeheartedly agree that the battles of Naseby and Langport were decisive, but Gardiner's analysis is infused by his partisan attitude towards the war, while Firth's charge of amateurishness is countered by the fact that Essex, Manchester and Waller attended the committee almost every day during May and early June. A careful examination of the documentary record rather than a reworking of the relevant pages of *The Great Civil War* produces a very different picture of the committee's achievements in the run-up to Naseby.[4]

The New Model Army opened the 1645 campaign in brave style. Oliver Cromwell, with most of the forces that had returned from the West

Country, some New Model Army, some not, took up a position to the east of Oxford on about 21st April, while Sir Thomas Fairfax with the infantry and the rest of the New Model cavalry moved from Windsor to Reading a few days later.[5] What followed was not a fourth Thames valley campaign. Instead, the objectives were twofold: to relieve Taunton, which was in danger of surrendering; and to prevent Rupert reuniting the scattered components of the king's field army. If Taunton fell, the likelihood of the Royalists taking the offensive with a fair prospect of victory would be much enhanced. In the first place, half the besiegers would most likely head northwards to reinforce the king. Second, the town's capture would increase the chance of the Prince of Wales's council successfully raising a new army in the four counties of the west of England. Finally, the council would be much better able to provide the king's forces with all manner of military supplies imported from the Continent. Less would be consumed locally, and more could be purchased using the revenues of the four counties, much of which had been consumed by operations before Taunton. Fairfax therefore set out from Reading for Taunton with about 10,000 men on 30th April. Gentles claims that this was all the New Model could muster at that date, but he failed to take into account troops that were committed to a second objective.[6]

The Committee of Both Kingdoms' other principal concern was that the principal aim of the king's strategy in 1645 was to invade the Eastern Association. However, the forces that Rupert and Maurice had collected in the Welsh borders, the nucleus of the king's field army, could do nothing without their train of artillery, which was at Oxford, and Sir George Lisle's infantry brigade, still at Faringdon guarding the road to Bristol. To prevent their uniting with the rest of the field army, Cromwell's horse and dragoons supported by infantry from Abingdon were ordered to cross the Cherwell and station themselves to the north and west of the city. They beat up some cavalry regiments under the Earl of Northampton at Islip on 24th April, forced the new garrison at Bletchingdon to surrender on the 25th, captured 300 veteran infantry belonging to Lisle's brigade at Bampton-in-the-Bush on the 27th, and then lay siege to the rest of the brigade in Faringdon itself for the next week. Cromwell's men also swept through the villages around Oxford requisitioning carthorses, without which the Royalist heavy guns could not set out on campaign. Rupert sent his brother with a thousand cavalry to rescue their uncle, but Maurice held back, which is scarcely surprising as Cromwell had four times as many troops under his command. A quick dash there and back to rescue the king might have been practicable, but not a return journey escorting the slow-moving train of artillery. Instead, General Goring was ordered to return to the Oxford area, bringing with him the rest of the field army cavalry from Somerset, some 3,000 strong, supported by 1,000 mounted infantry. He encountered Cromwell's forces at Radcot bridge near Faringdon on 3rd May. After a prolonged fight, the Parliamentarians gave way and retired to Abingdon, Reading and Newbury, allowing the king and the artillery train to leave the city, but Cromwell had nevertheless delayed the Royalist offensive by two weeks at a time when the rest of the New Model Army was still finding its feet.[7]

All the elements of the king's field army, apart from Gerard's brigade, came together at Stow on the Wold on 8th May, and the Committee of Both Kingdoms immediately went on the defensive. Fairfax, who had reached Blandford, received orders to return to Newbury and make contact with Cromwell, who was in the same general area. However, three regiments of New Model Army foot and one of horse under Colonel Weldon's command were to continue towards Taunton in the expectation that they would be strong enough to deal with the besiegers if they decided to fight, weakened as they were by the departure of Goring's 4,000 men. This was the best decision the committee could have made in the circumstances. The relief force reached the town on 12th May, having almost succeeded in taking the besiegers by surprise, who thought at first that they were Goring's men returning from Oxford. In the final few days, Hopton, who had replaced Sir John Berkeley and was in contention with Goring for the command of the new, enlarged Western army that would come into being once Taunton had fallen, assaulted the town remorselessly, setting fire to most of the houses and confining Blake's soldiers to the castle and a few strong points. When the relief force arrived, the garrison was down to its last barrel of gunpowder, and there is little doubt that, if the Committee of Both Kingdoms had required the whole of the New Model Army to return eastwards, Taunton would have been obliged to capitulate.[8]

While the Royalist army rested at Stow, the king presided over a council of war to discuss the best strategy for the field army in the 1645 campaign. It was quickly decided that invading the Eastern Association in early May was too much of a risk, presumably on the grounds that even if Fairfax did not return quickly from Somerset, the Committee of Both Kingdoms would be able to assemble a large enough force in the Ouse valley to delay the Royalists' return to Oxford until he arrived with the rest of the New Model.

However, there was a spirited debate between those who favoured marching into the West Country to attack Fairfax and those who favoured a northern campaign beginning with the relief of Chester, closely besieged for the second time by Sir William Brereton aided by a polyglot force drawn from Yorkshire, the northwest and the north Midlands. It did not take long for a compromise to emerge. The bulk of the army was to march towards Chester, while Goring and his brigades were to return to Taunton and bring the siege to a successful conclusion. From Sir Edward Walker onwards, this has been seen as the decision that led directly to the destruction of the king's armies at Naseby and Langport, but this is not so. Such an opinion is very clearly based on hindsight. Goring had clear instructions to rejoin the rest of the army when ordered to do so. Moreover, despite what Walker claimed, the king was not totally committed to a further advance north to attack the Scottish army and liberate Yorkshire. This is clear from a letter he sent to the queen from Droitwich on 12th May. All his options were still open. He might advance into the Eastern Association 'or if Fairfax be engaged far westwards, engage him there'.[9] Moreover, at the time the decision was taken, the New Model Army was itself divided and would remain so for the next month. The fatal strategic mistake came much further down the line.

The other criticism made of the strategic decisions taken at Stow is that if the Royalist field army had kept together and marched south rather than north, it could have destroyed Fairfax's corps of the New Model Army on its way back from Taunton or when it arrived at Newbury. This idea was also first put forward by Walker and is also wrong. However fast the king's army had marched, it could not have intercepted Fairfax before he joined Cromwell's horse and dragoons. Sir Thomas's return route was via Winchester, so that he was approaching Newbury from the opposite direction to that which the king's army would have taken, whereas Cromwell, who had remained to the south of Oxford after Radcot bridge keeping a watch on its movements, could easily have joined Fairfax as soon as he learned that Charles was heading in his direction.[10] Moreover, once the two of them had been reinforced by other troops in the vicinity, such as Waller's cavalry regiments that had not been incorporated into the New Model Army, the forces under Fairfax's command would have been much larger than Rupert's, and very strong in horse, normally the decisive element in a battle fought in open country like the downlands that stretched from Winchester to 12 miles north of Newbury on the road to Oxford.

The king's army duly set off northwards on 10th May and proceeded in a somewhat leisurely manner towards Chester through Worcestershire, Staffordshire and east Shropshire. Oliver Cromwell and Richard Browne, the commander of Abingdon garrison, with about 7,000 horse and foot were ordered to follow the king, but they kept at a respectful distance, reaching Coventry on the 18th, by which time the Royalist field army was about to cross into Shropshire. In the meantime, Fairfax's corps minus Weldon's brigade was resting at Newbury after its vigorous march into the West Country and back again. The Committee of Both Kingdoms tried to strengthen Cromwell with local forces in case the march towards Chester was merely a deception designed to lure him into a battle under unfavourable circumstances. At the same time, it ordered the Scottish army and Lord Fairfax's forces in Yorkshire to march to Brereton's support. It recognized that the siege of Chester would probably have to be abandoned, but was determined that Lancashire be defended given its known Royalist sympathies. However, the behaviour of the Scottish army, by that time in central Yorkshire, undermined everything. Brereton suggested a rendezvous at Barlow Moor, just to the north of the Mersey in what are now the suburbs of Manchester, presumably with the intention of attacking the Royalists as they attempted to cross the river, or else of pursuing them if, having relieved Chester, they started to return south. The committee agreed and sent instructions to other commanders in the north to join Brereton and the besiegers of Chester at Barlow Moor, but the Scots' reaction to the request that they should do the same was not to cross the Pennines into south Lancashire but to set off northwards by way of Ripon and Stainmore towards the Lake District. One reason that Leven gave for this bizarre behaviour was that the more southerly roads were not strong enough to carry his train of artillery; the other was that taking up a position in the vale of Eden on the other side of the Lakeland hills would make it easier to prevent the king sending a small 'flying army' into Scotland to link up with Montrose, who had just won a major battle at Auldearn near Inverness. Leven's advice to Brereton was to fall back on the Scottish army in Cumbria if put under pressure, but Sir William recognized this as a recipe for disaster. Once he had begun to retreat, the Royalists could send cavalry and dragoons in an outflanking movement through the open field country that ran parallel to the sea coast and capture the bridges over the Ribble, 30 miles to the north of Barlow Moor. Moreover, the morale of almost all the other troops assembled at Barlow Moor would be undermined if they withdrew northwards, as they would be abandoning their homes and families. Even the Yorkshire troops would be affected; Rupert in command of the Pennine passes could raid their county at will.

Brereton abandoned the siege of Chester on 21st May when the king's army was at Market Drayton, three days' march away, thus allowing the city to relieve itself. However, Rupert was not about to perform a repeat of the 1644 campaign and force his way across the Mersey (which was just as well, as the Barlow Moor rendezvous was miserably attended even by local forces). A letter written by Digby to General Goring two days earlier shows that a decision to march east rather than north had already been taken. Fearful that Fairfax was about to join Cromwell and Browne's shadowing force, the king required Goring to return, bringing as many troops as he could to Market Harborough in Leicestershire for 'the last blow in the business'. Reading between the lines of the tale told by a Royalist deserter, other messages to this effect had probably also been sent to Charles Gerard in South Wales and to the governor of Newark. However, within a day or so, the danger had passed. Instead of being joined by Fairfax, the shadowing force had broken up. A very large part of the cavalry and dragoons were riding towards Yorkshire under Commissary-General Vermuyden's command to strengthen the Scottish army for a possible battle with the Royalist field army if it marched north, while Cromwell and Browne were returning towards the Thames valley with the infantry to take part with Fairfax's corps in the Committee of Both Kingdoms' next initiative, the siege of Oxford. In the meantime, the king's army continued undisturbed on its march via Stone and Uttoxeter to Newark, the jumping-off point for the invasion of Yorkshire.[11]

The committee's decision to lay siege to Oxford has been roundly condemned by historians, but in doing so they merely repeat Gardiner's narrative, inflected as it is by his hero worship of Oliver Cromwell. To be fair, the generals were also against it. Fairfax disliked having to 'spend time unprofitably before a town whilst the king hath time to strengthen himself'. Cromwell was more circumspect, but in a letter sent from Coventry to a Staffordshire commander he expressed his reluctance to abandon his friends but wrote that he had to obey orders. However, the decision can be defended on strategic grounds. In the first place, the threat to Oxford achieved one of its objectives in that it enabled Parliament to regain the strategic initiative. The king's army put its march north on hold because of the threat to the Royalist headquarters. Second, by stopping in one place and placing the onus on the king to call his bluff, Fairfax avoided another 'dance across the Midlands', which had so severely damaged Waller's composite army the previous summer. Indeed, the march towards Coventry had already caused grumbling among Browne's troops. Third, confining the New Model Army firmly to the Thames valley at a time when the king was threatening to march into Yorkshire shook the Scottish generals and politicians out of their parochial attitudes. Their army was now in the firing line and outnumbered by the enemy. They therefore decided that the best course of action would be for their army to leave Westmorland and move south in order to combine forces with Lord Fairfax's and Sir William Brereton's troops and Vermuyden's cavalry and dragoons. Leaving Appleby no earlier than 1st June, the Scottish army had reached Doncaster on the Yorkshire/Nottinghamshire border by 14th June, when the battle of Naseby was fought. Finally, the siege of Oxford brought together the two largest components of the New Model Army, which had previously operated separately, Fairfax's corps and Cromwell's infantry. The only weakness in the committee's new strategic initiative was that Sir Thomas Fairfax probably had insufficient men to surround Oxford completely, and he certainly had the wrong types of artillery to batter down its fortifications.[12]

While the rest of the king's army marched north towards Chester, Goring and his cavalry and dragoons returned into the West Country. They failed by a day to prevent the relief of Taunton, which took place when they were between Marshfield and Bath, but despite an accidental fight between some of his own troops, Goring was able to prevent the relief force from escaping. For the next six weeks, he pinned it down in west Somerset while attempting what had always been his preferred plan for capturing Taunton, namely starving it into surrender. Assault was out of the question, as the defenders now comprised 4,000–5,000 men, most of whom were infantry.[13] Wisely, the Committee of Both Kingdoms decided against an immediate rescue mission, which would have disrupted military operations in the Midlands. However, by early June supplies in the besieged garrison were running low once more, and the committee began to assemble a new Western army to relieve the town out of cavalry left over from the New Model. This was to be under the command of the former governor of Gloucester, Edward Massey, who, as a major-general, came under Fairfax's direct authority. At about the same time, the committee sent Cromwell to Cambridge to prepare the Eastern Association for imminent invasion, his commission having been extended for forty days, which the Self-Denying

Ordinance permitted in exceptional circumstances. He was charged with raising 3,000 cavalry in the Association to reinforce the field army, and he was still usually addressed as lieutenant-general in recognition of his past command, but he did not hold that rank in the New Model.[14]

The supposed threat to the Eastern Association arose out of the change in the direction of the king's army's line of march, which was now south-eastwards into Leicestershire, culminating in the storming of the county town on the night of 30th/31st May. This was in response to Fairfax's siege of Oxford. Initially, the Royalist council of war had thought that Goring would be able to do something to assist the city. As a result, his first set of orders was changed on 26th May, and he was instructed to move to the Newbury area instead. However, there were doubts as to whether he would be strong enough to do anything more than observe what was happening until such time as the field army was able to join him. These doubts were more strongly felt by the sub-committee of the council of war at Oxford, which panicked, claiming that the city could hold out for only a fortnight, not the six or so weeks that Charles and Rupert estimated was needed for the northern expedition and a rendezvous with Goring. The attack on Leicester was the only way to distract the New Model quickly, but its effect was not immediate. The field army therefore turned southwards to Market Harborough as if it were now marching towards Oxford, but on arriving there, the king learned from Sir Edward Nicholas that the New Model had abandoned the siege and seemed to be retreating in a northeasterly direction towards Bedford, apparently to protect the eastern approaches to the Association.

At London the loss of Leicester, the importance of which was greatly exaggerated by some of the weekly journals, was blamed on the Committee of Both Kingdoms' decision to lay siege to Oxford rather than pursue the king's army. Rumours circulated that the decision reflected the influence of the army commanders displaced by the Self-Denying Ordinance who sat on the committee, and whose names were associated in the public mind with caution and lost opportunities in the past. Significantly, it was Sir Phillip Stapleton, the Earl of Essex's closest ally throughout the 1644 campaigns, who made the committee's case for the siege in the House of Commons. The rumour mongers may well have been partly right given widespread fears about Fairfax's inexperience (and possibly hot-headedness). The former generals on the committee may have decided that they had to do something to prevent Sir Thomas losing the war in a single day, and that laying siege to Oxford was the best option as it should also act as a curb on the king's activities. However, some of the members of the committee had another, secret reason for besieging Oxford, the Saville plot. Lord Saville, who had recently deserted the king, claimed to have contact with Royalists who were willing not only to surrender the king's headquarters if the New Model Army lay siege to it but also to arrange the wholesale surrender of the king's forces in the south of England once the city had capitulated. However, by early June it had become apparent that Saville was not telling the truth. The discrediting of the plot coincided with a petition from the city of London to the effect that Fairfax was missing the chance to exploit hopeful military opportunities because he was dependent on the permission of the committee, which might take several days to reach him. This met with a positive response from the House of Commons, and Fairfax was duly granted his strategic independence on 9th June. A suggestion from the army that Cromwell should become temporary commander of the cavalry was also approved a day later. The absence of any shouting from the ex-generals may have been because they knew that they had done all they could in the past eight days to ensure that Fairfax would not lose the next battle.

It has been shown that Gardiner's attack on the strategy pursued by the Committee of Both Kingdoms in April and May is largely invalid. It now remains to put to the test the claim that there is a direct causal link between Parliament's freeing of the New Model Army from the committee's 'leading strings' and the decisive victories at Naseby and Langport.[15] In fact, the argument that is its mirror image is more convincing, namely that the last week of the committee's control of strategy was the old generals' finest hour in that otherwise Fairfax would have found it much more difficult to defeat the king's armies. Between 2nd and 9th June, Manchester and Waller attended the committee every day. Essex was missing on only a single occasion, and that was when unimportant business was being conducted. During that week it ordered Fairfax to engage the king in battle and delivered the resources necessary for winning. It required the general to abandon the siege of Oxford the day after it received news of the storming of Leicester, chivvied him for spending precious time trying to capture Boarstall House as he withdrew, and then pointed him firmly in the direction of the western border of the Association and a decisive encounter with the king's forces. It also ordered the regiments under Vermuyden's command, the Eastern Association troops Cromwell was raising and Colonel

Rossiter's Lincolnshire regiment of horse to rendezvous with the New Model Army as quickly as possible. This they all succeeded in doing before the battle took place, giving Fairfax a significant numerical advantage in cavalry that he would not otherwise have had. Thus preparations for a decisive encounter with the king's field army were complete before the committee surrendered strategic control. All Fairfax had to do was to seek the king out and bring him to battle in favourable circumstances.[16]

The singlemindedness with which the Committee of Both Kingdoms prepared for battle had no equivalent on the king's side, where the need to react speedily to changing contingencies resulted in a series of understandable but seemingly contradictory decisions, the last of which proved disastrous. Capturing Leicester was probably a sound move. There was no other way of lifting the siege of Oxford, the casualties had been relatively light, new recruits flocked to the colours, and the reputation of the king's army as a fighting force had increased as a result. However, the decision to march south two days later is more questionable. In the first place, the Northern Horse regarded the king as having broken his promises to advance into Yorkshire and rode off in the direction of Newark. Charles managed to persuade them to turn back, but at the time and since writers have wondered whether this episode affected their performance at Naseby. Second, it wasted precious time. If the northern march was to succeed, Charles needed to catch the Scots unawares. The longer he spent in the Midlands, the more time would English regiments from the northwest, the northeast and the East Midlands have to join the Earl of Leven. On the other hand, the march to Market Harborough was no more than a feint. Charles had no intention of confronting the besiegers of Oxford head-on. This he likened to taking risks like a madman. However, having then heard that Fairfax had abandoned the siege, he could have returned north immediately. Instead, he continued to march south, taking up quarters in west-central Northamptonshire around the town of Daventry. This was the king's first incontrovertible mistake.

The reason for the move to Daventry was to ensure that Oxford was fully provisioned. While there, the king's army collected together large numbers of cattle and sheep, which were escorted to Oxford by a party of cavalry. The rest of the army rested at Daventry until the convoy returned with military supplies, but no reinforcements, on the 11th. In the meantime, however, nothing was done to ascertain the New Model Army's line of march. This is partly understandable, as the king's council of war normally relied on Sir Edward Nicholas at Oxford to provide them with intelligence about the movements of the enemy armies, but on this occasion his informants provided him with incorrect information. The New Model Army was not moving in a northeasterly direction towards Bedford, as they claimed. Instead, it was heading due north to Newport Pagnell and Olney, only 20 miles from Daventry. Fairfax's intention was to defend the line of the River Ouse against an enemy advancing from mid-Northamptonshire towards the Eastern Association, but when by 9th June there was no sign of this happening the New Model moved hesitantly towards Northampton, another possible Royalist target after the easy capture of Leicester. Fairfax's letter written from Wootton, close to the present outskirts of Northampton, on the 11th showed that he had less knowledge of the king's intentions than Charles had of his. On the following day, however, patrols of the two armies clashed in the village of Kislingbury, just to the west of the town.

Hearing of Fairfax's advance, the royal army occupied Borough Hill guarding the eastern approaches to Daventry. Although an excellent defensive site for an army that was numerically inferior to its opponent, it was waterless and therefore not a suitable place to be surrounded while waiting for reinforcements to arrive, for, unlike Fairfax, the king had not yet managed to unite his scattered army. Admittedly, the Newark garrison had provided him with 800 additional cavalry after the capture of Leicester, but there was no sign of George Goring or Charles Gerard. Surprisingly, Gerard was expected any day, even though he had yet to leave South Wales, a massive indictment of intelligence in Royalist-controlled Herefordshire and Worcestershire. However, his 2,000 troops would have done little to improve the prospects of victory over the New Model as they were primarily infantry. Goring, on the other hand, commanded 'the best horse in the king's army' according to Walker, and only five weeks earlier he had been able to make his way from Taunton to Oxford with 3,000 cavalry in only four days. Why had he not repeated the performance when his men were so desperately needed?[17]

The conventional view is that Goring received several orders to rejoin the field army but refused to obey them on the grounds that he could guarantee that Taunton would surrender within a few weeks, thus enabling him to bring a huge army into the Midlands to support the king. On the other hand, if he obeyed the king's commands and abandoned the siege, the Western Association troops would desert in droves, the enemy would overrun the counties of the southwest, and Weldon's corps would follow him closely, adding almost as many troops to Fairfax's army as he could to the king's. He therefore strongly advised Charles to remain on the defensive until the Western army arrived and in no circumstances fight the New Model Army before it did so. However, the king never received Goring's letters, all of which fell into enemy hands. Thus, while Charles waited expectantly for his crack cavalry to arrive, Fairfax knew they were still in Somerset and that he would be facing an enemy army with the odds heavily weighted in his favour. As a result, by refusing to obey the king's orders Goring bears a considerable responsibility for the allied victory in the Great Civil War.[18]

Some of this is true, but the conclusions drawn from it are not. There is no doubt that at least one of Goring's letters fell into enemy hands before it could reach the king, but the information it contained did not reach Fairfax until the eve of the battle at the earliest. Its contents would therefore, at best, have done no more than confirm the New Model Army's council of war in its decision taken some days before to fight the king's army at the earliest opportunity, provided that it did not march west (and by 13th June it was obvious that it was marching north). Second, we believe that there is sufficient evidence to show that the king was fully aware of Goring's intentions and whereabouts other than in mid- to late May, when Digby complained that no news had come from the west for some days. A packet of Digby's correspondence captured much later in the war contains a letter to Charles from the Prince of Wales's council written on 24th May to the effect that, with General Goring's complete approval, they had delayed his march. The reasons were set out as in the paragraph above, but begging the king's pardon for their disobedience. However, they were quite sure that if he had known what they knew, he would not have issued the order.[19] This letter would have been received by the king on about 29th May, but even if it did not arrive until much later, the fact that Goring was not coming would have been apparent from the postscript to one of a series of almost daily letters from Sir Edward Nicholas and the council at Oxford to Charles written on 8th June. This gave news of Goring's successes in the west, namely a series of engagements outside the walls of Taunton between 30th May and 1st June, as a result of which Weldon's troops had been driven back into the town. The fact that Charles wrote to the queen to the same effect on the 8th (and thus almost certainly before the letter from Oxford reached him) suggests very strongly that he not only knew that Goring was still in Somerset but approved of his being there. That the king had such information almost certainly explains why there is no mention of Goring at all in the three replies he sent to Nicholas on 9th, 11th and 13th June. Admittedly, his letter of 4th June stated in no uncertain terms that he was not prepared to march to Oxford while it was under siege until after either Gerard or Goring had joined him. However, the context of this comment is the second set of orders sent to Goring on 26th May, referred to briefly earlier in this chapter, to the effect that he was no longer to join the royal army in Leicestershire but to move to the Newbury area with as many troops as he could muster in order to assist the Oxford garrison. If unable to effect a relief or to distract Fairfax, he was to put his forces in a defensive posture until such time as the king's army arrived. However, the rendezvous would not take place until the king's army had relieved Pontefract Castle, defeated the Scots and, presumably, been reinforced by Gerard and by new recruits from Yorkshire.[20]

Thus, if the king knew that Goring was still besieging Taunton, the lack of concern about his whereabouts and intentions is fully understandable. However, after receiving news on 6th June that Oxford was no longer under siege, the king must have sent a third set of orders to Goring and the prince's council, as those issued on 26th May were now redundant. These were almost certainly a reversion to those of 19th May, namely that Goring was to bring his horse and foot into the central Midlands. A letter written to Digby from Bridgwater on 10th June by a member of the prince's council reiterates the earlier argument that the king should go on the defensive until Taunton had been captured. It was not intercepted by the enemy, as it is also among Digby's papers captured at Sherburn, but it may not have reached Charles until after the battle of Naseby. At about the same time, Goring wrote to the king in very similar terms, and it was this letter that came into Sir Thomas Fairfax's hands on 13th, 14th or 15th June.

What is very clear from all of this is that, even if Goring had obeyed his third set of instructions, he could not have reached the central Midlands with his mounted troops until 16th June at the earliest, that is two days after the battle of Naseby had taken place. His cavalry were further west than they had been in April, around Taunton rather than around Wells, and Leicester was two days' ride further north than Oxford. More importantly, the king and Rupert would have been fully aware of it. The final marching and countermarching of the field army in the day or so before Naseby cannot therefore be explained in any way by the expectation that Goring's troops might arrive at any moment.[21]

On 13th June, the day after its scouts had clashed with Fairfax's scouts outside Northampton, the king's army duly set out for the north, not for Oxford as Digby appears to have recommended. The deciding factor was probably a letter received at Oxford on 10th June to the effect that Pontefract Castle could hold out for only another ten days.[22] The army advanced rapidly from Daventry to Market Harborough with the intention of marching beyond Leicester to Belvoir Castle, one of the outer garrisons of Newark, but during the night it became apparent that Fairfax was in hot pursuit. Nevertheless, Rupert recommended that the army continue its march, choose a good defensive site and wait for reinforcements, which may suggest that the letter from Bridgwater had arrived. However, he was overruled. The Royalist army backtracked into the wold country of mid-Northamptonshire looking for a favourable place to offer battle. This decision has been blamed on the ill-founded optimism of the king's civilian advisers concerning the quality of the New Model Army, but Lord Astley and the rest of the military men must have had reservations about their ability to conduct a fighting retreat across the many miles of open field country that stretched northwards to Leicester and beyond. Some complicated manoeuvring on the morning of 14th June combined with faulty intelligence resulted in Rupert selecting one of the worst sites to fight an enemy army if things went wrong. There was no safe place of retreat within miles of the battlefield, and the time of day at which battle commenced would allow for at least eight hours of fighting before darkness fell. Moreover, the king's army was heavily outnumbered in both horse and foot.[23]

Notes

1 Hutton, *Royalist War Effort*, 166–74; Corbet, *Military Government*, 145–7; Kitson, *Rupert*, 224.

2 Wanklyn, *King's Armies*, 160–92; BL Additional ms 18982, 60; *Mercurius Aulicus*, 1586; Warburton, *Memoirs* III, 79–80, 82.

3 Baillie, *Letters and Journals* II, 286; CSP Domestic 1644–5, 230, 314, 339, 392; BL additional ms 18978, 173–4; Brereton, *Letterbooks* I, 54, 11, 128–31; Juxon, *Journal*, 80.

4 Gardiner, *Great Civil War* II, 211–13, 238; Firth, *Cromwell*, 125.

5 CSP Domestic 1644–5, 419, 433; TT E292 27; Whitelock, *Memorials*, 143.

6 Gentles, *New Model Army*, 53–4.

7 Abbott, *Writings and Speeches* I, 192–4; Symonds, *Diary*, 163–4; Warburton, *Memoirs* III, 77–81; Walsingham, *Hector Britannicus*, 110.

8 CSP Domestic 1644–5, 459; Bodleian Clarendon ms 24, 148; TT E284, 7, 9, 11.

9 BL Harleian ms 7379, 41.

10 Walker, *Historical Discourses*, 125–6; Clarendon, *Great Rebellion* ix, 29; Warwick, *Memoirs*, 314–15.

11 Brereton, *Letterbooks* I, 491, 495, 516, 532, 643; CSP Domestic 1644–5, 459, 521, 535; HMC Portland ms I, 224–5; HMC Appendix to the 1st Report, 9.

12 Bell, *Memoirs*, 228; Walker, *Historical Discourses*, 127; Brereton, *Letterbooks* I, 573, 583; LJ VII 379; CJ IV 146–7; Terry, *Leven*, 362; CSP Domestic 1644–5, 537, 551.

13 Wanklyn, *King's Armies*, 209–28.

14 CSP Domestic 1644–5, 525–6, 585; Rushworth, *Historical Collections* VI, 20, 34; Whitelock, *Memorials*, 148–50.

15 BL Harleian ms 7379, 42; Walker, *Historical Discourses*, 127; CSP Domestic 1644–5, 578; BL Harleian ms 166, 210; Crawford, 'Saville affair', 79; Bodleian Clarendon ms 24, 166; Kishlansky, *New Model Army*, 54–6; Gardiner, *Great Civil War* II, 207–13, 238, 261–3.

16 CSP Domestic 1644–5, 562–7, 573, 578, 611, 613. Vermuyden resigned after returning from the north and was replaced by Ireton.

17 Walker, *Historical Discourses*, 128–9; Evelyn, *Diary* IV, 148; Rushworth, *Historical Collections* VI, 40; Symonds, *Diary*, 184–8; TT E292 27; Wanklyn, *King's Armies*, 154, 195.

18 Bulstrode, *Memoirs*, 124–5; Firth, 'Bulstrode', 273–4; Woolrych, *Battles*, 109–10, 125, 138; Young and Holmes, *English Civil Wars*, 245, 269; Reid, *All the King's Armies*, 207. This was very much my argument in 'King's armies', but placing the onus on the prince's council rather than on Goring.

19 Rushworth, *Historical Collections* VI, 49; Bulstrode, *Memoirs*, 124–5; Firth, 'Bulstrode', 273; Bodleian Clarendon ms 24, 166; CSP Domestic 1644–5, 522.

20 Evelyn, *Diary* IV, 148–52; Symonds, *Diary*, 190; HMC Appendix to the 1st Report, 9; Powell, *Robert Blake*, 61.

21 CSP Domestic 1644–5, 581–2.

22 Wilts CRO 413/444B, 37; HMC Appendix to the 9th Report II, 437.

23 *Ibid.*, 520; Symonds, *Diary*, 186–93; Walker, *Historical Discourses*, 129–30; Rushworth, *Historical Discourses* VI, 41; HMC Appendix to the 1st Report, 9; Evelyn, *Diary* IV, 150–1; Wilts CRO 413/444B 37.

chapter XXI

The battle of Naseby

The two armies drew up along parallel ridges, Red Hill and Dust Hill, in a small tract of open country between the villages of Naseby and Sibbertoft, five miles to the south of Market Harborough. The battlefield was hemmed in on the west by a patchwork of enclosures and on the east by a belt of gorse bushes and scrub concealing a steep slope. As a result, outflanking movements were out of the question. Rupert deployed the Royalist army on Dust Hill with Prince Maurice commanding the right wing and Sir Marmaduke Langdale the left. In total they amounted to just over 3,000 cavalry, with the Northern Horse reinforced by a regiment from Bristol being slightly more numerous than Maurice's 'old horse' of the king's field army strengthened by a regiment from the English army in Ireland. In the centre were seven small brigades of infantry totalling no more than 4,000 foot interspersed with another 800 cavalry drawn up in squadrons. The cavalry reserve comprised about 1,000 horse, two brigades from Newark on the wings and the king's lifeguard in the centre. Stationed between them were the infantry reserves, the king's and Prince Rupert's regiments of foot.[1]

Facing Maurice were just over 2,000 New Model Army troopers under Henry Ireton's command, supported by several hundred Eastern Association horse. On the other wing, Oliver Cromwell had well over 3,000 men in three lines, 600 or more of whom belonged to auxiliary regiments. There was no cavalry reserve. The New Model Army infantry was drawn up in three lines, the first containing five regiments, the second three, and the third half a regiment. The front line alone outnumbered the king's infantry by several hundred men, with the result that the regiment at the extreme right of the formation did not have a Royalist brigade in front of it. All the Royalists

Map 6 The Central Midlands, 1644–45

could see of the New Model infantry was the front line, the rest being hidden by Red Hill. This was not deliberate deception on Sir Thomas Fairfax's part but was forced on him by the confined space and the fact that the second line was still deploying when the battle began.[2]

Streeter's plan of the battle suggests that the New Model Army was drawn up in an offensive formation, but it was the Royalists who attacked first along the whole of the front and without the usual preliminary, an artillery bombardment. Rupert may have hoped to overcome the king's army's disadvantage in numbers by catching the New Model off-guard, but his plan was almost certainly more complex than that. His diary shows that crucial to its success was first for Maurice's wing to win a quick victory over Ireton

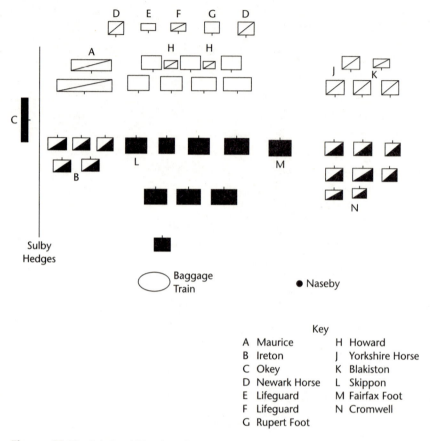

Figure 17 The battle of Naseby, about 11a.m.

Key

A	Maurice	H	Howard
B	Ireton	J	Yorkshire Horse
C	Okey	K	Blakiston
D	Newark Horse	L	Skippon
E	Lifeguard	M	Fairfax Foot
F	Lifeguard	N	Cromwell
G	Rupert Foot		

(which explains why Rupert himself joined it for the initial charge) and second that the reserve should keep together and not be committed too early.[3] Possibly the intention was that Maurice's regiments, having defeated Ireton, should swing around the back of the enemy army and attack Cromwell's wing from the rear while Langdale kept their front line in check. However, the cavalry fight on the Royalist right lasted half an hour, with the result that when Rupert returned to Dust Hill to resume control, it was too late. Moreover, even though the right wing had achieved its initial object-ive, it could not immediately attack Cromwell's wing, as the valley behind Red Hill was crowded with enemy infantry.[4] This probably explains why it responded by attempting to capture the Roundhead baggage train, which

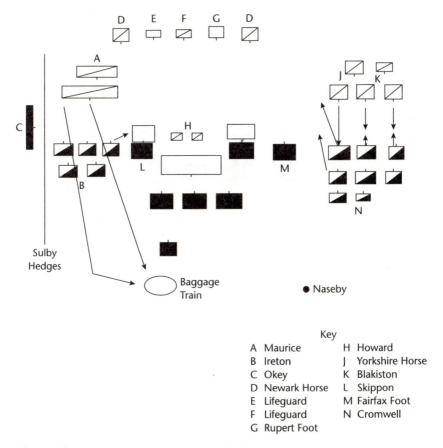

Key

A Maurice	H Howard
B Ireton	J Yorkshire Horse
C Okey	K Blakiston
D Newark Horse	L Skippon
E Lifeguard	M Fairfax Foot
F Lifeguard	N Cromwell
G Rupert Foot	

Figure 18 The battle of Naseby, about 11.30a.m.

lay behind the New Model Army centre blocking another possible route to the enemy right wing.

Rupert had probably calculated that his left wing would be able to hold its own for some time because of the nature of the ground over which Cromwell's men would have to advance, a rabbit warren and plenty of gorse bushes.[5] However, the very success of some of the Yorkshire horse against the squadron on the left of the New Model first line forced Cromwell to commit second-line troops against them as they puffed up Red Hill. This, together with the gradient, was sufficient to cause the Yorkshiremen to turn tail, as they received no help whatsoever from the regiments in the second line supposed to support them. Soon afterwards, the rest of Langdale's

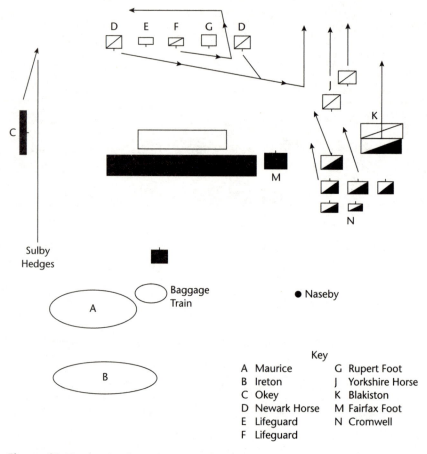

Figure 19 The battle of Naseby, about 12.15p.m.

Key

A	Maurice	G	Rupert Foot
B	Ireton	J	Yorkshire Horse
C	Okey	K	Blakiston
D	Newark Horse	M	Fairfax Foot
E	Lifeguard	N	Cromwell
F	Lifeguard		

formation also gave way as the pressure on them increased. More and more New Model cavalrymen were pushing their way through the rabbit warren, and their right flank had now been exposed by the flight of their colleagues.[6] The king therefore ordered the cavalry reserves to move forward, but the Newark horse seem to have been caught up in the general rout of the left wing, while the lifeguard lost formation when their order to charge was countermanded. However, as at Marston Moor, Cromwell's horse stopped in their pursuit of the enemy, who lurked impotently in the rear until the final stage of the battle.

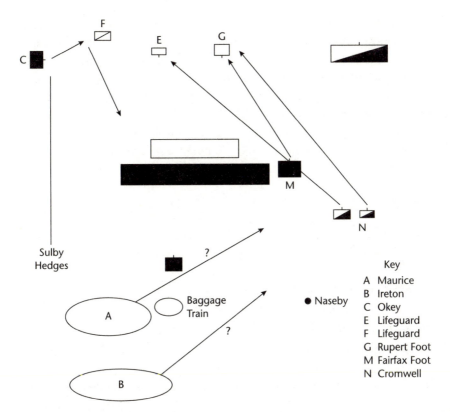

Figure 20 The battle of Naseby, about 1p.m.

In the centre the Royalist infantry, although heavily outnumbered and advancing uphill, was initially successful, but determined resistance put up by Major-General Skippon's regiment on the extreme left of the New Model front line, and the unexpected sight of a second line when they reached the top of the hill, caused the attack to grind to a halt.[7] The Royalist infantry reserve did not move forwards, possibly because Rupert, downcast by the disaster that had occurred on the left wing, thought it best to leave them where they were to protect the army's retreat. However, if this was his intention, it was overtaken by events as Fairfax launched his uncommitted right-wing cavalry and infantry against both regiments. Rupert had no cavalry left with which to support his infantry reserves, and they were over-whelmed after a very fierce fight. As a consequence, the main body of the

Royalist infantry found itself with enemy troops to the front and the rear.[8] Although Maurice's horse were now beginning to return to the battlefield shadowed by the New Model cavalry they had defeated, they were in no state to rescue anybody, whereupon the king's infantry, veterans and impressed men alike, surrendered. While this was happening, Rupert and the king were doing all they could to put their scattered cavalry in order, but when Fairfax led forward the whole of his army to confront them, they simply fled in the direction of Leicester pursued by Cromwell's horsemen.[9]

Notes

1 BL Additional ms 16370, 63; Sprigg, *Anglia Rediviva*, 1st edn; Warburton, *Memoirs* III, 105; Symonds, *Diary*, 165–6, 186, 193; Slingsby, *Diary*, 150–1; Walker, *Historical Discourses*, 130.

2 Sprigg, *Anglia Rediviva*, 1st edn; TT E288 25, 38.

3 Walker, *Historical Discourses*, 130; Wilts CRO 413/444A 45.

4 *Ibid.*; Staffs CRO DW 1778 Ii, 56; Carte, *Letters*, 128.

5 Slingsby, *Diary*, 150–2; Walker, *Historical Discourses*, 130–1; Symonds, *Diary*, 193.

6 Sprigg, *Anglia Rediviva*, 39–40; Slingsby, *Diary*, 153; Clarendon, *Great Rebellion* ix, 36; Wilts CRO 413/444A 45; Walker, *Historical Discourses*, 131.

7 *Ibid.*, 130; TT E288 25; Young, *Naseby*, 87.

8 Sprigg, *Anglia Rediviva*, 43; TT E288 26; TT E289 3.

9 Walker, *Historical Discourses*, 130–1; Slingsby, *Diary*, 152; HMC Ormonde ms II ns, 386; TT E288 28, 37, 38.

chapter XXII

Langport and beyond

Sir Thomas Fairfax followed up his victory at Naseby not by pursuing the defeated king but by laying siege to Leicester. As a result, Charles was able to make his way safely across the Midlands, arriving at Hereford on the following day. Soon afterwards, he was joined by Charles Gerard and his corps from southwest Wales. Possibly as many as 4,000 horse had escaped from Naseby, which meant that, even after he had sent what was left of the Newark and Midlands horse back to their garrisons, the king was still in command of an army of 5,000–6,000 men. This he had every intention of using in an offensive capacity. Sir William Vaughan was sent into Shropshire, where he won a notable victory over the local Parliamentarians at High Ercall, capturing their commander and over 200 men, while Prince Maurice was sent to secure Worcester and its bridge over the Severn, the most important staging post on the way to Bristol or Oxford. On 23rd June, the council of war decided to 'form the body of a new army' by raising 6,500 infantry in South Wales and the border counties and adding to them 800 men already raised in North Wales.[1] Soon afterwards, it was agreed that the best strategy for turning the tables on the New Model was to assemble as many troops as possible in the west of England, where Goring still had a force of 5,000 foot and 4,000 horse besieging Taunton. Gerard's corps and the newly raised infantry were to be transported across the Bristol Channel to join him, while the cavalry that the king had with him, now under Gerard's command as lieutenant-general of horse, were to take the overland route via Worcester to Devizes in Wiltshire, where they were to await further orders. Rupert himself then went first to Barnstaple to discuss strategy with the Prince of Wales's council and then to Bristol to prepare

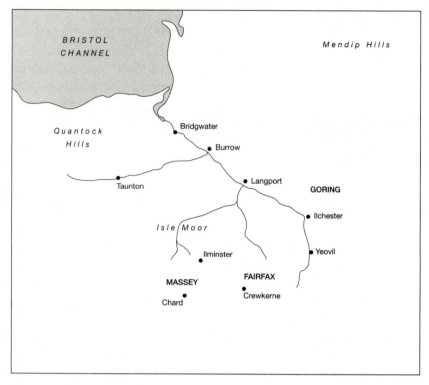

Map 7 The Langport campaign, July 1645

the garrison for a possible siege if that should be Fairfax's next destination, but also for the king's arrival once all the other pieces on the chessboard were in place. This frantic activity probably helps to explain the mood of optimism that pervades the letters written by Rupert, Digby and the king in late June, but even if Wales did produce infantry in the numbers anticipated, it is difficult to see how they could have been armed at such short notice. Hutton writes confidently about Richard Foley's ironworks turning out weapons for them, but his furnaces and forges in Shropshire and Worcestershire could supply only pike heads and cast iron objects like cannonballs, not muskets. Rupert was concerned (wrongly) about munitions and wrote to this effect to an unknown correspondent on 5th July, but he nevertheless expected there to be an army of 8,000 foot and 7,000 horse in Somerset shortly. However, success also depended on the speed with which Parliament and its general understood, and then responded to, the new strategic plan.[2]

After the surrender of Leicester on 18th June, Fairfax had two possible courses of action for keeping up pressure on the Royalists. He could follow the king into the Welsh borderland and seek to destroy what was left of the field army, or else he could relieve Taunton and in the process draw Goring's army into a set-piece battle. Fairfax's initial preference, as expressed in a letter to Massey written before Naseby, had been to attack Goring after defeating the king, but with Charles in the Welsh borderland with a substantial force, and the Royalists in control of Worcester bridge, advancing into the west of England would involve an element of risk. He therefore asked for Parliament's formal approval. In the meantime, the New Model moved rapidly southwards, but in such a direction as to keep both options open. As the days passed and no instructions arrived from Westminster, so Fairfax became less sure of himself, conceding in a letter written from Lechlade that it might be best to march towards Wales. Parliament's reply did not arrive until 30th June, by which time the New Model had reached Marlborough, but it did endorse Fairfax's original plan. The delay in responding may have been caused by some elements in Parliament trying to regain control over day-to-day strategy, but the more important reason was the lack of accurate intelligence. By the end of June the situation had clarified. It was clear that the king intended to reinforce Goring rather than march into the Midlands, thus making the southwest even more clearly the location for the next major clash between the two sides. Nevertheless, the Scottish army was on the march to Hereford to ensure that the principal route out of South Wales for the king's cavalry was firmly blocked. However, Parliament also hedged its bets. Fairfax was to advance into the west in such a manner as not to leave the south and east of England open to attack.[3]

By late June, the other measure for the relief of Taunton was making better progress. Massey had reached Shaftesbury in Dorset with a force of between 2,000 and 3,000 horse and dragoons and was heading for Lyme, presumably to pick up some infantry from the garrison there. In response, Goring abandoned the siege and was advancing to Chard to attack him when he learned that the New Model was approaching. He then withdrew to a position on the other side of the Rivers Yeo and Parrett, which run in a southeasterly direction across central Somerset from Bridgwater to Yeovil. The river line could be crossed in only a limited number of places, most of which were guarded by Royalist garrisons, but even when it had been crossed, the tributaries of the two rivers, and the extensive areas of marshland on both banks, gave great advantage to the defence. By 5th July the

New Model had reached Beaminster, only 25 miles from Taunton, with Massey nearby at Axminster. On the 6th, the combined armies advanced to Ilminster and Crewkerne, where they met Weldon's force, which had escaped from Taunton. This raised the number of soldiers under Fairfax's command to 17,000 or more, almost twice the number Goring could muster, as troops from South Wales were only just beginning to cross the water. However, it was difficult for Fairfax to secure victuals for his two armies in south and west Somerset because of the large number of soldiers that had been quartered there from March onwards. It was therefore in Sir Thomas's best interests to engage Goring in battle as quickly as possible and move elsewhere.[4]

The Royalist army in Somerset, on the other hand, was keen to avoid battle at all costs. The king's new strategy for winning the war required two or three weeks' grace to give time for all the new infantry regiments to be transported across the Bristol Channel. Goring was therefore to fall back slowly towards Bridgwater, the port through which most of the troops were to be shipped, rather than into the enclosed country around Tiverton or over the Mendip Hills to Bristol.[5] For several days, the Royalist general successfully used the rivers and wetlands of the vale of Taunton to wear down the two armies facing him. However, on 9th July his main position at Yeovil was outflanked when some of his cavalry brigades were taken by surprise and routed on Isle Moor by General Massey, reinforced by some New Model cavalry and dragoons. With Parliamentary troops now between Taunton and Bridgwater, Goring's army base was open to attack from the west, whereupon the Royalist army retreated from Yeovil to Langport with the intention of moving to Burrow the following day. However, a surprise attack by a commanded party of musketeers under Colonel Rainsborough assisted by three troops of New Model horse drove the Royalists from their position as they were in the process of withdrawing. Goring's infantry escaped to the west bank of the River Parrett, breaking down Langport bridge behind them, but his cavalry were unable to cross the river and as a result were very severely beaten up in the pursuit. After the battle, Parliamentary sources claimed that, although few Royalists had been slain and only two cannon captured, between 1,000 and 2,000 cavalrymen had been taken prisoner. The disaster would have been even greater had Fairfax made more imaginative use of Massey's force. If it had been ordered to advance on Bridgwater from the southwest rather than move in an easterly direction to reinforce the New Model, it could have intercepted and destroyed the Royalist foot

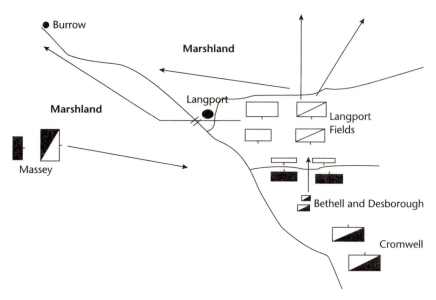

Figure 21 The battle of Langport 1

before they reached the town, as both formations were on the same side of the Parrett.

Two days after the encounter at Langport, Goring ordered what was left of his army, 2,500 horse and 3,000–4,000 infantry, to retreat westwards to Barnstaple rather than eastwards towards Bristol. This was probably the best course of action, as it was twice as far to the safety of the Mendips as it was to that of the Quantocks. Moreover, although the country people attacked his troops as they retired, Goring had at least retained a balanced army of some size. In his letter to Lord Digby reporting the battle, Goring claimed to be confident of defending Devon and Cornwall from the New Model, provided that it did not pursue him too rapidly and that he was able to draw on the support of Sir Richard Grenville's troops besieging Plymouth.[6] The king's advisers went along with this strategy, particularly when it became clear that Fairfax had decided to lay siege to Bridgwater, not pursue Goring. The town was expected to hold out for a number of weeks, but it surrendered on 23rd July after a number of vigorous assaults by the New Model Army. As a result, the Royalists lost large quantities of military stores, Goring's artillery train and another thousand soldiers.[7]

The king ordered a halt to the movement of cavalry overland into the west of England on hearing of the setback at Langport. After the fall of

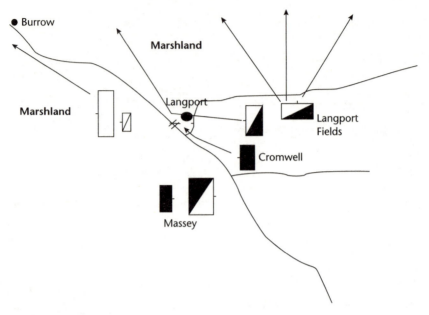

Figure 22 The battle of Langport 2

Bridgwater, he decided that it would be too dangerous for him to cross the Severn estuary to Bristol, as Fairfax's next move might be to lay siege to the city. However, there was no point in remaining in South Wales. The landed gentry of Glamorgan had begun to distance themselves from the Royalist cause and were making difficulties about raising more men. Putting the infantry that had been raised into Bristol and the Welsh borderland garrisons, the king turned northeastwards early in August, heading for Yorkshire in the hope of finally putting into effect Rupert's plans for the spring campaign. Avoiding the Scottish army, which by then was besieging Hereford, he reached Doncaster on the 17th but with fewer than 3,000 men under his command had to fall back on the garrison at Newark after three days in the face of a revitalized Northern army under a professional soldier just returned from the continent, Sydenham Poyntz, who had replaced Lord Fairfax. He was also threatened by a force of 4,000 Scottish cavalry under David Leslie, which had set off from Herefordshire on 13th August, not primarily to chase the king but to return to Scotland and put an end to Montrose's army. Fearful that the Scots were in hot pursuit, Charles's little army hurried south from Newark to Oxford. On its way, it at last invaded the Eastern Association. For two days the Royalist cavalry plundered the countryside around Huntingdon, but it was not strong enough to cause any serious damage and resumed its march on receiving intelligence that local forces were approaching from the direction of Cambridge.[8]

Fairfax's capture of Bridgwater was as fundamental to his own grand strategy as its retention had been to the king's. Parliament's general had appreciated that with the town in the hands of the New Model Army he was a long way towards establishing a chain of garrisons across the narrowest part of the southwestern peninsula, which would make it difficult for Goring to break out or for the king to attempt a break-in, especially if Massey's forces were quartered along the Dorset/Somerset border, thus fulfilling a similar function to that of the Scots' army in the Wye valley. The capture of Bath and Sherborne in late July completed the chain. With its western flank secure, the New Model Army could return east and deal with the remaining important Royalist garrisons in southern England without having to worry about Goring attacking it from the rear. Over the next two months, Bristol fell to an assault very similar to that which Rupert had launched against it in 1643, while Devizes, Winchester and Basing House surrendered on terms or were stormed. By mid-October, the New Model was ready to invade Devon and Cornwall in a campaign that was to last five months. In the final year of the war, the armies did not go into winter quarters.[9]

Long before the king's return to Oxford on 28th August, the Great Civil War was to all intents and purposes over. Rupert had recognized this a month earlier when he wrote to the Duke of Richmond with the intention that his views reach the king's ear via a friend rather than an enemy. Rupert's advice was that Charles 'hath now no way left to preserve his posterity, kingdom and nobility than by a treaty'. In one respect, the military one, he was right. From the resources he still possessed in England and Wales, the king could not assemble an army large enough and proficient enough to defeat the New Model Army, and the prospect of obtaining more troops from Ireland, never more than hopeful, was now very remote indeed. The English forces there had already been stripped to the bone, and the Irish Catholic rebels had set terms that were too high for Charles to accept.[10] Rupert also had severe reservations about the king's going to Scotland to join Montrose. Not only did he have misgivings about Charles's chances of reaching there, he also felt that news of the king's departure would discourage his English and Welsh supporters.[11] What he did not mention were the queen's efforts to gain military support on the Continent, probably because he saw them as mere fantasy. France, the most hopeful prospect given Henrietta Maria's parentage, was fully occupied fighting Spain, and in the closing stages of the Thirty Years War mercenary brigades could obtain easier employment in Germany than in England.[12]

Rupert was right to be sceptical that any good could come out of Scotland. Up to the time he wrote to Richmond, Montrose's string of victories had had a good impact on Royalist morale but little indirect and no direct effect on the progress of the war in England and Wales. Admittedly, fears about Montrose had been the principal factor delaying the Scottish army's participation in the 1645 campaign in England, but Fairfax had been able to defeat the king's forces at Naseby and Langport without its assistance. Five months later, Leven's troops suffered the ignominy of being on the receiving end of the last, albeit small, Royalist strategic triumph. As the king's cavalry headed north once more in early September, this time to relieve the besieged garrison at Chester, the Scottish general kept well out of their way, claiming that he was defenceless as most of his cavalry were in Scotland with General Leslie. However, this has to be weighed in the balance against the fact that Leslie's cavalry brought an end to the king's Scottish strategy by destroying Montrose's army at Philiphaugh in the Borders on the 13th of the month.[13]

However, politically Rupert was wrong, because he did not take into account the ideological dimension. The English Civil War was not a war for territory but for principles. Neither the king nor Parliament could accept a peace in which they had to concede more than they had put on the table at Uxbridge in February, and if anything Parliament's position had hardened. The Scots seemed more amenable to concessions insofar as the powers of the Crown were concerned, but they demanded a Presbyterian Church in England, which would run its own affairs independent of royal authority. However, Charles would not agree to a Presbyterian Church, on the grounds of both constitutional principle and theological conviction. In his reply to Rupert, the king recognized that by any rational criteria his military position was hopeless.

you had full reason for your advice. For I confess that speaking as a mere soldier or statesman, I must say there is no probability but of my ruin. Yet as a Christian I must tell you that God will not suffer rebels and traitors to prosper, nor this cause to be overthrown, and whatever personal punishment it shall please him to inflict on me must not make me repine, let alone give over this quarrel.[14]

Charles's only hope, therefore, was for a miracle, and his strategy for the rest of the war, being predicated on the supernatural, lost touch with reality. Despite Montrose's overthrow, Digby persisted in arguing for a military incursion into Scotland. He got his way, but his military career and that of what was left of the Northern Horse ended at Annan Moor near Dumfries in early November. The Irish strategy, on the other hand, was on the cards insofar as Charles was concerned until the war's end. As a result, most of what was left of the field army was quartered in the Welsh borders in the late autumn and early winter of 1645 and was employed in a series of increasingly hopeless attempts to prevent Chester surrendering to Sir William Brereton. When the city finally fell in February 1646, the royal army, reinforced by what the remaining garrisons in the Midlands could spare, tried to make its way over the Cotswolds to Oxford but was caught by local forces at Stow on the Wold on 20th March and destroyed. A week earlier the Western army, back under Hopton's command once more after Goring had left for France in November, surrendered to the New Model Army at Truro in Cornwall after losing a final battle at Torrington in February. In his final campaign of the Great Civil War, Fairfax showed that he was better at the cut and thrust of active warfare than the dogged pursuit of a demoralized enemy. Gentles attributes his slowness to lack of resources, the winter weather and the small size of the force he had at his disposal, little larger than that of the enemy, but the fumbling way in which the siege of Exeter was conducted points to exhaustion.[15]

Less than a month after the battle of Stow the king surrendered to the Scottish army, which at the time was besieging Newark. In recognition that the war was over, he ordered his remaining garrisons to surrender. Not all obeyed. As a result, hostilities dragged on into 1647, when the last castles on the mainland of England and Wales, Holt and Harlech, gave up the struggle in January and March, respectively, by which time divisions within the victorious alliance were preparing the way for a second civil war.

Notes

1 Walker, *Historical Discourses*, 116; *Mercurius Aulicus*, 1661–3; Warburton, *Memoirs* III, 119–21.

2 Bell, *Memoirs*, 235; BL Harleian ms 6802, 56; BL Harleian ms 6852, 120; BL Additional ms 18738, 80; Evelyn, *Diary* IV, 153; Staffs CRO DW1778 Ii 55; Warburton, *Memoirs* III, 145–6.

3 Bodleian Firth ms C8, 300–1; Ellis, *Letters*, 3rd series 4, 259; Gardiner, *Great Civil War* II, 255; CSP Domestic 1644–5, 610, 617, 652; Rushworth, *Historical Collections* VI, 1; BL Harleian ms 166, 220–1; LJ VI 263.

4 Warburton, *Memoirs* III, 125; Sanford, *Great Rebellion*, 625; Bodleian Clarendon ms 24, 200; Sprigg, *Anglia Rediviva*, 61–7; TT E292 16.

5 BL Harleian ms 6804, 52; *ibid.*, Harleian ms 6852, 120, 280–1; Bell, *Memoirs*, 235; Carte, *Letters*, 131.

6 BL Additional ms 18982, 70; BL additional ms 18978, 204; Bodleian Firth ms C8, 301–2; *ibid.*, Wood Pamphlets, 378 9.

7 Sprigg, *Anglia Rediviva*, 81–2.

8 Symonds, *Diary*, 210–11; Bell, *Memoirs*, 239; CSP Domestic 1645–7, 62; BL Harleian ms 6852, 80–1; HMC Portland I, 259–60, 263, 271–3; Hutton, *Royalist War Effort*, 183–5; Symonds, *Diary*, 211–18; HMC Ormonde ms II ns, 387.

9 Gentles, *New Model Army*, 70–2, 76–8.

10 Warburton, *Memoirs* III, 149, 151; Petrie, *Letters of Charles I*, 155.

11 Staffs CRO DW 1778 Ii 57; Warburton, *Memoirs* III, 149.

12 Nevertheless, her schemes alarmed Parliament from time to time between October 1644 and March 1646 (CSP Domestic 1644–45, 154; Sanford, *Great Rebellion*, 624; Gentles, *New Model Army*, 83).

13 Birch, *Military Memoir*, 23–30; Symonds, *Diary*, 232; Hutton, *Royalist War Effort*, 186–7; Barrett, *Cavaliers*, 147–50.

14 Petrie, *Charles I and Rupert*, 9; Rushworth, *Historical Collections* VI, 132.

15 CSP Domestic 1645–47, 220; Gentles, *New Model Army*, 78–82; Rushworth, *Historical Collections* VI, 133–4.

PART VII

Tactics

chapter XXIII

Triumph on the battlefield

The commanders on both sides during the Great Civil War were fully aware of the military reforms described in Chapter III, adapted them to English circumstances and then modified them in the light of experience. Our objective in this chapter is not to compare battlefield tactics and check them against the major and minor innovations associated with Dutch and Swedish military practice, interesting though that may be, but to ascertain the extent to which tactical developments on their own were responsible for Parliament's victory and the king's defeat.

As Parliament had control of the royal arsenals and the ironworks of the Weald of Kent, it was able to equip its armies with large numbers of good-quality cannon from the start of the war. The Earl of Essex, for example, took at least thirty-seven with him on the Edgehill campaign and lost forty-two at Lostwithiel. The king lagged behind initially, but by the time of the Gloucester campaign he too had a formidable train of artillery. However, on the battlefield the generals were never able to lure enemy forces into a position in which they could pound them into submission using the concentrated fire of their cannon.[1] Thus artillery on its own was no more a winner of battles in the Great Civil War than elsewhere in Europe at the time, and this is reflected in contemporary comment. Cannon 'caused more terror than execution', opined one Parliamentary commander, and in the words of another seventeenth-century writer, 'great artillery seldom or never hurts'.[2] As for killing power, a Royalist officer at the first battle of Newbury commented on the rareness of the sight of six dead enemy infantrymen, whose heads had been taken off by a single round.[3]

Bombardments by heavy cannon preceded the battles of Edgehill and Marston Moor and the second battle of Newbury, but they had no positive impact on the outcome of any of them. Indeed, it could be argued that Waller's decision to spend up to an hour bombarding the western flank of the Royalist position at Speen before attacking brought nightfall that much closer and possibly saved the king's army from being overwhelmed. At the first battle of Newbury a preliminary bombardment would have been counter-productive, as Essex wanted to conceal his troop movements from the enemy for as long as possible. At Naseby, on the other hand, the generals on both sides decided that an initial softening up by the heavy cannon was not needed. After the battle, a Parliamentarian wrote that 'the ordnance began to play, but that [as] at Marston Moor and other places it was but a loss of time', while the Royalists did not deign to reply, so anxious were they for the fighting to begin (although afterwards Lord Digby described this as a stupid mistake in an attempt to discredit Prince Rupert).[4] Only at Langport was cannon fire of some significance. A bombardment by Fairfax's artillery train knocked out two cannons guarding the top of a lane along which he intended the New Model Army cavalry to charge.

The most interesting use of artillery in a major engagement in the Great Civil War was at the first battle of Newbury, where, for the first and only time, both sides were able to use roads and tracks to move light and heavy cannon quite rapidly into the central part of the battlefield once the fighting had begun. Indeed, if Essex had not been able to establish an artillery position defending the northeast corner of Wash Common, his vanguard might have been unable to repulse the massed Royalist assaults on their position and been pushed back in defeat into the valley of the Kennet. The battle also provides the first example in the war of small artillery pieces operating with infantry and cavalry units in the Swedish manner. The red regiment of the London trained bands, for example, suffered badly from the artillery fire that accompanied Royalist cavalry attacks and could do nothing about it because its own field pieces were slow to arrive, while several small cannons were lost at the top end of Wash common when one of Essex's infantry regiments retreated.[5] Similarly, at Cheriton, Waller used light cannon to reinforce the mixed force of infantry and cavalry that he had moved into Cheriton wood and its surroundings to outflank the Royalist advance guard, but they were not flexible enough to defend it when Hopton altered the direction of his attack. Later, however, assaults by the Royalist cavalry brigades on the centre of Sir William Waller's position seem to have been blunted in part by artillery fire; and at the end of the day it was Waller's bringing forward of his cannon to bombard the hill to which the enemy had retreated that caused their final withdrawal.[6] However, the length of time it took to move the cannon to their new position gave Forth and Hopton the breathing space in which to plan a structured and, in the event, very successful withdrawal.

Infantry tactics drew heavily on continental models. At Edgehill, after a heated discussion, the king's generals decided to draw up in the Swedish manner rather than the Dutch. However, at that stage in the war, their musketeers cannot have acquired sufficient training and experience for all six ranks to fire a simultaneous volley. On the other hand, requiring them to rotate firing by rank in the Dutch manner may have caused even greater confusion. Another possible reason for preferring the Swedish model was that muskets were in short supply in some of the king's regiments, and the Swedish formation incorporated a higher ratio of pikemen to musketeers (although for a quite different reason). However, the five large battalions thus formed were incapable of giving one another supporting fire once the fighting started, as the two second-line battalions moved forward to fill the gaps between the three to their front, thus creating one continuous line. The Earl of Essex drew up his infantry in three large bodies, each containing about 3,000 men, an antiquated type of formation, which also probably reflected a lack of confidence in his foot soldiers' level of training. However, half an hour after the fighting began, what was left of his infantry also formed up in a line, and, to the amazement of the future King James II, the musketeers of both sides spent the rest of the encounter firing almost continuously at one another in the open rather than taking cover.[7]

Thereafter, Royalist and Parliamentary generals showed considerable flexibility in fitting their tactics to the landscape and considerable expertise in moving battalions around during the course of a battle, particularly in encounter-type engagements like Cropredy Bridge, where armies did not have the time or the space to draw up in the orthodox cavalry–infantry–cavalry formation. From the start, however, the Parliamentary field armies proved more competent in combining infantry and cavalry units in the continental manner to destroy parts of the opposing army. Sir William Balfour and the Earl of Essex showed the way at Edgehill with the attack on Sir Nicholas Byron's brigade. A similar process can be seen at work in the destruction of Prince Rupert's regiment of foot at Naseby, and on a much larger scale at Marston Moor, where the cavalry and infantry of the Eastern

Association army combined with some Scottish cavalry and dragoons in the closing stages of the battle to destroy the Royalist infantry that remained in the field. But combined operations did not always work. Balfour's attack on the Royalist left wing at the second battle of Newbury, for example, although initially successful, was repulsed with heavy losses before night fell.

The king's commanders, on the other hand, tended to show greater imagination in the use of the infantry on its own. Commanded parties of musketeers were used as shock troops in battles as well as during the course of campaigns, at first unsuccessfully, as in the initial attack on Round Hill during the first battle of Newbury, but later with much greater success, as in the Newark[8] and Severn valley campaigns in March and June 1644 and in the capture of Cheriton Wood. However, the most effective use of musketeers on their own in the entire war was by Fairfax at Langport, where the battle was won as much by the efforts of Rainsborough's men driving back the Royalist foot opposing them from hedge to hedge and then breaking into the ranks of the Earl of Cleveland's brigade of horse, as by the more spectacular eruption of three troops of New Model cavalry into the midst of Goring's army. Evidence of the skill of the king's infantry after two years of war can be seen in the successful defence of Shaw House by Sir George Lisle's brigade against overwhelming numbers during the second battle of Newbury. The king's veteran infantry have also been praised for their performance in the opening stages of the battle of Naseby,[9] where they pushed back the first line of the opposing foot, which outnumbered them, inflicting heavy casualties. However, the veterans would not have been able to win the battle by their own efforts had the cavalry engagements on the wings taken longer to resolve. When they came unexpectedly upon a second line of enemy infantry, their attack faltered. But there were battles in the Great Civil War that were won by the infantry. The engagement at Nantwich in January 1644 between Lord Byron's troops and a scratch force of northerners led by Sir Thomas Fairfax was decided almost entirely by a series of infantry engagements in a countryside dominated by small fields and watercourses where cavalry were at an obvious disadvantage.[10] At Cheriton, however, Waller's infantry managed to win a major encounter in more open country when the Parliamentarians pushed the outnumbered Royalist foot back relentlessly on the right wing and on the left, bypassing the cavalry of both sides caught up in a vast *melée* in the centre of the battlefield.

In the Great Civil War, the cavalry of both sides were very largely harquebusiers like those of Gustavus Adolphus, although other types do occur. At Edgehill, the charges of Essex's lifeguard, the *jeunesse dorée* of the Parliamentary army mounted on the best horses, showed what cuirassiers could do if given the opportunity to play to their strengths, that is short periods of violent activity interspersed with long periods for rest and recovery.[11] On the other hand, the experience of Sir Arthur Haselrig's 'lobsters' at Roundway Down in July 1643 showed that cuirassiers were as easily routed as the rest of Parliament's horse at the time, and although the regiment performed better at Cheriton, it was not incorporated into the New Model Army in 1645. Indeed, by the last year of the war, neither side had any more than the odd troop of cuirassiers still in arms.

There were no lancers in the English field armies, but the Scottish army contained several regiments armed with lances, which played an important, possibly crucial, role in the allied victory at Marston Moor. However, they were certainly not heavy cavalry, as they were mounted on ponies and can have worn only a small amount of body armour. It was well understood at the time that they could not stand up to harquebusiers in equal combat, which explains why they were in the reserve line, and also why the Scots quickly abandoned the lance when they acquired decent-sized horses in any numbers.[12]

Both sides employed dragoons in considerable numbers at the start of the war, but as time passed those regiments that survived tended to be converted into infantry or cavalry units. There was a single regiment of dragoons in the New Model Army, whose colonel claimed they performed well at Naseby, but there were no Royalist dragoons in the main field army in 1645. Prince Rupert seems even to have lost interest in his own regiment, which remained in the west of England with George Goring.[13]

However, the two sides diverged in the ways in which they used cavalry on the battlefield. In none of the major battles did the Parliamentarians station a cavalry reserve of any size behind the army, or station any horse in the centre as direct support for the infantry. Instead, the reserves formed up behind the two wings in every major battle in open country. At Edgehill, the fact that Balfour's and Stapleton's troops acted as a form of central reserve was probably an illusion. Insofar as the former were concerned, it was probably an accident that they were where they were at the start of the battle, whereas the latter may have been kept out of the way because of their poor performance at Powick bridge.[14] The king's generals, on the other hand, failed to win a decisive victory at Edgehill because they kept all their horse on the wings, with the result that the reserve squadrons in the second line ignored their orders to remain where they were and chased after the victorious first line of horse. That mistake was never made again. At Roundway Down, Lord Wilmot and Prince Maurice kept their reserves in the rear and used them to very good effect to stop a counter-charge.[15] At the first battle of Newbury, there was plenty of cavalry action in which the horse were sometimes substituted for infantry in assaults on enemy positions, but the Royalist horse was not drawn up in the orthodox manner, that is flanking the infantry, because of the shape of the Parliamentary attack. Insofar as there was a cavalry reserve, it was stationed on the green as a precaution against the enemy left wing attempting to break through defences in the Kennet valley. However, at Marston Moor Prince Rupert adopted a more thorough-going Swedish model, that is strong forces on both wings but a single cavalry brigade in the centre with the infantry and another placed in reserve behind the army with the prince's lifeguard of horse, which could be used wherever it was needed on the battlefield. Despite the Royalist defeat, the way in which the cavalry had been deployed must have been regarded as a success, as the cavalry were to have drawn up in a very similar manner in the battle that never happened, the third battle of Newbury. At Naseby, Rupert went a stage further with the reserve in the third line increased to almost 1,000 men and the brigade stationed among the infantry in a support role split up into two or three divisions. In his diary, the prince gives only the haziest indication as to why he used so complex a formation, but whatever the plan it failed completely, as he was not present when the reserve was brought into action. Against his orders, its components were fed into the battle in penny numbers and, unlike at Marston Moor, it did not succeed even temporarily in stemming the enemy advance.

From the start, Rupert trained his troopers to take an active role on the battlefield. In the words of Richard Bulstrode, who fought with the king's lifeguard of horse at Edgehill:

Prince Rupert passed from one wing to the other, giving positive orders to the Horse to march as close as possible keeping their ranks with sword in hand . . . without firing either carbine or pistol, till we broke in amongst the enemy and then make use of our firearms as need should require, which order was punctually obeyed.[16]

This reflected Swedish practice, but the length of the charge and the speed at which it was delivered suggests Polish or French influences. It remained Royalist practice to charge the enemy in this manner for the rest of the war when they were given the opportunity, but they were also capable of biding their time, as on the left wing at Marston Moor, where Goring timed his charge so that it hit the enemy as they were making their way across a patch of difficult ground. One significant change in Royalist tactics during the war, which had strong Swedish precedents, involved stationing small bodies of musketeers among the cavalry on both wings, thus increasing their firepower if they were not intending to charge. The casualties among his cavalry caused by the Royalist musketeers was a matter of comment in Fairfax's account of Marston Moor, but he did not himself employ them in that manner at Naseby, a sure sign that he intended to charge the Royalists, not wait to be charged. De Gomme's plans of the Royalist battle formation at Naseby show Rupert deploying musketeers among the horse on the right and left wings as at Marston Moor, but they do not appear in Streeter's plan. Possibly it was Rupert's original intention to do so, but the decision to attack on both wings meant that they would have served no useful purpose, while weakening the infantry formation.

The orders given to the Parliamentary horse at Edgehill were very different. The right wing was to remain stationary in the hope that the fire of its dragoons and musketeers would blunt the Royalist charge. The left may have been on the move as Rupert charged, but they fired their pistols and carbines at too great a distance to have any real effect.[17] Both suggest Dutch practice, and both were completely unsuccessful.[18] However, despite what had happened at Edgehill, army commanders in the south of England were reluctant to change. Although individual units charged or counter-charged during a battle when the opportunity offered, the wing as a whole tended to wait for the Royalist attack and then to fire on them as they approached. Essex's horse behaved in this way at the first battle of Newbury, and Waller's at Roundway Down[19] and Cheriton. It was not until the second battle of Newbury that both wings advanced on the enemy rather than waiting to be attacked.

The deployment of cavalry on the battlefield in a defensive formation had come to an end a year earlier in the north of England, and it is to Oliver Cromwell's credit that the Eastern Association horse were the first to abandon the Dutch model, although Sir Thomas Fairfax was very quick to follow suit. Insofar as Cromwell was concerned, the penny seems to have dropped almost by accident at the battle of Grantham in May 1643. He describes the moment of enlightenment as follows:

After we had stood a little above musket shot the one body from the other . . . for the space of half an hour or more, they not advancing towards us, we agreed to charge them . . . and came on with our troops at a pretty round trot, they standing firm to receive us, and our men charging fiercely upon them by God's providence they were immediately routed and ran all away, and we had the execution of them two or three miles.

However, Cromwell did not slavishly copy Prince Rupert's Swedish model with a Franco-Polish gloss. Cromwell was concerned with keeping his troops in formation from the very beginning. He almost certainly saw the drawbacks of the charge taken at the gallop in terms of maintaining close order and controlling his men. He also never employed musketeers interspersed with his horse squadrons, as they could easily get in the way and disrupt the cavalry formations' close order. Finally, he never positioned a cavalry reserve behind the infantry to be used as appropriate. This may have been an accidental consequence of his never being in overall command of an army during the Great Civil War with *carte blanche* to place his cavalry where he wished. On the other hand, he did claim that Fairfax left him in complete charge of the cavalry at Naseby.

At the next engagement, at Gainsborough two months later, both sides charged, but Cromwell's men, although surprised, were able to deploy quickly from column into line while 'keeping close order', that is each man keeping cheek by jowl with his neighbour, thus creating an equine battering ram that would gain momentum as the horse picked up speed in the charge. Once the main body of enemy horse had been routed, Cromwell allowed most of his cavalry to pursue the enemy, but he successfully recalled three troops of his own regiment and used them to rout the Royalist reserves. These are the first sign of Cromwell's training of his men having an effect on the outcome of an action.[20] At Winceby, the third battle to take place in Lincolnshire in 1643, Cromwell was unhorsed when both sides charged. As a result his account of the engagement lacks detail, but Fairfax's Yorkshire horse seem to have won the engagement by charging the enemy in the flank while they were engaged in a *melée* with the Eastern Association horse. A Royalist account of the battle described Cromwell's men as absorbing the initial shock with great success and as being 'very good and extraordinarily armed'. Oliver himself was very sound

on the latter point: 'If a man has not got good weapons, horse and har-
ness, he is naught'.[21]

Cromwell commanded an entire wing of between 3,000 and 4,000
horse at Marston Moor in what was probably the biggest cavalry engagement of the war. There, despite being charged in the flank, he not only
routed the Royalists facing him in a fight lasting half an hour, he also stopped
his men pursuing the enemy. They then turned to the right and attacked
those regiments of enemy horse that were still on the battlefield in a manoeuvre closely resembling one that the Duke of Enghien had used to
destroy the Spanish cavalry at Rocroi the year before.[22] In the process,
Cromwell turned a near disaster into an undoubted victory.

Given that all Cromwell's horse had been committed in the first stage
of the engagement, it is difficult to understand how he could have kept
them together to such an extent that they were capable almost immediately of marching off in a different direction in good order. All that we can
imagine is that when the Royalist right wing fled, Cromwell's cavalry were
at a virtual standstill. If so, this makes it highly likely that Scottish claims
that David Leslie's three regiments of lancers, drawn up in reserve immediately behind the Eastern Association horse, charged the Royalists in the flank
and put them to flight are correct.[23] Otherwise, if the enemy horse had
broken slowly or rapidly, Cromwell's formation would have splintered as
one Royalist troop after another turned tail.

Cromwell's triumph at Naseby was far less spectacular, and also far
less of a personal achievement, given the New Model Army's strength in
cavalry and Rupert's orders for the Northern Horse to leave their good
defensive position and advance to attack him on an uphill slope. On this
occasion, despite numerous claims to that effect, Cromwell did not first
rout the enemy horse and then turn on the enemy infantry. The first and
part of his second line defeated the Northern Horse, and the Newark
brigade sent to their support. The assault on the enemy infantry reserves
that followed was carried out by the rest of the second line, supported by
the third line. The first regiments to charge were almost certainly no longer
in close order and therefore unlikely to have been able to make a successful attack on the Royalist infantry. The conflict had been quite lengthy, there
had been numerous casualties, and the ground over which they had fought
– a rabbit warren, furze bushes, and steep, though short, inclines – must
have disrupted their formation. However, the discipline of those who had
routed the Northern Horse was such that they did not pursue the enemy

over the horizon but stopped in a position where they could watch their movements and ensure that they took no further part in the fight.

As battlefield tacticians, Royalist cavalry generals have been compared unfavourably with Cromwell in one important respect. Although their horse often routed the enemy wing facing them, the commanders were unable to control their men, who rode off in pursuit of the fleeing Parliamentarians or in search of plunder instead of regrouping and turning their attention to the enemy infantry formations. Not surprisingly, this opinion was first publicized by Clarendon, the originator of so many errors and half-truths about the Royalist army and its commanders.[24] Barratt has recently challenged this, and we agree with his rather tentative conclusions.[25] At Marston Moor, the second line of the Royalist left wing did almost exactly what Cromwell's wing did at Naseby. While the first line followed the enemy to prevent their reforming, it turned on the enemy infantry. At Naseby, the victorious Royalist right wing is alleged to have lost complete control as at Edgehill and attacked the New Model baggage train instead of reordering itself and returning to the battlefield. We have suggested that it may have done this because Parliamentary infantry regiments were blocking the most direct route for an attack on the rear of Cromwell's wing, but we also acknowledge that they were unlikely to have been able to do much against the enemy other than hope to take them by surprise, as the length of the encounter must have meant that they were no longer in close order.

Insofar as tactics are concerned, it therefore seems most unlikely that Parliament would have won the Great Civil War as soon as it did without the change in cavalry tactics introduced by Oliver Cromwell. Similarly, it is becoming increasingly clear that the relative failure of the Royalist horse on the battlefield from Cheriton onwards was not because they combined lack of discipline and training with slavish adherence to what had worked at Edgehill. What the king's generals lacked above all else at Marston Moor, and even more so at Naseby, was sufficient cavalry to defeat a large, well-trained and well-motivated enemy, and that was the result of poor strategy, not poor tactics.

However, it is certainly not our intention to downplay Cromwell's contribution to winning the war. His achievement was to combine elements from the Dutch and the Swedish traditions to create a formula for cavalry attack that was appropriate for English conditions: disciplined, controlled charges delivered at a brisk trot, which developed an impressive momentum as the formations were still in close order when they struck the enemy. Finally,

Cromwell used sound training and religious zeal as mutually reinforcing elements to create the most dedicated cavalry on either side in the Great Civil War.[26] By encouraging those ideologically committed to religious reform to join his regiments, and by promoting men for their competence and their commitment rather than their social class, he created cavalry formations that could only experience an incremental enhancement of both characteristics as victory followed victory and they saw themselves more and more clearly as God's instruments in a holy war. Here, too, he was building on the work of Gustavus Adolphus, who had tried to create a godly army renowned for its military virtue and its piety, but he failed ultimately because he had to employ mercenaries in order to bring his army up to a competent size. Cromwell, however, succeeded. In the words of Michael Roberts, he 'united in his own person the military and moral heritage of the Swedish king'.[27] In the process, he also created a cavalry arm that would serve in his eyes and those of many of his radical Protestant contemporaries as the humble instrument of the divine will. His were literally the 'shock troops of God'.[28]

Notes

1 Young, *Edgehill*, 103.

2 Quoted in Carlton, *Going to the Wars*, 139–40.

3 Gwynne, *Military Memoirs*, 53.

4 TT E288 26; Staffs CRO DW 1778 Ii, 56.

5 TT E 69 12, 15.

6 HMC Portland III, 109. In the rest of the chapter, evidence concerning what happened in the main battles will be referenced only when the reference is not cited in the relevant chapter.

7 Roberts, *Gustavus Adolphus and the Rise of Sweden*, 110; James II, *Life*, 13. However, it is difficult to square King James's description with what other accounts have to say about the infantry encounter, unless James, who was on the slope behind the centre of the Royalist army, was looking down on Charles Gerard's brigade, which may not have come to push of pike at any time in the engagement.

8 *Mercurius Aulicus*, 794.

9 E.g. Kenyon, *Civil Wars*, 145; Kitson, *Rupert*, 244.

10 Phillips, *Memoirs of the Civil Wars*, 127, 132–3.

11 Ludlow, *Memoirs*, 39.

12 TT E54 19; TT E811 2.

13 *Ibid.*, E288 38; TT E292 27.

14 Ludlow, *Memoirs*, 41–2.

15 Byron, Relation, 130.

16 Bulstrode, *Memoirs*, 81.

17 TT 669 f6 184.

18 See especially Jones, *Role and Efficiency of Cavalry*, 112–15, 189, 208–9.

19 Adair, *Roundhead General*, 94; Washbourne, *Bibliotheca Gloucestrensis*, 243–4; Byron, *Relation*, 130.

20 Carlyle, *Letters and Speeches*, 124, 142–3. Firth mentions that Cromwell armed his cavalry with pistols rather than carbines, which very strongly suggests that he did not intend them to be employed in a defensive role, but he does not provide a reference, so it may not have been his practice at the start of the Lincolnshire campaign. He also claims that Cromwell urged his men to take great care in grooming and feeding their horses, which may explain his own concern not to use them in battle if they were tired, as in October 1643 just before Winceby (Firth, *Cromwell*, 92–3; TT E71 5).

21 Carlyle, *Letters and Speeches*, 163–5; TT E71 22; Jones, *Role and Efficiency of Cavalry*, 113.

22 Holmes (ed.), *Oxford Companion to Military History*, 779.

23 TT E54 19.

24 Clarendon, *Great Rebellion* ix, 41. Bulstrode made the point more forcibly, but he was not at Naseby. Also, he was writing some years later and could have had access to a copy of *The Great Rebellion* (Bulstrode, *Memoirs*, 123; Firth, 'Bulstrode').

25 Barrett, *Cavaliers*, 29–30.

26 Firth, *Cromwell*, 92.

27 Roberts, *Gustavus Adolphus*, 245.

28 Woolrych writing in Morrill, *Oliver Cromwell and the English Revolution*, 97.

chapter XXIV

Reflections on the military history of the Great Civil War

Parliament won the Great Civil War when it did for two reasons: first, the Committee of Both Kingdoms' success in gathering together its scattered brigades in north Buckinghamshire, thus giving Sir Thomas Fairfax's New Model Army a distinct numerical advantage over the king's army; and, second, the performance at Naseby of the cavalry motivated and trained by Oliver Cromwell. Charles lost the war because of strategic errors and a battle plan predicated on the idea that the New Model was indeed the 'New Noddle'.[1] Thus it was operational factors that made the difference between the two sides. In the summer of 1645, the disparity in resources between them was not such that the allies were bound to have won. Indeed, if the Royalists had behaved with greater circumspection in the days immediately before the battle, the war could have continued for much longer, particularly if widening divisions within the allied ranks had coincided with worsening administrative problems.

By the same token, it is important not to forget that the war could have ended much earlier than it did. A rapid advance on Shrewsbury in early October 1642, when Essex's army was still far larger than the king's, could have been decisive. The earl could possibly have inflicted fatal damage on the Royalist army at Edgehill if his fourth infantry brigade had been on the battlefield instead of scattered across the West Midlands. In such circumstances, he might have wiped out all the king's infantry brigades before Rupert's cavalry returned, leaving Charles without the body of an army. Manchester and Waller in their turn could have won a decisive victory at Newbury in October 1644 had they not wasted time on a preliminary bombardment and then misread the king's intentions for the following day. The king, on the other hand, might have won at Edgehill had the cavalry regiments in his second line obeyed his instructions, and at the first battle of Newbury had his army had more ammunition. A Royalist victory at Cheriton would have been significant only if Hopton and Forth had managed to destroy the enemy cavalry, half of which belonged to Essex's army. Without Balfour's regiments, the earl could have done little more than take up a defensive position covering London until, hopefully, assistance arrived from the north. Marston Moor, despite recent remarks to the contrary, was not a decisive battle.[2] The allied armies failed to destroy Rupert's army and were so badly shaken by their near-defeat in the first hour of the battle that they were unable to pursue and destroy the forces he had managed to rescue from the battlefield. Thereafter, all three generals were distracted from leaving the north of England by issues of regional security. At Naseby, however, circumstances conspired to deliver the king's army up on a plate to Fairfax and Cromwell, somewhat to their surprise.

However, it should be realized that although some of the decisions taken by the king's council of war early in the Naseby campaign, most particularly to send Goring back into the West Country, turned out to be ill-advised in retrospect, there was plenty of time to neutralize their effects. On 8th May, the king's council of war was merely following the example of the Committee of Both Kingdoms.[3] For the first half of May, the New Model was operating as if it were two armies, one under Fairfax trying to relieve Taunton and the other under Cromwell charged with keeping a watch on the king. Later in the month, the two corps joined together for the siege of Oxford, but Vermuyden was sent as far as the Trent valley with several thousand cavalry and dragoons to encourage the Scottish army to march south, whereas Weldon with another 3,000 men was still trapped in Taunton. However, unlike in previous years, it was the king's enemies, not the king, who managed to regroup in time for the next battle. This was due to decisions taken by the Committee of Both Kingdoms just before Fairfax assumed greater strategic control of the New Model Army on 10th June. It was probably the last service rendered to Parliament by the generals who had resigned as a result of the Self-Denying Ordinance, and it was based on the lessons they had learned from the campaigns of 1642–1644.

The failure of the king to achieve the same measure of success is partly explained by his habitual tendency to allow commanders in the regions the freedom to disobey royal orders, however firmly worded.[4] Even so, the king still had some room for avoiding a disaster by returning to Oxford.[5] This escape route was available until as late as 12th June, two days before Naseby, but he chose instead to follow the advice of his generals and order the field army to march north, with all the risks that this entailed of being trapped between the New Model Army and the Scots and starved into surrender.

Given their numerical inferiority in cavalry in a battle fought in open country on a long summer's day, it is difficult in retrospect to see how the Royalists could have won at Naseby, or even achieved a draw. Rupert's only real hope would have been to attack on the right wing only, relying on the good defensive position on Dust Hill to blunt any assault by the New Model Army on his infantry and the Northern Horse until such time as Maurice's cavalry had done their work. However, his decision to attack along the whole line of battle made matters worse. Fairfax handled his army well, but it was the New Model Army troopers who played the truly decisive role by routing the Royalist left wing, holding the right until it was too late for Maurice's men to have an impact on the outcome of the battle, and then destroying what was left of the enemy reserves.

After Naseby, it is most unlikely that the Royalists could have won the war or achieved honourable terms by their own efforts with or without the assistance of troops from the other two kingdoms. The most Montrose was able to do was to distract the Scottish army from its limited strategic role in England. So, as in the previous year, the fate of the Royalist cause depended on the enemy generals making mistakes, but on this occasion they were not as obliging as they had been in 1642 and 1644. Fairfax marched rapidly into the West Country and prevented the king reassembling his field army in Somerset by forcing Goring to flee before the other corps could arrive. However, Sir Thomas's conduct of the Langport campaign allowed most of the Western army to escape, thus prolonging the war in the southwest by at least six months.

The emphasis in this book has been very strongly on the significance of purely military factors on the outcome of the Great Civil War, largely because we regard them as having been seriously neglected by the historical establishment over the past forty years. That is not to say that we deny that the kinds of factors listed by determinists are worthy of serious consideration. Most were vitally important in preventing Parliament losing the war in 1643. Nevertheless, we have a sneaking feeling that demography might have given Parliament victory in the end had the war dragged on inconclusively for several more years. The fact that the king very effectively drew recruits from the less highly populated parts of England in 1642 meant that his supporters who remained at home had difficulty retaining territory against their local rivals, most particularly in Wales and northwest England, which had supplied so many regiments for the field army. In the southeast quarter of England, on the other hand, the male population was large enough both to provide Parliament with a field army and to defend its home territory against the local Royalists. Ultimately, inability to hold on to territory would have reduced the size of the king's field army by cutting it off from potential recruits. However, that point had not been reached in 1645. The achievements of Rupert in Lancashire in June 1644 and of Rupert and Maurice in the Welsh borderland in the spring of 1645 showed what could still be done in terms of recruitment by a corps of the field army even in an area no longer totally controlled by the Royalists. However, the absence of Charles Gerard's brigade from the spring campaign in the Midlands was caused by a higher imperative, the need to reconquer the brigade's home territory.

Our final comments are designed to show how important it is to look at all sides of an argument by critically examining the most recent restatement of the determinist case.[6] In his conclusion, Barratt emphasizes Parliament's greater resilience in defeat because of its more copious resources of men and material. As evidence of this he contrasts the ease with which Essex's army recovered after Lostwithiel with the experience of the Royalist armies after being defeated in 1644 and 1645. However, he is not comparing like with like. Essex's cavalry escaped from Lostwithiel, while Essex's infantry, although deprived of their weapons, were not taken captive like the Royalist foot at Marston Moor and Naseby but allowed to return overland to Southampton. Second, he maintains that even if the king had destroyed Parliament's main field army at any stage in the war and advanced on London, the city could have been supplied by sea using the navy, while troops still at large disrupted the Royalists' siege operations by attacking their rear areas. However, seventeenth-century London was situated on a river, not an estuary. Thus the king's artillery train could have prevented boats getting through to the city in the same way as they had managed to thwart the Earl of Warwick's attempts to relieve Exeter in August 1643. Finally, he claims that dwindling resources explain why the king's armies found themselves outnumbered in battles from 1644 onwards. However, with the possible exception of the first battle of Newbury, the king's army was out-numbered in every major encounter during the Great Civil War. Also, with respect to the decisive factor in most encounters, battle-hardened cavalry, it was strategic mistakes, not lack of resources, that caused the disparity between the two sides at Naseby. One can only guess at the outcome of a battle in mid-June 1645 between the king's army and the New Model if Goring had joined the king in Leicestershire. The contents of Fairfax's letter to the House of Commons written on 11th July 1645 suggest that Sir Thomas would have avoided a conflict until more reinforcements arrived, but if he had decided to fight there is little doubt that the Royalists would have stood a better chance of winning.

However, that said, we must emphasize that we do not claim that the determinist argument is fatally flawed. We are merely concerned with redressing the balance. Indeed, in Chapter II we have singled out some positive or potentially positive elements in the determinist case that deserve fuller investigation. We have also been highly critical of some established orthodoxies in the operational argument, such as the idea that Parliament's giving Fairfax strategic independence in June 1645, or the king's decision to divide his army at Stow on the Wold in the previous month, were crucial factors in Parliament's decisive victories at Naseby and Langport. Our intention in this book is to initiate a revisionist debate, not to stifle it.

Notes

1 Wanklyn, 'Royalist strategy', 70–4; TT E272 27.

2 E.g. Barrett, *Cavaliers*, 217.

3 This was the view of Gardiner (*Great Civil War* II, 210). It is also implicit in Woolrych, *Battles*, 106.

4 Wanklyn, 'Royalist strategy', 74.

5 HMC Appendix to the 9th Report II, 477.

6 Barrett, *Cavaliers*, 215–18.

Postscript: The Second Civil War

Civil war broke out again in England in the spring of 1648, but it was very different in nature. In 1642, the two sides had been very much on equal terms insofar as readiness for war was concerned. Six years later, Parliament started with a huge advantage as the New Model Army was still under arms and commanded by the duo of generals that had won the earlier war, Fairfax and Cromwell. Also, the king was not a free agent, being confined to open prison on the Isle of Wight, where he had fled just before hostilities broke out in the mistaken belief that the island's governor would support him. As a result, there was no central structure of command. To make matters worse, the various centres of royalist military activity were separated from one another by considerable distances – West Wales, North Wales, the Anglo-Welsh border counties, Kent and Essex, and parts of the north of England. This meant that the New Model Army had to be split, with Fairfax taking charge of operations around the capital and Cromwell having a roving mission that took his corps first to West Wales, then to Lancashire and finally to Yorkshire. Moreover, the uprisings were not coordinated, a weakness compounded by the fact that before the event Fairfax appears to have stationed contingents of the New Model Army in parts of the country where he expected trouble to occur. More significantly, the only really sizeable Royalist force, an army raised from scratch in Scotland by the Duke of Hamilton and some other members of the Scottish nobility, did not invade until the Welsh uprisings had been suppressed and the rebels in the southeast confined to the town of Colchester. The only early battles were scrappy affairs at Maidstone and St Fagans, in which the king's supporters were quickly routed. However, Fairfax allowed the Kentish Royalists to escape across the Thames into Essex, where they formed the backbone of Colchester's resistance. The town's dogged defence did nothing to increase Fairfax's reputation, but Cromwell, for the first time in independent command, gained significantly in prestige by eliminating the Scottish army and its English supporters in a string of engagements in Lancashire between 17th and 19th August. From then onwards it was only a matter of mopping up, with Pontefract Castle being the last fortress to surrender, in March 1649. The consequences for the defeated Royalists were more serious than in the first war. Those, like Sir Charles Lucas, who had sworn not to take up arms again, were put up against a wall after the surrender of Colchester and shot. The Duke of Hamilton was similarly despatched after a state trial, but the most important casualty was the king, who was held personally responsible for the thousands killed in the second war. The Royalists had for the most part fought bravely; the Scots less so for their hearts were not in it; but none of the uprisings stood a chance given the scattergun strategy and the failure of London and moderate Parliamentarians from the first war, or indeed many former Royalists, to support the cause in any numbers. There was no third civil war.

Bibliography

Manuscript primary sources

Public Record Office

SP 23 (Royalist compounding papers).

British Library

Additional ms 16370, 18738, 18778–9, 18978–83, 21506, 27402, 34253, 36913.
Egerton ms 785.
Harleian ms 166, 252, 986, 2125, 6802, 6804, 6851–2, 6988, 7379.
Sloane ms 1519.

Bodleian Library, University of Oxford

Carte ms X, XI, XII.
Clarendon ms 21–25, 28.
Dugdale ms 19.
Fairfax ms 32, 36.
Firth ms C6–8.
Tanner ms 60.2.

Cheshire Record Office

Quarter-sessions files.

Hampshire County Record Office

53 M 67/1 (survey of the manor of Cheriton, 1612).
Isaac Taylor, map of Hampshire and the Isle of Wight, 1759.

Newbury Museum

J. Rocque's map of Berkshire 1761.

Staffordshire County Record Office

Earl of Dartmouth mss DW 1778 Ii 40, 52–7.
Duke of Sutherland mss, *Letterbook* 3.

Shropshire County Record Office

445/277 An account of the battle of Marston Moor by Ferdinando, Lord Fairfax.
445/278 A version of Leonard Watson's account of the battle that appears to predate the one printed in London (Thomason Tracts E2 14).

William Salt Library, Stafford

WS 2007 Minute Book of the Prince of Wales's Council, March–April 1644, unfoliated.

Warwickshire County Record Office

Earl of Denbigh ms.

Wiltshire County Record Office

413/444a Prince Rupert's 'diary' of the Civil War.
413/444b Typed copy of notes made by the seventeenth-century compiler of the diary to supplement the narrative, but not included in the text of 413/444a.
P5/1626/1111b Constable's accounts of Fisherton, 1644–5.

Printed primary sources

Contemporary biographies, diaries and memoirs

Robert Baillie (1841) *Letters and Journals 1637–1662*, D. Laing (ed.), Ballantine
    Publications 72, 73, 77.

Joseph Bamfield (1993) *Apologie written by himself and printed at his desire*, J. Loftis
    and P. Hardacre (eds) London and Toronto: Associated Universities Press.

Richard Baxter (1931 edn) *Autobiography*, London: Dent.

Sir John Byron (1953) Relation of the Late Western Action, P. Young (ed.),
    Journal of the Society for Army Historical Research XXXI.

Sir Richard Bulstrode (1721) *Memoirs and Reflections upon the Reign and Government of Charles I and Charles II*, London.

Margaret Cavendish, Duchess of Newcastle (1872 edn) *The Lives of William Cavendish, Duke of Newcastle and of his wife Margaret, Duchess of Newcastle*, London: J.R. Smith.

Sir Hugh Cholmley (1890) Memorials Touching the Battle of York, *English Historical Review* V.

Robert Codrington (1646) *The Life and Death of the Illustrious Robert, Earl of Essex*, London.

John Corbet (1835) 'An historical relation of the military government of Gloucester from the beginning of the Civil War between King and Parliament and the removal of Colonel Massey from that government to the command of the Western forces', in *Bibliotheca Gloucestrensis*, J. Washbourn (ed.), Gloucester.

John Cruso (1972) *Militarie Instructions for the Cavallrie*, P. Young (ed.), Kineton: Roundway Press.

Sir William Dugdale (1827) *Diary, Correspondence etc.*, W. Hamner (ed.), London: Harding, Lepard.

John Evelyn (1877–9) *Diary*, W. Bray (ed.), Oxford University Press.

Thomas, Lord Fairfax (1815) Short Memorials of the Northern Actions, *Select Tracts relating to the Civil Wars in England*, Francis, Lord Maseres (ed.), Vol 1., London: R. Wilkes.

Richard Gough (1878) *Human Nature Displayed in the History of Myddle*, Shrewsbury: Adnitt and Naunton.

John Gwynne (1967) *Military Memoirs: The Civil War*, N. Tucker and P. Young (eds), London: Longman.

Denzil Holles (1815) Memoirs 1641–1648, *Select Tracts relating to the Civil Wars in England*, Francis, Lord Maseres (ed.), Vol. 1, London: R. Wilkes.

Ralph, Lord Hopton (1902) Bellum Civile, C. Chadwyck-Healey (ed.), *Somerset Record Society* 18.

Lucy Hutchinson (1808) *Memoirs of the Life of Colonel John Hutchinson*, London: Longman.

Edward Hyde, Lord Clarendon (1888) *The History of the Rebellion and Civil Wars in England*, W. Macray (ed.), Oxford: Oxford University Press.

James II, King of England (1816) *Life of James II collected out of memoirs written by his own hand*, Vol. 1, J. Clarke (ed.), London: Longman.

Thomas Juxon (1999) Journal 1644–47, K. Lindley and D. Scott (eds), *Camden Society* 5th series 13.

Edmund Ludlow (1894) *Memoirs 1625–1672*, I, Sir Charles Firth (ed.), Oxford University Press.

Sir Samuel Luke (1947, 1950, 1952–3) Journals, 3 vols, I. Phillip (ed.), *Oxfordshire Record Society* 29, 31, 33.

Sir Samuel Luke (1963) Letterbooks, H. Tibbutt (ed.), *Historical Manuscripts Commission Joint Publications* 4, HMSO.

Thomas Malbon (1889) Memoirs, J. Hall (ed.), *Lancashire and Cheshire Record Society* 19.

William Maurice (1845) Notebook, R. Williams (ed.), *Archaeologica Cambriensis*, I.

The Monckton Papers (*c.* 1884) *Philobiblion Society*, Miscellany XV.

Sydenham Poyntz (1908) A True Relation of these Warres in Germany 1624–36, A. Goodrick (ed.), *Camden Society* 3rd series 14.

. . . Roe (1873) Military Memoir of Colonel Birch, J. Webb (ed.), *Camden Society* new series VII.

Sir Henry Slingsby (1836) *Diary*, D. Parsons (ed.), London: Longman.

Walter Slingsby (1902) Accounts of the campaigns in the south of England 1643–44, *Somerset Record Society* 18.

Joshua Sprigg (1844 edn) *Anglia Rediviva*, Oxford University Press.

Richard Symonds (1859) Diaries of the Marches of the Royal Army during the Great Civil War, C. Long (ed.), *Camden Society* LXXIV.

Sir Henry Townshend (1920) Diary, J. Willis Bund (ed.), *Worcestershire Historical Society*.

John Vernon (1644) *The Young Horseman or the Honest Plain-dealing Cavalier*, London.

John Vicars (1647) *England's Worthies under whom all the Civill and Bloedy Warrs 1642 to 1647 are related*, London.

Sir Edward Walker (1705) *Historical Discourses*, London: S. Keble.

Sir Robert Walsh (1679) *The True Narration and Manifest*, Holland?

Edward Walsingham (1644) *Britannicae Virtutis Imago*, Oxford (Thomason Tract E53.10).

Edward Walsingham (1645) *Alter Britannicae Heros*, Oxford.

Edward Walsingham (1910) Hector Britannicus: the Life of Sir John Digby, G. Bernard (ed.), *Camden Society* 3rd series 18.

Sir Phillip Warwick (1813) *Memoirs of the Reign of King Charles I*, Edinburgh: Ballantyne.

Bulstrode Whitelock (1732) *Memoirs of the English Affairs*, London: J. Tonson.

Edited collections

Abbott, W. (ed.) (1937) *The Writings and Letters of Oliver Cromwell*, Vol. 1, Harvard University Press.

Beaumont, W. (ed.) (1864) A Discourse of the Warr in Lancashire, *Chetham Society* lxii.

Bell, R. (ed.) (1841) *Memoirs of the Reign of Charles I*, London: Richard Bentley.

Carlyle, T. (ed.) (1846) *Letters and Speeches of Oliver Cromwell*, Vol. 1, London: Chapman & Hall.

Bruce, J. and Masson, D. (eds) (1875) 'Manchester's quarrel: documents relating to the quarrel between the Earl of Manchester and Oliver Cromwell', *Camden Society* new series XII.

Calendar of the Clarendon State Papers (1869) Oxford University Press.

Calendar of State Papers Domestic 1644, 1644–45, 1645–47, 1625–49 addenda, London: HMSO.

Calendar of State Papers Venetian 1642–43.

Carte, T. (ed.) (1739) *A Collection of Original Documents and Papers 1641–60 Found amongst the Duke of Ormonde's Papers*, Vol. 1, London: J. Buttenham.

Coleman, J. (ed.) (1898) Wyndham's letter – a Royalist account of the withdrawal of the king's forces from Taunton, *English Historical Review* XIII.

Cooper, W.D. (ed.) (1853) 'The Trelawney Papers', *Camden Society* LV.

Day, W. (ed.) (1879) *The Pythouse Papers*, London: Bickers & Son.

Dore, R. (ed.) (1983–4 and 1990) Sir William Brereton, Letterbooks I–IV, *Lancashire and Cheshire Record Society* 123 and 128.

Ellis, Sir Henry (ed.) (1847) *Original Letters Illustrative of English History 1400–1793*, 3rd series, London: Richard Bentley.

Firth, Sir Charles (ed.) (1898) Prince Rupert's Marches, *English Historical Review* XIII.

Firth, Sir Charles and Rait, R. (eds) (1911) *Acts and Ordinances of the Interregnum 1642–1660*, London: HMSO.

Gardiner, S.R. (ed.) (1871) The Fortescue Papers, *Camden Society* new series I.

Gardiner, S.R. (ed.) (1906 edn) *The Constitutional Documents of the Puritan Revolution 1625–1660*, Oxford: Oxford University Press.

Green, M. (ed.) (1857) *Letters of Queen Henrietta Maria*, London: Richard Bentley.

Historical Manuscripts Commission (HMC) London: HMSO.

Appendices to the 1st Report (House of Lords), 2nd Report (Lord Leigh), 4th Report (Earl de la Warre, Earl of Denbigh), 5th Report (Duke of Sutherland), 6th Report (House of Lords), 7th Report (Verney), 9th Report part II (A. Morrison), 10th Report VI (Lord Bray), 12th Report II (Earl Cowper), 12th Report IX (Duke of Beaufort), 13th Report I, III (Duke of Portland), 14th Report VII (Marquis of Ormonde).

House of Commons Journals II, III.

House of Lords Journals V, VI, VII.

Petrie, Sir Charles (ed.) (1935) *The Letters of King Charles I*, London: Cassell.

Petrie, Sir Charles (ed.) (1974) *Charles I, Prince Rupert and the Civil War*, London: Routledge & Kegan Paul.

Phillips, J. (ed.) (1874) *Memoirs of the Civil War in Wales and the Marches*, Vol. 2, London: Longman.

Roy, I. (ed.) (1964 and 1975) Royalist Ordnance Papers, *Oxfordshire Record Society* 43 and 49.

Rushworth, J. (ed.) (1721) *Historical Collections*, Vols V and VI, London: D. Browne.

Sanford, J. (ed.) (1858) Appendix to *The Great Rebellion*, London: Bickers & Son.

Scott, Sir Walter (ed.) (1809–15) Somers Tracts, IV.

Toynbee, M. (ed.) (1961) The Papers of Captain Stevens, Wagon-master, *Oxfordshire Record Society* 42.

Trevelyan, Sir Walter and Sir Charles (eds) (1872) The Trevelyan Papers, *Camden Society* CV.

Warburton, E.B.G. (1849) *Memoirs of Prince Rupert and the Cavaliers*, 3 vols, London: Richard Bentley.

Washbourne, J. (ed.) (1825) *Bibliotheca Gloucestrensis*, Gloucester.

Collections of newspapers and pamphlets

Bodleian Library, Wood Pamphlets 376–378.

British Library, Thomason Tracts (TT) E2–350.

British Library, Thomason Tracts (TT) 669 f6.

Printed secondary sources

Books

Adair, J. (1973) *Cheriton 1644: The Campaign and the Battle*, Kineton: Roundway Press.

Adair, J. (1982) *John Hampden, the Patriot 1594–1643*, London: MacDonald & Jane's.

Adair, J. (1997) *Roundhead General: The Campaigns of Sir William Waller*, 2nd edition, Stroud: Sutton.

Andriette, E. (1971) *Devon and Exeter in the Civil War*, Newton Abbot: David & Charles.

Ashley, M. (1957) *The Greatness of Oliver Cromwell*, London: Hodder & Stoughton.

Ashley, M. (1975) *The English Civil War*, London: Thames & Hudson.

Ashton, R. (1978) *The English Civil War: Conservatism and Revolution 1603–1649*, London: Weidenfeld & Nicolson.

Aylmer, G. (1963) *The Struggle for the Constitution*, London: Blandford.

Aylmer, G. (1987) *Revolution or Rebellion: England from Civil War to Restoration*, Oxford University Press.

Barratt, J. (2000) *Cavaliers: The Royalist Army at War 1642–46*, Stroud: Alan Sutton.

Barratt, J. (2003) *The Battle for York: Marston Moor 1644*, Stroud: Tempus.

Bennett, M. (1995) *The English Civil War*, London: Longman.

Bennett, M. (1997) *The Civil Wars in Britain and Ireland 1638–1651*, Oxford: Basil Blackwell.

Burne, A.H. (1996 edn) *Battlefields of England*, London: Penguin.

Burne, A.H. and Young, P. (1959) *The Great Civil War: A Military History of the First Civil War*, London: Eyre & Spottiswood.

Carlton, C. (1992) *Going to the Wars: The Experience of the British Civil Wars 1638–1651*, London: Routledge.

Carte, T. (1851) *Life of the First Duke of Ormonde*, Oxford University Press.

Cotton, R. (1889) *Barnstaple and the Northern Part of Devon in the Great Civil War*, London.

Coward, B. (1994 edn) *The Stuart Age*, London: Longman.

Cust, R. and Hughes, A. (eds) (1997) *The English Civil War*, London: Edward Arnold.

Devereux, W. (1853) *Lives and Letters of the Devereux, Earls of Essex*, II, London: John Murray.

Dupuy, T. and Dupuy, R. (eds) (1993) *The Collins Encyclopaedia of Military History*, 4th edition, London: Collins.

Edgar, F. (1968) *Sir Ralph Hopton*, Oxford University Press.

Edwards, P. (2000) *Dealing in Death: The Arms Trade and the British Civil Wars, 1638–1652*, Stroud: Alan Sutton.

Everitt, A. (1966) *The Community of Kent and the Great Rebellion 1640–60*, Leicester University Press.

Firth, Sir Charles (1962) *Cromwell's Army*, London: Methuen.

Firth, Sir Charles (1904) *Cromwell*, London: Putnam's.

Fissell, M. (1994) *The Bishops Wars: Charles I's Campaigns against Scotland 1638–40*, Cambridge University Press.

Fletcher, A. (1981) *The Outbreak of the English Civil War*, London: Edward Arnold.

Foard, G. (1995) *Naseby: the Decisive Campaign*, Whitstable: Prior Publications.

Gardiner, S.R. (1991 edn) *History of the Great Civil War*, 4 vols, Moreton in the Marsh: Windrush Press.

Gaunt, P. (1997) *The British Wars*, London: Routledge.

Gaunt, P. (ed.) (2000) *The English Civil War*, Oxford: Basil Blackwell.

Gentles, I. (1992) *The New Model Army in England, Ireland and Scotland 1645–1653*, Oxford: Basil Blackwell.

Gush, G. (1982) *Renaissance Armies 1480–1650*, George Gush.

Gush, G. (1984) *Army Lists 1420–1700*, George Gush.

Hexter, J.H. (1961) *The Reign of King Pym*, Cambridge, Mass.

Hill, J.E.C. (1961) *The Century of Revolution*, Edinburgh: Nelson.

Hirst, D. (1999) *England in Conflict 1603–1660*, London: Edward Arnold.

Holmes, C. (1974) *The Eastern Association in the English Civil War*, Cambridge University Press.

Holmes, R. (ed.) (2001) *The Oxford Companion to Military History*, Oxford University Press.

Hughes, A. (1987) *Politics, Society and Civil War in Warwickshire, 1620–1660*, Cambridge University Press.

Hughes, B. (1997) *Firepower: Weapon Effectiveness on the Battlefield 1630–1850*, London: Basil Perrott.

Hutton, R. (1982) *The Royalist War Effort 1642–1646*, London: Longman.

Jones, A. (1987) *The Art of War in the Western World*, Oxford University Press.

Kenyon, J. (1988) *The Civil Wars of England*, London: Weidenfeld & Nicolson.

Kenyon, J. and Ohlmeyer, J. (1998) *The Civil Wars: A Military History of England, Scotland and Ireland 1639–1660*, Oxford University Press.

Kishlansky, M. (1979) *The Rise of the New Model Army*, Cambridge University Press.

Kitson, Sir Frank (1994) *Prince Rupert: Portrait of a Soldier*, London: Constable.

Lynch, J. (1999) *For King and Parliament: Bristol and the Civil War*, Stroud: Stutton.

MacInnes, A. (1991) *Charles I and the Making of the Covenanting Movement*, Edinburgh; John Donald.

Mackay, W. (1939) *Little Madam: A Life of Queen Henrietta Maria*, London: Bell.

Malcolm, J. (1983) *Caesar's Due: Loyalty and King Charles I*, London: Royal Historical Society.

Morrah, P. (1976) *Prince Rupert of the Rhine*, London: Constable.

Morrill, J. (1973) *Cheshire 1630–60*, Oxford University Press.

Morrill, J. (ed.) (1990) *Oliver Cromwell and the English Revolution*, London: Longman.

Newman, P. (1981) *The Battle of Marston Moor 1644*, Chichester: Phillimore.

Oman, Sir Charles (1937) *The Art of War in the Seventeenth Century*, London: Methuen.

Parker, G. (1996) *The Military Revolution: Military Innovation and the Rise of the West 1500–1800*, 2nd edition, Cambridge University Press.

Porter, S. (ed.) (1996) *London and the Civil War*, London: Macmillan.

Powell, J.R. (1972) *Robert Blake: General-at-Sea*, London: Collins.

Reid, S. (1998) *All the King's Armies*, Sevenoaks: Spellmount.

Roberts, M. (1958) *Gustavus Adolphus: A History of Sweden 1611–1632*, Longman: London.

Roberts, M. (1973) *Gustavus Adolphus and the Rise of Sweden*, London: English Universities Press.

Rogers, C.J. (ed.) (1995) *The Military Revolution Debate: Readings on the Military Transformation of Early Modern Europe*, New York: Westview Press.

Rogers, H. (1968) *Battles and Generals of the English Civil War*, London: Seeley Press.

Russell, C. (1990) *The Causes of the English Civil Wars*, Oxford.

Russell, C. (1991) *The Fall of the British Monarchies*, Oxford.

Seel, G. (1996) *The English Civil Wars and Republic 1637–60*, London: Routledge.

Smith, D. (1998) *A History of the Modern British Isles 1603–1707*, Oxford: Basil Blackwell.

Snow, V. (1970) *Essex the Rebel: The Life of Robert Devereux, the Third Earl of Essex*, University of Nebraska Press.

Stoyle, M. (1996) *From Deliverance to Destruction: Rebellion and Civil War in an English City*, University of Exeter Press.

Sunderland, F. (1926) *Marmaduke, Lord Langdale*, London: Jenkins.

Terry, C. (1899) *Life and Campaigns of Alexander Leslie, Earl of Leven*, London: Longman, Green.

Thomas-Stanford, Sir Charles (1910) *Sussex in the Great Civil War and the Interregnum 1642–1660*, London: Chiswick Press.

Tincey, J. (1990) *Soldiers of the English Civil War 2: Cavalry*, London.

Toynbee, M. and Young, P. (1970) *The Battle of Cropredy Bridge*, Kineton: Roundway Press.

Tucker, N. (1963) *Sir John Owen, Royalist Major General*, Rhyl.

Wagner, E. (1979) *European Weapons and Warfare 1618–1648*, translated from the Czech by S. Pellar, London.

Wedgwood, C.V. (1958) *The King's War*, London: Collins.

Wheeler, J. (2002) *The Irish and British Wars 1637–1654, Triumph, Tragedy and Failure*, London: Routledge.

Woolrych, A. (1961) *Battles of the English Civil Wars*, London: Batsford.

Young, M. (1997) *Charles I*, London: Macmillan.

Young, P. (1967) *Edgehill: The Campaign and the Battle*, Kineton: Roundway Press.

Young, P. (1970) *Marston Moor 1644*, Kineton: Roundway Press.

Young, P. (1973) *English Civil War Armies*, Men at Arms series, London.

Young, P. (1985) *Naseby*, London: Century Press.

Young, P. *et al.* (1964) *Newark-upon-Trent: The Civil War Siege Works*, London: HMSO.

Young, P. and Holmes, R. (1974) *The English Civil Wars*, London: Eyre Methuen.

Essays and journal articles

Auden, J. (1936) 'My case with the Committee of Salop', *Transactions of the Shropshire Archaeological and Natural History Society* 48.

Beats, L. (1977–8) 'The East Midlands Association 1642–1644', *Midland History* IV.

Bennett, M. (1986) 'Contribution and assessment: financial exactions in the English Civil War, 1642–1646', *War and Society* 4.

Crawford, L. (1975) 'The Saville Affair', *English Historical Review* XC.

Danskin, N. (November 1992) 'The Battle of Wittstock 1636', *Military Illustrated* 54.

Davies, G. (1921) 'The battle of Edgehill', *English Historical Review* XXXVI.

Davies, G. (1934) 'The Parliamentary army under the Earl of Essex 1642–1645', *English Historical Review* XXXIX.

Firth, Sir Charles (1895) 'The "memoirs" of Sir Richard Bulstrode', *English Historical Review* X.

Firth, Sir Charles (1899) 'The raising of the Ironsides', *Transactions of the Royal Historical Society* XIII.

Firth, Sir Charles (1904) 'Clarendon's History of the Great Rebellion', *English Historical Review* XIX.

Malcolm, J. (1978) 'A king in search of soldiers: Charles I in 1642', *Historical Journal* XXI.

Malcolm, J. (1979) 'All the king's men: the impact on the crown of Irish soldiers in the English Civil War', *Irish Historical Review*.

Parrott, D. (1992) 'The military revolution in seventeenth-century Europe', *History Today*.

Phillips, C. (1978) 'The Royalist North: the Cumberland and Westmoreland Gentry 1642–1660', *Northern History* XIV.

Roy, I. (1962) 'The Royalist Council of War, 1642–46', *Bulletin of the Institute of Historical Research* 35.

Roy, I. (1975) 'The English Civil War and English society', in *War and Society: Military History Yearbook 1*, Bond, B. and Roy, I. (eds) London: Croom Helm.

Roy, I. (1978) 'England turned Germany? The aftermath of the Civil War in its European context', *Transactions of the Royal Historical Society* 4th series 28.

Russell, C. (2003) 'James VI and I's rule over two kingdoms: an English view', *Historical Research* LXXVI.

Stoyle, M. (1996) ' "Sir Richard Grenville's creatures": the new Cornish tertia, 1644–46' *Cornish Studies* 4.

Tibbutt, H. (1948) 'The life and letters of Sir Lewis Dyve', *Bedfordshire Record Society* 22.

Wanklyn, M. (1981) 'Royalist Strategy in the South of England 1642–1644', *Southern History* 3.

Wanklyn, M. and Young. P. (1981) 'A king in search of soldiers: a rejoinder', *Historical Journal* XXIV.

Young, P. (1953) 'The Royalist army at the battle of Roundway Down', *Journal of the Society of Army Historical Research* XXXI.

Young, P. (1955) 'The Royalist army at Edgehill', *Journal of the Society of Army Historical Research* XXXIII.

Theses

Jones, F. (2000) The Role and Effectiveness of Cavalry in the English Civil War, M.Phil., Wolverhampton.

Roy, I. (1963) The Royalist Army in the First Civil War, Ph.D., Oxford.

Wanklyn, M. (1966) The King's Armies in the West of England 1642–46, M.A., Manchester.

Wanklyn, M. (1976) Landed Society and Allegiance in Cheshire and Shropshire in the First Civil War, Ph.D., Manchester.

Maps

J. Ogilby, *Britannia, or an Illustration of the Kingdom of England and the Dominion of Wales*, 1665 (1939 edn).

Ordnance survey maps of the British Isles, 1st edition.

Index